ALLEN COUNTY PUBLIC LIBRARY

m 3 1833 01041 6

D0501545

914.70385 B51L W 7052980
BINYON, MICHAEL, 1944—
LIFE IN RUSSIA

914.70385 B51L W 7052980
BINYON, MICHAEL, 1944—
LIFE IN RUSSIA

WAYNEDALE BRANCH LIBRARY
2200 LOWER HUNTINGTON ROAD
FORT WAYNE, INDIANA 46819

ALLEN COUNTY PUBLIC LIBRARY

FORT WAYNE, INDIANA 46802

You may return this book to any agency, branch,
or bookmobile of the Allen County Public Library.

DEMCO

LIFE IN RUSSIA

LIFE IN RUSSIA

MICHAEL BINYON

PANTHEON BOOKS, NEW YORK

ALLEN COUNTY PUBLIC LIBRARY
FORT WAYNE, INDIANA

Copyright © 1983 by Michael Binyon

All rights reserved under International and Pan-American
Copyright Conventions. Published in the United States by
Pantheon Books, a division of Random House, Inc.,
New York. Originally published in Great Britain by
Hamish Hamilton, London, 1983.

Library of Congress Cataloging in Publication Data

Binyon, Michael, 1944–
Life in Russia.
Includes index.
1. Soviet Union—Social life and customs—1970
2. National characteristics, Russian. I. Title.
DK276.B48   1983   947.085′4   83-19377
ISBN 0-394-53339-9

Manufactured in the United States of America

First American Edition

W 7052980

Contents

AUTHOR'S NOTE

Much of the material in this book has appeared, in one form or another, in *The Times* between 1978 and 1982. I am grateful to *The Times* for sending me off to Moscow as its correspondent, for giving me time off to write this book and for allowing me to draw on some of my published articles.

LIFE IN RUSSIA

Introduction

Sooner or later every Western tourist to Russia is confronted with the
same problem. You decide to leave your tour group and go out one
evening with your husband or wife to an ordinary Russian restaurant – a
chance, perhaps, to meet the people, to see how the average Muscovite
enjoys himself away from the Intourist guides. You pick one of a dozen
restaurants recommended at the hotel service desk, ask them to make a
booking, and set off for the evening's adventure. But when you get there,
things are not quite what you imagined. A heavy wooden door with a big
glass panel is firmly shut. Beyond it is another door leading into the
restaurant itself, with a net curtain covering the glass. In the little lobby
between the two sits an old man in a crumpled uniform and cap who
periodically gets up and scowls at the motley group of people hanging
around outside. He appears not to understand your signs to him to open
the door, and shouts out something you cannot understand. What do
you do?

There are three approaches. You can insist on your rights and make a
scene: look, I have a booking here. Kindly open this door immediately. I
am a Western tourist and I insist you let me me in. The grumpy doorman
becomes downright surly. He shouts out something again, then sits
down and takes no further notice of you. Or you can appeal to his better
nature: please, I do want to go in. And you shuffle about uncomfortably
as you plead with him. He seems impervious to wheedling, and gestures
you away haughtily. Or you can stand firmly in front of the door, and
when he opens it a crack state calmly and authoritatively that you have a
booking and intend to keep it. You smile back politely at his objections,
remain where you are, exude an air of patient immovability, give him a
moment or two to make a further protest until you step past with a
courteous nod as he grudgingly opens the door. You have learned how to
negotiate with the Russians.

All nations are made up of the people they comprise, and behave
according to the traditions, values and outlook of that people. Unfortu-

nately the West seems to have forgotten this truism in dealing with the
Soviet Union. Politicians and the press have been distracted by the
power and the ideology into thinking of the Soviet Union as an abstract
political entity. They look at a military superpower, at a system they fear
and dislike, at a rival whose behaviour is analysed and judged according
to Western experience and viewpoints. The idea of Russia, to most
people, is a political idea: we do not think of individual Russians,
Georgians, Armenians, Tadzhiks, Lithuanians and all the dozens of
peoples who live in the Soviet Union. We have even started talking about
the 'Soviets' – a word that itself is a political term and somehow
depersonalizes the people we are referring to.

Of course the Russians are as much to blame for this as anyone else.
They choose to present themselves as the guardians of an ideology, as a
powerful anonymous bloc, as an impersonal opponent of capitalism.
The collective and politicized idea of the 'Soviet people' has officially
replaced the warmer and more comprehensible picture of a society of
individual human beings.

But Russians are people. It is extremely foolish when dealing with
them on an international level to forget this. Branding the Soviet Union
as an 'evil empire' can easily be taken to mean, both in the West and the
East, an empire of evil people, something grossly insulting and dangerously inciting. And the West, so used to thinking of the Soviet Union in
political terms, then fails to see why such remarks provoke such a furious
reaction in the Kremlin. The Russians and their leaders react as people,
not as political opponents.

Applying the lessons of everyday life in Russia to an interpretation of
how the USSR will react as a nation to this or that event in the world is
sensible and important but peculiarly difficult for Westerners, as so few
have any experience of living in Russia. (I should really say the Soviet
Union, but the use of the word 'Russia' to refer to all the country instead
of just one of its fifteen republics is so widespread in the West that it
would seem silly to quibble.)

Even if you have spent some time in the country, you get to know it
only slowly and with difficulty. I spent four and a half years as a
correspondent in Moscow, but led a very artificial life, very different
from that of ordinary Russians. I enjoyed special shops and services,
privileged access to theatres, the chance to jump the queue almost
everywhere, to travel abroad and stock up with clothes and consumer
goods. In many ways I was isolated – intentionally – from everyday
realities, living in a foreigners' ghetto with other journalists and diplo-

mats, restricted in my movements and with limited contacts with Russians.

No Westerner is ever permitted to learn more than a fraction of what goes on in such an obsessively secretive society. It takes a long time to establish friendships and trust, and even in Moscow I found it hard to get behind the propaganda façade, to discover what people thought and felt, what the real pressures on them were, how they reacted when no foreigners were present. It was perhaps a little easier to do this when I spent a year teaching English at a pedagogical institute in Minsk on a British Council teachers' exchange scheme in 1967–68. But even then I was secluded in a hotel, and was placed apart from the mainstream of ordinary life simply because I was a foreigner – and what is more, a Westerner.

Nevertheless, you can see and experience things at second hand – through conversations with friends, through plays, television, radio and newspapers, by comparing notes with other foreigners in Moscow. Tourists find this difficult. They tend to go home with an undefinable sense of dissatisfaction, a feeling they have been fooled and seen only the surface of things. Were they misinformed or simply naive? Were all the things they read back home exaggerations, cold-war myths? Or was the guide a little too smooth-talking, too pat with her answers? There is no helpful reply. Of course Intourist does its best to show only the best, to conceal awkward facts, to impress visitors. Which tourist agency does not? But even those who have lived a generation in the Soviet Union – and there are one or two – never fully understand the country. It is aptly symbolized by those painted wooden dolls you find in any souvenir shop; you open one and there is another inside. When you are confident that you really know how Russians think and react, that is the time to beware, for you can be mightily deceived.

Tourist impressions are not altogether false, though they may be superficial. What you find impressive may not be what you expect, but it is not necessarily just a charade set up by Intourist to empty your pockets of hard currency while filling you with friendly sentiments. And tourists can learn valuable lessons from such everyday experiences as the encounter with the restaurant doorman. That experience teaches a lot about power and face. Russians do not like to be made to lose face, or back down, even if – or perhaps especially if – the other side is right. It is no use, either on a personal level or in international dealings, threatening the Russians, trying to pressurize them into backing down while loudly and publicly denouncing them. They only become, like the doorman, more obstinately determined to resist. Equally, it is a waste of time abjectly appealing to them from a position of weakness. Russians respect power and authority, and most have a bully's instinct to walk all over anyone who is servile and obsequious. The best way of doing business is to make your position and determination clear from the start, negotiate toughly but politely and ensure that face is not lost. When you win your point, you allow the other side the courtesy of a dignified retreat. In international politics this would seem to suggest that steely-nerved détente is the best approach. Threatening rhetoric and subservience – all too prevalent in the West and the East respectively – are self-defeating.

It might seem odd to emphasize the importance of human qualities and individual personalities in a system that is so vast, so monolithic, so rigidly governed by prescribed rules and anonymous authority. But precisely because of its size and overwhelming impersonality, the Russians feel a strong need for humanity, for face-to-face contact and personal dealings. One of the most successful American diplomats I knew in Moscow was a man of Mediterranean origin who had spent most of his career in the Arab world. He approached the Russians on the human, individual basis that is so typically Eastern. Rather than dealing with Soviet officials formally (and nobody can be stiffer or more impenetrably impersonal than a Russian who feels he has to act in a formal capacity), he used to put an arm on their shoulder, give them a 'I-know-you-know-I-know' look, take them to one side and ask them what they as individuals thought of this or that.

The system is indeed vast. It is hard for a Westerner, especially a European, to comprehend the sheer physical size of the Soviet Union, harder still to understand how a single political and economic system can encompass so many different climates and landscapes, peoples, languages, races, religions and cultures. The Soviet Union is a world of its own. But it is a world its rulers ever fear will fly apart into disparate fragments unless they keep a very tight grip. The rigidity of the bureaucracy, the draconian nature of the rules and the oppressing omnipotence of authority all stem from this almost impossible attempt to hold together such a heterogeneous entity. There cannot be any exceptions, any room for flexibility, lest the chinks be discovered and exploited, the fissures become great rifts and the whole system fall apart. That, at any rate, is – and always has been – the reasoning of Russia's rulers.

The result is that the ordinary individual feels very small and powerless against so vast a system. He cannot change it and does not try. Russians have an understandably fatalistic approach to life. They also have a very poorly developed sense of personal responsibility and initiative. Indeed, many have deliberately suppressed whatever inclinations they had to take decisions and show initiative – this is politically safer, and anyway the system will not penalize them for not making that extra effort.

Many things follow from this that strongly affect the way Russians behave and their outlook on the world. One is that the system itself is extremely inefficient. Things cannot work smoothly and easily when no one is willing to take responsibility, when no one fears the consequences of his own actions, or lack of them, and when no one has much idea of what is going on higher up, lower down or far away from him. The system does indeed provide the people with much that is essential: with jobs, security, cheap food and housing, a health service, reasonable salaries and a slow but gradual improvement in the standard of living. But the system cannot respond with speed or flexibility to new circumstances. It cannot satisfy individual wants and ambitions. It works at the speed of the slowest.

Russians know this well. They joke about it. They complain about it, privately and officially. They draw up schemes to make the system work better. But the system is too big, too entrenched to change. And so most people's reaction is forthright: beat the system. And so they do. This comes as a surprise to Westerners, who think of Soviet society as disciplined, cowed, regimented, somehow like our image of Nazi Germany. Nothing could be further from the truth. Instead, most visitors complain of the chaos, lackadaisical pace, haphazard organization and general disregard for a thousand rules and regulations. In a country where so much is forbidden, almost everything seems to be possible. ('The land of unlimited impossibilities,' as one witty Austrian diplomat once remarked to me.) But thank goodness for such human responses to the system. Otherwise it would be unworkable – and unbearable. 'It's like a fence,' a Russian who had lived most of her life in Germany told me, holding up her fingers and opening them to make gaps here and there. 'There's always a way through if you look. It's not like that in East Germany. There are no gaps in the fence there.'

It is these gaps that are the fascination, the joy and the despair of Russia. The authorities do their best to hide them: the age-old sense of inferiority, the gnawing concern about Russia's backwardness that has motivated rulers for generations to huff and puff, building Potemkin villages and pulling the wool over foreigners' eyes, the worries that ideological enemies will find out the weaknesses and trumpet them abroad to discredit Russia and undermine its people's faith in their rulers – all this has conditioned Russians to draw back instinctively from frank discussion with outsiders, to prevent strangers from probing and nosing around their country, to present a blank, grey mask to the world that hides both the human foibles and the brilliant flashes of light that illuminate the society behind the mask.

Not everything can be hidden. And the more sophisticated newspaper editors and party officials now realize that not everything should be. There is slightly less worry now than there used to be about what outsiders think, more self-confidence and more interest in highlighting mistakes and ridiculing wrong-doing in order to try to instill some sense of discipline, to ward off criticism of the system as a whole. The papers regularly report the most bizarre goings-on, and in doing so reveal a great deal about life in the Soviet Union and the attitudes of bureaucrats as well as the concerns of the leadership. As a correspondent I drew heavily on such stories in the press – first because they were often very funny, secondly because they were the only way often of knowing what went on in remote areas I was not allowed to visit, and thirdly because it is far wiser and more tactful to let the Russians make their own criticisms of their society than to judge them and pontificate as an outsider with different assumptions and outlook. For the same reason I have based many of the incidents and anecdotes in this book on published press reports.

Almost every day you can find something to amaze you in Soviet newspapers. Perhaps one of the more ironic stories recently was one about a newspaper itself, which was published in Birlyusy in Siberia. For a whole month the paper did not appear, and the local party committee, whose organ it was, never noticed its absence. No inhabitant of the town remarked on it either, and it was only when a visiting journalist from the provincial capital asked for it that it was discovered that a typesetter had been withdrawn, the staff had gone on holiday and the editor had decided it was too difficult to find replacements.

I remember dozens of other incidents: the case of the factory where the workers had dug a tunnel to smuggle in bottles of vodka and the management could not understand why they were perpetually drunk; the case of an inventive pavement sweeper who devised a machine to clear snow from pathways and spent the best part of thirty years trying to get his contraption – which did the work of a dozen stout old men –

patented and put into production by the state; the case of the ambulance drivers whose sick passengers turned out to be factory canteen managers smuggling quantities of meat, salami and eggs out of the kitchens and on to the black market; the doting grandmothers who sent illegal vodka to their grandsons in the army by disguising it as syrup in jars of preserved fruit or hiding it in hot water bottles; the builders who erected a block of flats with balconies that had no railings and sloped outwards so that each resident had to barricade the windows leading on to these death-traps; the old woman who declared a miraculous likeness of Christ's head had suddenly appeared on her living-room wall and attracted crowds from miles around who besieged her house day and night, singing hymns and hoping for a cure, until a scientific commission urgently dispatched by the worried local committee of atheists found the likeness was nothing more than a patch of mould; the railway wagons that were so rusty that when they reached their destination every single lump of coal had fallen through to the line on the way.

Encounters in daily life are just as peculiar and revealing. A friend once went into Moscow's main record shop to buy some typical Russian music. At home she was astonished to find that the entire record, labelled as balalaika music, consisted of pirated recordings of Abba, which some enterprising workers in the record factory had evidently hoped to manufacture on the side and sell for fat sums on the black market. She went back to the shop, bought half a dozen more such records and gave them away to grateful Russian fans of pop music.

When the Soviet Union introduced summer time for the first time in 1981, the confusion was so great that one diplomat's Soviet maid asked her employers the day before what she should do when she came in an hour earlier the next morning. 'For us it will be nine o'clock, but you'll still be in bed I suppose as this change is only for Soviet people, and for you it will still be eight o'clock,' she explained.

On a famous occasion one summer, confusion and inefficiency culminated in an almost disastrous diplomatic incident. The ambassador of Chad was taken to hospital suddenly and died of a heart attack. Unfortunately the hospital did not inform more than one of his wives, and when the others appeared on Monday morning they were distressed to find their husband had passed away on Friday. But the funeral arrangements were even more embarrassing. Aeroflot refused to fly the corpse and the multitude of dependents home without payment in Western currency in advance. After a hasty diplomatic hat had been passed around to raise the cash, the airline agreed to fly to Chad via

Nigeria. At the stop-over there, the mourning relatives decided to check that the coffin was all right and found it missing. Urgent telexes were dispatched to Moscow, and an unfortunate secretary at the Chad embassy drove out to the airport only to find the coffin with his ambassador's body inside broiling on the tarmac in the summer sun. He had to use all his cash and powers of persuasion to get some workmen to take it inside.

The depths of disorganization are often hard to appreciate. One English friend was strikingly reminded of this after a long journey on the Trans-Siberian railway. He arrived at a remote hotel where he was supposed to stay to find it deserted and dilapidated. After several minutes calling and banging the desk he saw an ancient figure with a walrus white moustache shuffling in. 'It's no use your banging like that,' the old man grumbled reproachfully. 'It won't make any difference.' He paused. 'Russia is one big mess.'

It is equally hard to realize the lengths to which the party and central authorities go to try to enforce control. Conformity is instilled into every Russian from birth. The swaddling of babies, the clucking and fussing of grandmothers to ensure their charges do not slip their hands or frolic unchaperoned, the insistence at school on prescribed patterns of behaviour and learning by rote, the harsh discipline of the army – all this would seem enough to make any people pliantly conformist. But it is not. The Russians, it is true, have a marked collective instinct, a group mentality that baffles more independently minded Westerners. Sour-faced old grandmothers – *babushki* as they are universally known – have no hesitation at all in delivering stern lectures of reproach to complete strangers who they think are not behaving in a way they regard as seemly. But not everything can be controlled. And the party is ever fearful of exuberance, spontaneity, individualism or the setting up of any group, be it as innocent as a chess club or drama circle, where it does not supervise and organize what goes on.

The battle between order and chaos, control and freedom, discipline and corruption swings back and forth. But there is no mistaking the present trend, the crack-down that has marked the rule of Yuri Andropov. Things had slipped very far in the last torpid days of the Brezhnev regime. Consolidation had hardened into fossilisation, conservatism into brittle rigidity. The good life which détente had seemed to usher in receded ever further away as the economy stagnated and hopes for change were frustrated by the caution of an elderly leadership unwilling to risk radical steps to deal with the mounting social and economic problems. The era was plainly drawing to a close. In Moscow the prevailing mood was one of apathy. Old slogans and tested formulas were brought out to patch and botch the creaking system, but their effectiveness was lost in the face of falling industrial growth, a series of agricultural disasters, widespread corruption and a demoralized work-force. Time stood still for Russia.

This was the *fin de siècle* I observed as a correspondent. It was rather a depressing time because it was clear that change, when it came, would be painful. There was a malaise that showed itself in an astonishing growth of corruption at all levels, a cynicism that undermined all enterprise, a drift that led to sloppiness and shabbiness. The calls for a strong leader, for discipline and law and order became ever more insistent, especially among the ordinary people who were angered by food shortages and the blatant privileges of senior party officials and those with connections.

Western observers at the time could only guess that the next party secretary would be Yuri Andropov, and even then they had to rely on arcane hints, veiled signs and the simple elimination of other possibilities: such is the closed world of Soviet politics. But we could predict with greater certainty that whoever came after Brezhnev would have to act swiftly and firmly to establish his authority and would make the worsening economy and the general laxity his top concern. That has proved true. Andropov has changed the tone, reimposed firm control at the top with a series of well-publicised moves. Within a few months of taking office he ordered regular 'raids' on shops, bath-houses, cinemas and hairdressers to pounce on the thousands who were illegally skiving from work, imposing on-the-spot fines and setting a sombre example for others. He also ordered shops to stay open longer in the evenings to eliminate the need for office-hours shopping. He sacked dozens of elderly and incompetent bureaucrats, shook up the lethargic party apparatus, publicly laid the blame for shortcomings at the doors of senior ministers. He took steps to keep people better informed about the concerns of the leadership, issuing bulletins after the regular weekly meetings of the politburo, though keeping his own shadowy presence in the background. But above all he tightened up control: political, economic and ideological. Artists and the intelligentsia have been served warning that experiments are over, that loyalty and commitment to the party are publicly demanded. Factory managers have been warned that greater checks will be kept on what goes on in their enterprises. Dissidents, already the target of Andropov's relentless campaign against them as head of the KGB security police, have been all but silenced.

For Russia these measures promise a harsher, tougher climate. The intelligensia is nervous, fearful of a return to strict orthodoxy. But even those who now look back with regret at the relative liberality of the later Brezhnev years, recognize that something had to be done. And if Andropov is really to force through the economic changes and the new realism he appears to favour, he has to do so with an iron grip on all spheres of Soviet life.

But beneath the surface of these important new political accents, I wonder how much has changed in Andropov's first year or will change. Life in the Soviet Union is so slow-moving, so settled in its pattern and framework that it would take a political earthquake to make even a slight jolt in the habits and thinking of Russians. And these habits are older than ideology, more deeply rooted in Russian history and culture than most outside observers realize. It is only when you read the tales of travellers a hundred years ago that you fully appreciate the phrase 'eternal Russia'. So much has changed on the surface, so little deeper down.

What has been important in recent years has not always been noticed in the West. We have tended to concentrate on the protests of the dissidents, on human rights and individual liberty. It reflects our own concerns, but these are not the issues that are changing Soviet society. Partly for this reason I personally spent less time following the dissident scene, depleted as it was by exile, imprisonment and recantation, than many other Western colleagues. But partly also I felt more attention should be paid to the people pressing for change within the system: they might have greater effect in the long run. This is especially the case in the social field. Soviet officials now make no secret of their worries about the low birth-rate in European Russia, the soaring number of divorces, the family instability and the breakdown of traditional values. Perhaps only in the last five years has the press begun to discuss the sexual revolution that has crept up upon the country and taken its prudish leadership by surprise. And yet this, together with the influence of the West, is what is shaping Soviet youth today.

There are other areas of Soviet life which I have touched on only briefly but which are of crucial importance. One is military affairs. All information is hard to obtain in Russia, but military information is also dangerous. Sometimes Russians told me about their lives in the army, about the way they would drain brake fluid from tanks and filter it to make alcohol, about the difficulties with Central Asian conscripts who spoke little Russian and were resented by ethnic Russians, about the privileges of the officer class. But I never asked. Russians appear ready to believe that all foreigners are potential spies, and any journalist who tries to find out what really goes on in the civil defence exercises, what kind of political instruction is given in the army or the daily routine of a conscript would arouse immediate suspicion.

Similarly I have left out material on the political establishment and institutions. The structure of the party tells us far less about what actually happens than Soviet propagandists maintain, and in any case has been expertly analyzed in dozens of scholarly books. As for the KGB and the *nomenklatura*, as the senior officials of the party apparatus are called, their lives are secluded behind the fences of private dachas, within unmarked buildings. They are shadowy sources of power and authority which take care not to let outsiders, and especially foreigners, into their world. The KGB, of course, is everywhere in Russia and many was the contact and even the occasional friend whom I suspected of informing on me, keeping a check on whom I saw and what I did. The Soviet Union is a totalitarian state and as the enforcers of political repression the KGB is a feared and fearful organization. Ironically however this does not mean that it does not attract some of the brightest talent – especially in Andropov's Russia – or number among its members the most urbane, intelligent and sophisticated officials, the kind of people I found stimulating and worthwhile talking to because only they had the self-assurance and authority to speak frankly – or reasonably frankly – and drop the mumbo-jumbo of propaganda clichés. But it was impossible officially to enter into the real world of the senior party officials and the KGB. For them, contact with foreigners was absolutely taboo. They had too much to fear from exposure, were instructed not to allow public revelation of their perks and privileges – special shops, closed performances of forbidden Western films, private polyclinics to serve the Kremlin élite, lives where everything is regulated by rank and power down to the amount of imported liquor that can be purchased in the unmarked party stores. It does not tally with the propaganda picture of Marxist egalitarianism. It draws unwelcome attention to the gap between rulers and the ruled. It raises questions that are anathema to the party about the popularity and legitimacy of its rule, the basis for its monopoly of power and the overriding concern of the *nachalstvo* – the bosses – to keep themselves in power.

My contacts were with the less privileged, with people far from power who knew little and cared less about politics. Of course all those I met on a regular basis were within the magic circle of people permitted – or tolerated – to meet foreigners. Few Russians run the risk of strolling past the police posted at the entranceway to every foreigners' compound, and Russians who did not hold senior positions or carry official invitations had to be escorted in and out of our ghetto if they were not to be stopped and asked to produce their papers. (That occasionally happened after they had left, in any case.)

Many of those I talked to were people I met on chance encounters – on trains (a favourite Russian place for gossip, where you can spend hours talking to complete strangers about their lives), in the offices of bureaucrats, on picnics, on visits around the country. They were almost always fascinated to meet a Westerner, appeared anxious to be hospitable and demonstrate goodwill and warm feelings, but were invariably cautious. There was always that tell-tale glance over the shoulder, that reluctance to be overheard talking to someone who looked and sounded like an outsider. The habits of a generation brought up under Stalin do not die quickly. I quickly understood that the spontaneous invitations were often better not taken up, that an evening of fascinating and uninhibited conversation with chance acquaintances could not be repeated.

Yet from almost all those I knew or met I had the impression that a great political and cultural gulf separates our two worlds. To reach through to the warmth of human feelings of many Russians (I emphatically do not include the hypocritical and self-righteous propagandists and those whose job it is to 'look after' foreigners) is not difficult; to understand and sympathize with their way of thinking is infinitely harder.

My wife and I left Moscow with genuine nostalgia: we experienced some of the pain Soviet exiles feel when they know they will never return to the self-enclosed world they both love and hate. Russia is a country that demands constant effort. It demands patience, tolerance, and a sense of humour. It is a country of hardship, frustration and oppression, insecure at home, encircled by enemies abroad, facing an uncertain future and grappling with political and economic difficulties that look awesomely intractable. But it is also a country where life has an intensity and sharpness that few know in the West. Shorn of the affluent ease that cocoons us in the West, personal relationships seem stronger, values, emotions and choices harsher and more real.

One has only to look back and see that none of this is new. Similar problems, dilemmas and preoccupations have occurred again and again in Russian history. And the Russian people have reacted in ways that seem determined by their own peculiar experiences, their turbulent past. It is the pattern of life that moulds the Russian's outlook that we know so little about in the West. From this, it seems to me, we can learn a hundred times more about Soviet behaviour on the international stage than we can from a whole library of dusty declarations by Tass.

CHAPTER ONE

The Tyranny of the Plan

Shortly before I left Moscow a small item appeared in one paper to the effect that a factory in the Ukraine had been severely reproved for producing 13,000 pairs of sunglasses so dark that you could not see the sun through them even when looking directly at it, and manufacturing thousands of children's plastic balls that burst like soap bubbles as soon as they were kicked. The bland report seemed to sum up the problems of the Soviet economy and the monumental task awaiting Yuri Andropov and those who wish to introduce reform. Why did the factory start production of items clearly so badly designed? Why had it continued producing such quantities of goods of no use to anybody? Why was there no quality control? How did the factory make any profits?

To a Westerner the most astonishing thing is the waste involved. But to a Russian this is neither surprising nor unusual. Almost every day he encounters the results of an economic bureaucracy that seems designed to generate waste and defy logic. One can take random examples from daily observation or from the press. Over half of all the milk sold in cardboard cartons in Moscow was bad or sour, one paper noted, because the packaging machinery, crudely repaired with improvised spare parts, tore a hole in most of the cartons. One dairy plant received 7,000 complaints in the first half of 1981 but ignored them all. Another example – on any summer evening tanker trucks prowl around the big cities washing the streets – and continue doing so even during a thunderstorm. Or again, each day a fully loaded freight train from Moscow takes concrete roof beams to construction sites in Leningrad, passing on its way a train from Leningrad carrying concrete beams to construction sites in Moscow.

Communism at heart is an economic system, one that its ideologists maintain is better, fairer and more productive than capitalism. Yet it is clear to most Russians, and certainly to experts who see the figures, that the Soviet economy is in a mess. The system has become so unwieldy that it is almost impossible for planners in Moscow to keep track of what is going on and to oversee the operations of individual factories some 2,000 miles away. Yet any change in the structure of the economy is difficult, for it immediately raises ideological hackles, and is seen as a threat to the principles of collective ownership and central planning. Many a well-read expert has called for decentralisation, greater flexibility, even moves towards a market economy, realistic prices corresponding to manufacturing costs, limited private enterprise and even some form of unemployment in all but name. But the Brezhnev regime, having seen its early attempts at reform in 1965 run into a bog of bureaucratic opposition, lost heart, and instead issued decrees that simply tightened up existing regulations or urged greater incentives without giving factories the freedom to implement them. Mr Andropov, almost on assuming office, was more candid than his predecessor was in years in stating that the economy was not performing properly, and changes had to be made.

But two things frustrate all efforts to squeeze better results from what is one of the world's biggest economies: the lack of real incentives and the tyranny of the Plan. The factory manufacturing the impenetrable sunglasses did not need to compete with rivals to capture a share of the market; it needed only to turn out the number of items assigned to it under its yearly Plan. If it failed, there would be penalties, party reprimands and possible sanctions against the bosses; if it succeeded in going beyond the targets set, there would be a bonus for all the workers. For almost every factory, fulfilling the Plan is the only criterion, and quality control is lost in the scramble to turn out the requisite number of products.

But earning the precious bonuses is not easy. The State Planning Committee periodically raises the targets in an effort to make industry more efficient; and bottlenecks in the supply of raw materials and components means that on many days most factories are unable to work at full capacity. The result is that when supplies finally arrive – and often they have to be winkled out of suppliers by desperate factory directors offering substantial bribes and employing full-time *tolkachi* (pushers) to speed the flow of deliveries – there are only a few days to fulfil the monthly targets. The factory works round the clock, there is no time to check or control anything and the finished articles are so sloppily made that at least half are defective. But this does not matter: retail outlets have little legal redress, and the consumer has virtually no alternative, so the products enter the market. The end of the month rush is called 'storming the Plan', and has become a vicious circle, as most factories are for ever waiting for deliveries from another, which in turn waits for suppliers from elsewhere. Russians try to avoid buying things made at the end of the month as they are bound to be faulty.

Sometimes a harassed plant manager knows he does not have the slightest chance of achieving an unrealistic yearly target. But in the Soviet Union there is always a way of beating the system however draconian its regulations. One factory, for example, divided the annual target into one huge portion for December and eleven modest monthly totals. From January until November the targets were easily overful-filled, giving the workers regular monthly bonuses. But in December the factory had no hope of achieving a fraction of its target, and so that month was written off. But at least everyone had earned more than they would have if the year's total had been divided into twelve equal portions.

Because of the serious consequences of failing to fulfil the Plan, every manager tries to hoard whatever tools, materials and labour he can in case of a breakdown or unexpected interruptions in supplies. Enormous quantities of perishable materials lie around, often rusting or spoiled by being left outside in the rain. So many extra workers are employed to ensure an adequate workforce in each plant – as well as to compensate for endemic absenteeism, drunkenness and the need to send workers out to help in the fields at harvest time – that there is actually a labour shortage in most parts of the country, in spite of the inefficient use of manpower.

It is not only manufacturing industries that are governed by the Plan. Every aspect of the economy has its target – restaurants have so many meals to serve, painters so many square metres of wall to cover, taxi drivers so many journeys to make and so on. This produces particularly bizarre results in transport, as empty trains rattle round the network to achieve the requisite monthly mileage. An example from the small republic of Moldavia, near the Romanian border, serves to illustrate some of the problems.

In August 1979 responsibility for the line from Kishinyov, the Moldavian capital, to the nearby port of Odessa in the Ukraine was divided. On the first day of the new agreement a train set out from Kishinyov, crossed the border into the newly independent Odessa administrative zone and disappeared. When the locomotive failed to return to its home depot in Moldavia, the alarm was raised. Inquiries were made, there were telephone calls and telegrams. Matters were becoming urgent. Moldavia had just harvested a large crop of fruit and vegetables which had to be shipped quickly before they went bad, and a full complement of locomotives was needed to transport them to Siberia and the Far East.

It turned out that the train had not just disappeared. It had been captured. The moment it crossed into the Odessa railway zone, the railway workers had seen their chance. They commandeered the engine and set it to work on their line. Now they could not only fulfil their plan, but overfulfil it and win a handsome bonus. It was not the only locomotive to disappear: all the subsequent trains to Odessa also failed to return. So the Moldavians appealed to the locomotive factory for help, and it responded by sending three of its newest models. The snag was that the line to Moldavia passed through the Odessa network. Not surprisingly, locomotives ZTE 10V numbers 0001 to 0003 never turned up, having been also kidnapped en route.

The Moldavians then phoned the head of the Odessa system. 'I'll look into it,' he said, and immediately put the matter out of his mind. So in despair they contacted the Ministry of Transport in Moscow. And that brought a reaction. A telegram was dispatched to Odessa with a warning that unless the three new locos were sent to Moldavia within twenty-four hours, the matter would be referred to 'the highest authorities'. Nothing happened. The Moldavians waited in vain for their trains, and sent more urgent telegrams to Moscow. There was consternation at the Ministry: it was unheard of to ignore an order that had come from 'the highest authorities'. Ministerial thunder reverberated in Odessa, and locomotive 0003 was eventually released. But all the others remained prisoners. And it was only after a raid into Odessan territory that the Moldavians eventually found them, carefully hidden away on branch lines, helping the Odessans get ahead with their freight targets.

Pravda, which recounted this story with glee, asked the pertinent question how it was possible that ministerial decrees could be so brazenly flouted. But in fact this happens all the time, and sometimes it is the ministers themselves who disobey orders from higher up. A Soviet deputy oil minister was sacked in a blaze of unusual publicity for knowingly allowing millions of roubles worth of imported chemicals and machinery for the vital oil industry to go to rust, and for falsifying figures to cover up his negligence in failing to carry out a government order to increase oil production. Periodically high officials are named and chastised for the poor performances in their departments. But such publicised reproofs – *pour encourager les autres* – are really only a search for scapegoats. No minister is able to guarantee that his orders will be carried out or are even feasible further down the line. A story from Minsk illustrates the point.

Some years ago an enterprising director of the Minsk Regional Electricity Authority, won over by calls for new initiative in technology, decided to install a computer. Hoping to win acclaim from his superiors, he ordered one of the largest models, and after much persuasive talk the ministry in Moscow sanctioned the expensive purchase. However, nobody in the Authority knew much about computers, so they wrote for advice to the Institute of Power Plant Construction in Novosibirsk, 2,000 miles away. The Institute asked about the nature of the Authority's functions, and then expressed surprise that it had bought such a complex machine capable of handling thirty-one different tasks when in fact no more than eight were needed. It offered nevertheless to write the required programmes. But the director could not wait for them all, and requested only five. Of those, three were incorrectly drawn up, so the authority was left with two: a weekly print-out to check that what was actually carried out corresponded to the director's orders, and a computerised estimate of the cost of new power stations.

After a few months dissatisfaction began to reverberate through the workforce. No one welcomed the daily print-out, which told the director what had not been done by his subordinates. And so they began to feed the computer misleading information so that its results would not look so bad. And the other programme simply doubled the workload, as the director of the section did not trust such a new-fangled machine, and as a safeguard made his staff do all the calculations in the traditional manner as well. Soon the discontent became general, and it was agreed by the director that they would be better off without the computer. But he could not scrap it without harming his newly-earned reputation as a go-ahead innovator. So he cut back the staff in the computer section from twenty-seven to seven, hoping it would simply wither away, and one day the Authority put a discreet advertisement in the local paper announcing 'One computer for sale, complete with spare parts.'

The authorities see the erratic performance in manufacturing industries as a problem of labour discipline. Workers do not work properly, they complain, and the measures to make them do so are not tough enough. They arrive late, often drunk, ignore instructions and frequently go absent. 'It used to be possible to sack a person who worked poorly,' the editor of an industrial magazine told a round-table conference on the problem in 1982. 'Nowadays such a decision is more costly: you have to hire someone new and train him, and your work unit will suffer. Just try to sack an excavator operator today! You'll think twice before taking such a step.'

But low morale on the shop floor is often the result of managerial incompetence, for in the Soviet Union there is little proper management training. Dzhermen Gvishiani, the silver-haired Georgian son-in-law of former prime minister Alexei Kosygin, is one of the few enterprising officials who has any real concept of management in the competitive, efficient Western sense. As deputy head of the State Committee on Science and Technology, he has tried to promote the kind of all-round training that management institutes offer in the West. But most bosses simply rely on coercion and administrative fiat. And they have little interest in setting an example. The press is full of stories of wild office parties during working hours held at the smallest excuse – birthdays, anniversaries, the registration of a new flat, even, according to one press account, the end of the salted cabbage season, which was marked in one enterprise in the Far East with a huge binge costing several thousand roubles.

Attacks on such carousing and drinking by factory directors and their cronies are most effectively made in the form of satire – for which Russians have a keen appreciation – and one memorable article by a leading satirist, Ustin Malapagin, stands out in my mind. He wanted to write a piece defining working time, and to find out what was accomplished in a typical factory. So for three days he telephoned a selected factory to make an appointment with the director. Each time a pleasant female voice answered that Boris Mikhailovich was out – he had just left, he had not yet arrived, he would be in after lunch, he was called to head office, he was opening something, meeting a delegation, heading a delegation – anyway, call again please. Malapagin decided the best thing was to go to the director's office in person and catch him.

It turned out the owner of the pleasant voice was a lady of uncertain age, hair colour and occupation who rejoiced in the name of Flora. Her main task was to pick up the various different coloured phones on her desk and tell callers Boris Mikhailovich was out. (Soviet offices do not have internal switchboards. Instead, the more senior the official, the more phones he has on his desk. I remember seeing at least five in the ante-room to Brezhnev's study in the Kremlin.) For the rest of the day she was engaged in four simultaneous occupations: typing, talking, listening and knitting. She did the work of a whole brigade of secretaries. In one day she told seventy-six callers that the director was not in, knitted a maxi-pullover and then a mini-dress, purchased – over the phone – a kilo of mincemeat, two much sought-after shirts (exchanging one for three ties), and collected 20 kilos of waste-paper for the city's recycling scheme, obtaining in return two volumes from a series of popular novels. During the lunch break, leaving the patient journalist by the phones, she hurried off to the museum to have a look at the exhibition of Spanish art treasures. And on the dot of six o'clock she took her mince and two jars of pickled peppers out of the office refrigerator and bade farewell.

The next day the pattern was repeated, only on this occasion Flora knitted a pair of trousers and instead of peppers she took home jars of pineapple. On the third day Malapagin made some progress: twice he spotted the director's fur hat, and three times heard his voice over the intercom, but there was no time to catch an interview. After a few more days the office staff got used to him: the porter no longer asked to see his pass when he appeared in the mornings, and he was persuaded to buy three office lottery tickets. At the end of the week he had already begun to take part in the daily morning exercises.

The gymnastics, intended to keep all citizens fit and healthy, take place in Soviet factories at 11.00 and 1.00, when the windows are thrown open and everyone swings his or her body around in time to the music on the radio. But things were more relaxed in this office. At 11.00 they turned on the radio, opened the windows and then went into the corridor to smoke. Here the real business of the day was transacted. Standing for half an hour under the slogan 'One minute of work saves an hour', the office staff discussed who was getting married, changing jobs, what had been on television and other such important topics. Malapagin decided to put his question about working hours. Did smoking constitute work or not? Opinion was divided. One person opined that if the smoker stood on the steps of his factory, this constituted work, but if he smoked in the street, that was his free time. Another said the smoking interval was overtime and should be paid double. The discussion was just heating up when Flora announced the director had arrived.

Now or never, he thought. He nipped across the road to get some chocolates and carnations, and in a mood to brook no argument, pressed them on Flora. 'Oh you shouldn't have,' she said. 'Is it very, very urgent that you see Boris Mikhailovich? In that case, here are the directions how to get there.' Malapagin asked which ministry he was in. Flora looked astonished. 'Ministry? No, no, he's in the steam bath.' She then explained that he was not in any ordinary bath, but in one decorated with Brazilian marble – like Pelé's. There were angled showerheads, a bidet large enough for three and bath essence. 'Who goes to the baths nowadays to wash himself?' she asked. 'People go there for cultural enrichment and conversation.' No self-respecting factory was without its own baths, she went on. They had lost all sanitary significance and were now 'an interdepartmental centre for co-operation in various economic sectors'.

No enterprise, however small, could function without its own baths, or, as Boris Mikhailovich more fashionably termed them, saunas. She professed astonishment at the journalist's lack of understanding of Soviet business etiquette. Most transactions were nowadays conducted in the sauna, which was replacing the more traditional Russian steam baths 'as samples and equipment do not rust in the sauna's dry heat'.

Malapagin's interview with the director was conducted on the highest level: the top bench of the sauna. 'Working time?' he mused. 'Well, supposing you were a director and an inspector arrived from the ministry, or a budget controller. You understand his function? So where would you take him to create a good impression, the right psychological atmosphere? In your office? I personally have a reflex action to shout at anyone I see in my office. In a restaurant? That might be misunderstood by those sitting near. You need a neutral place like a sauna, where there's no pomposity, no hint of bribery.' In any case, the director added, in the heat, the fresh aromatic air, the sparkling tiles, with the music of Abba playing gently in the background, any high official began to 'melt'. It was also a scientific fact that two naked people understood each other better than two clothed people. And afterwards, he explained, you arrange a fine feast of fish and delicacies in the cooling-off room, tell a few jokes and time stands still – even working time. Whatever problem the inspector brought down to the factory then soon disappears.

Malapagin confessed he was nonplussed, and found it harder and harder to define working time. He wondered whether any factory could get along without a man like Boris Mikhailovich. He took a cold shower, and decided to ask kindergarten children how they would define working time.

His delicious satire, true in more details than any factory director would care to admit, throws light on the Soviet equivalent of the expense-account lunch. (I indeed have seen a splendid sauna, complete with new tiles and imported fitments, attached to the administrative headquarters of a model collective farm in Estonia.) The satire also explains why so little ever seems to get done in a Soviet office, as there are countless Floras all over the country who genuinely believe that such a life constitutes a normal working day.

I discussed the problem of getting Russians to work hard with a young friend who spoke passionately and despairingly about his countrymen's attitudes. 'We have first to change the whole mentality of our people,' he said. 'They don't work because they don't need to. Wages are not high, but all basic commodities are very cheap, and our state looks after our people. No one will starve if he doesn't work, no one will be unemployed. Nothing will happen to him if he gets drunk, or doesn't turn up on time. Our workers have no incentive, but also no fear of being sacked. I want to work – I want to do well. But most people have no interest in their jobs and too much security. We should be much harsher.'

He said this only a few months before Brezhnev's death, and anticipated similar sentiments, voiced officially, by the new regime. For many years those in positions of power have advocated tougher measures to combat labour indiscipline. Perhaps the most daring is an outspoken professor at Moscow State University, Gavriil Popov. In 1980 he came close to issuing an open call for a system of unemployment – something the Russians boast they have not known for fifty years. He argued that only by creating a pool of temporarily unemployed workers would the state be able to reduce the overmanning in industry while releasing much-needed labour for reassignment to Siberia and other priority development areas. At the same time, he said, the threat of dismissal would galvanize lazy workers into greater productivity. He called for an extension to the vaunted Shchekino experiment, which was an attempt to stop industry hoarding labour. Instead of receiving the usual overhead payments based on the size of the workforce – which means the more people a factory employs, the more clubs and amenities it can afford – a chemical plant at Shchekino, a town about 100 miles south of Moscow, was given a bonus for every worker it dismissed. The bonuses were used to increase the wages of those remaining and to introduce automation to make it possible to get rid of more workers. Meanwhile a parallel plant that was starting up took on those who had left the chemical works.

Much has been written about this system, officially declared a success after six years, but so far its application is limited to about 1,000 factories. The drawback, of course, is that to avoid unemployment there has to be a guaranteed job nearby for the redundant workers to go to. Professor Popov called for something much more radical: a pool of

temporarily unemployed men, paid only the minimum wage of 80
roubles a month, who could be used as extra casual labour repairing
streets and working on farms until they found a new job suited to their
qualifications. Factories would then have no qualms about sacking bad
workers, and this would have the salutory effect of spurring people to
work harder. Popov admitted that this was harsh medicine, but quoted
Lenin – always a safe way of backing up any argument – who declared in
1921 that only those who work should eat. Popov also wanted to see
much greater differentials in wages, so that those who worked well could
be properly rewarded, while drunkards would earn no more than their
idleness merited.

Such suggestions are still too radical for a system deeply suspicious of
anything that smacks of capitalism. But there are moves in that direction.
A decree in 1980 laid down firmer punishment for idlers and drunkards,
and ordered factory directors to be less tolerant of absenteeism, the bane
of all Soviet enterprises. Sociologists who have studied the way people
take time off illegally from work to do their shopping, wait in queues and
arrange their personal affairs, find the loss of productive time runs into
millions of man-hours. Another factor preventing the formation of a
stable workforce is the high turnover rate. From 1940 until after Stalin's
death it was a criminal offence to leave one's place of work without
official sanction. But since 1956 people have been allowed to quit their
jobs voluntarily, and since then the annual turnover rates have hovered
between 19 and 20 per cent. If 'acceptable' reasons for leaving are
included, such as military service, retirement and the ending of temporary work, the rate goes up to 30 per cent; that is, almost one in every
three workers leaves his job each year. In the construction industry this
figure is as high as 60 per cent.

Experts have estimated that it takes people a month before they start a
new job, and then up to three months before reaching the production
levels of their colleagues. The waste in working time and in money spent
on training is considerable. The 1980 decree offered extra holidays,
bonuses and higher pensions to those staying in their jobs provided they
were not regularly absent during working hours. But it did nothing to
create any real career structure for a young worker in most factories, nor
induce real loyalty to people's places of work. Most workers know that
when they get bored they can leave, and they will still find another job.

The fundamental difficulty in changing this attitude is the underlying
assumption about work. It is officially regarded not as a way of getting
rich and getting ahead, as communist ideologists maintain is the case in

the West, but as the social duty of each citizen to the community. By law every Russian who is employable, apart from women with young children, has to hold a job or else face prosecution as a 'parasite'. Work, according to communist thinking, is essentially altruistic, for the benefit of everyone. Countless slogans extol 'heroic labour', and the dignity of work in an attempt not just to make people work harder, but to link the idea of work with patriotism, selflessness and other noble qualities. Good workers are not rewarded with the chance to become rich, but with honour and public praise. Every Soviet factory has a display board with the photographs of 'our outstanding workers', and often in parks in city centres you come across a tableau that looks like a rogues' gallery – assembled portraits, always unsmiling, of those who have overfulfilled their plans by some spectacular percentage.

None of this provides much incentive however. Unfortunately paying higher wages is not much help either. Money has ceased to have much real value in many people's eyes. There are too many roubles in circulation and not enough to spend them on. The result is an extraordinary amount of money in savings banks and a general indifference to wage rises – unless they are very large, such as the salaries paid to attract workers out to Siberia.

The average wage is still only about 170 roubles (£113) a month, which is low by Western standards. But basic commodities, and services, such as rent, fuel, transport, medicine and food are either free or heavily subsidized, and families where both adults work often accumulate money which they do not know how to spend. Deposits in savings banks, the only kind of banks open to the ordinary citizen, now amount to more than 130,000 million roubles, 131 times more than in 1950. In those days the average deposit for each person was just over 10 roubles; now it is more than 500. Many people have expressed concern that this money, earning 2 per cent interest a year, is dislocating the economy. The steady growth of savings has affected money circulation, and the conversion of money into savings and back into cash makes it difficult to balance consumer demand with available goods.

Since straight bonus payments are of only marginal use as incentive payments, a 'socialist competition' scheme has been instituted, which pits different factories against each other and rewards the most efficient with bonuses that are paid not just in straight cash but in coupons which entitle the bearer to shop in some of the special outlets carrying better goods and a range of imported consumer items and food. The disadvantage of this scheme as a general incentive is that by definition it rewards only a few, thus excluding large numbers who know they have no hope of winning and no interest therefore in working harder.

The answer everyone comes up with is always the same: boost the output of consumer goods to give people something to spend their money on. But this is not going to happen for a long time. Some experts have therefore suggested soaking up roubles in other ways, with more co-operative housing (where the owners have to pay sums ranging from 10,000 to 20,000 roubles, and actually buy their flats), more country dachas and garages, two-tier consumer services where customers would pay a premium for priority in buying air tickets, car repairs, express cleaning and so on. At present there is an unofficial premium in that the only way to get any priority service is to pay a fat bribe to the sales assistant, booking clerk, and garage mechanic. If money replaced unofficial 'favours' as a way of obtaining things in short supply, the basis for the all-pervasive corruption and bribery would be weakened. But again, adopting such capitalist market mechanisms as rationing by price is ideologically too difficult.

Both carrots and sticks are used to boost productivity. Factories try to buy the loyalty of workers by improving conditions, sometimes with re-markable success. A piston factory in the Crimea suffering from the usual turnover, absenteeism and noisy, dirty surroundings decided to raise the low morale of the mainly female workforce by making them look and feel better. It set up a hairdresser's saloon in the factory, offering hair-dos and manicure during working hours. The effect was immediate: women exhausted by housework and with no time to look after themselves used to be moody and quarrelsome, but after regular coiffeuring began to take pride in themselves and their surroundings and the atmosphere improved. The factory then opened a bookshop and employed a librarian to organize discussions, lectures and social evenings. Talk on the shop-floor changed from routine exhortations to fulfil the plan to debates on style and taste. The director brought in a seamstress to run up some elegant working clothes. Next came a shoe repair section, evening classes, physiotherapy units, a dentist, cake shop, café, fruiterer, fishmonger and so on. The labour turnover began to slow down as staff loyalty grew. Absenteeism fell twenty times over a decade and produc-tion increased. The factory built comfortably furnished hostels for its young workers and even employed someone whose sole job was to scour the local shops, using his wits and connections to obtain for the workers goods that were in short supply.

The moral of this idyllic tale, publicized in the press, is that a

commitment to the welfare and personal lives of workers can pro
good results. Indeed I have visited some factories that seem al
Japanese in their provision for their employees – comfortably furnished
relaxation rooms, crèches and kindergartens, large reception halls for
weddings and parties, and health clinics with special baths, massage
rooms and other apparatus for 'prophylactic care' which Russians take
so seriously. Well-off factories and collective farms spend large sums on
social amenities, putting on concerts and film shows, sponsoring ath-
letics clubs and football teams, arranging discothèques and parties for
young workers. Experiments have begun giving long-distance lorry
drivers two or three hours rest in specially equipped relaxation rooms in
an attempt to improve their mood and performance. One steelmill wrote
to *Pravda* to say how ten old-fashioned samovars had been bought to
serve tea in a relaxation room where workers could cool off after shifts.
This had proved more popular than the bar serving beer, and helped cut
down drunkenness.

Such attempts to generate worker loyalty are usually the initiative of a
few far-sighted individuals and local party bosses. But social and welfare
issues are generally the responsibility of the trade unions. Indeed, they
have little other independent function. The Soviet constitution gives the
unions an official role along with management in running an enterprise,
in formulating labour law and in working out quotas for individual
factories. But in practice this means telling the workers what the
management – and more particularly the party, which controls the
management – has decided and making sure that this is implemented. In
theory the unions are meant to protect their members' interests against
the management, but in fact they never challenge party policy. Not one
of the estimated 130 million Soviet trade unionists has ever gone on
strike.

Where the unions do have limited room for independent manoeuvre
is in dealing with individual cases. A worker who gets the sack can appeal
to the union to have his case reviewed; factory managers who break
safety regulations, notoriously lax by Western standards, can be taken to
court by union officials, provided of course the party concurs in such an
unusual step. And the payment of bonuses is often left to the unions to
determine. But all unions spend most of their time and money arranging
sports and recreation facilities, holidays to the sanitoria and Black Sea
resort homes for members, who pay only a quarter of the cost, and
organizing summer camps for children.

Surprisingly, union membership is not compulsory, though workers are strongly urged to join, and those that do not will soon find they get nowhere in their jobs. Membership is on the principle of everyone in a single factory belonging to one union, and each union embraces workers in a particular branch of the economy – machine builders, or workers in the food industry, for example. Trade unions have the right to nominate candidates for election to the Supreme Soviet, the equivalent of parliament in name but not in function. They also frequently call shop-floor meetings, where attendance is compulsory, where party policies are explained and poor workers publicly reprimanded. This political activity means little to the average worker, who regards the meetings as a dull obligation; and the elections are a foregone conclusion.

Lenin saw the unions as 'transmission belts', passing on party policy to the workers, and certainly did not envisage any independent political activity by them. It came as a rude shock to the authorities in 1977 when a number of disgruntled workers who had been sacked from their jobs got together to form an 'independent' union. The KGB moved quickly to suppress the organization. The leaders were exiled from Moscow, questioned, harassed, arrested and a few of them, including the unofficial initiator, Vladimir Klebanov, were sent to psychiatric hospitals. But things became much more serious three years later when Solidarity was born in Poland. The Russians saw this as a dangerous challenge to their own docile unions as well as a threat to their political system. They had already been shaken by workers' protests at the giant truck and car factories on the Volga – though these hardly amounted to all-out strikes as the Western press reported at the time.

The Soviet response was to try to galvanize the moribund unions into at least the appearance of independence and activity. The colourless head of the Central Trade Union Council, Alexei Shibayev, was peremptorily sacked a few days before the opening of the five-yearly congress of the trade unions in 1982, being replaced by a younger and apparently better qualified union official, Stepan Shalayev. Brezhnev launched a blistering attack on union officials for laziness and indifference to their members' needs, and there were warnings that union officials who connived with management to impose illegal conditions on workers faced prosecution.

But in fact the party has no intention of giving trade unions powerful weapons to oppose management; instead, the unions are being urged behind closed doors to get tough on labour discipline, to redouble efforts to get higher productivity, cut waste and improve the quality of output. Workers who raise inconvenient objections or attempt to oppose management will get short shrift, and with the general toughening up as the economy falters, trade unions are cracking down on their members.

Ever since the Revolution, the Soviet economy has been able to register high growth by large investment and regular additions to the workforce. But this era is now at an end. With the demands of defence and agriculture, investment money for industry is tight, and labour is already short. All future growth will have to come from increased efficiency, as the message at the 1981 party congress made bluntly clear. And this means cutting waste. That will be very difficult for the Russians, brought up with little conception of waste or the real cost of things. They are used to turning the gas stove on to warm the kitchen, leaving hot taps running, throwing away food (even when it is in short supply), and feeding fresh bread to their ducks and hens. It is all the more difficult to husband resources on a national scale, as no one thinks of state property as having any value. Little care is taken to clean and maintain equipment, protect machinery from rain or dirt, make timely use of a product before it spoils. Western businessmen have many stories of expensive equipment lying rusting outside because no one has bothered to move it indoors, of imported machinery remaining packed in boxes for two or three years because it is neither understood nor needed. An investigation in the Ukraine once discovered huge mountains of fertiliser that lay beside each railway station because the collective farms for which it was intended had never bothered to send lorries to the stations to pick it up.

Stealing from the state is scarcely regarded as stealing, and no one worries at the huge losses resulting from careless handling and breakages – millions of gallons of hot water pouring out of broken pipes, fruit rotting after being piled up with a shovel, bags of cement powder being left out in the rain. There are countless instances of bureaucratic waste – flats being expensively decorated and repaired a few months before the entire block is demolished, houses built so hurriedly to meet the target date that the walls and plaster crack and major repairs are needed within the first few months. Shortly before I left Moscow in 1982 Soviet television caused an unexpected sensation. During the evening news a correspondent was interviewing a manager of a Japanese factory where robots were widely used, something the Russians are now considering as a serious answer to the labour shortage. He asked the manager how long the system had been installed. Ten years, he replied. What did they do, the reporter asked, when the system broke down? The Japanese looked uncomprehending: it did not break down. The reporter in turn thought he had misunderstood, and tried again: what arrangements were made for the annual overhaul and replacement of defective parts? Again, the manager insisted this had never happened. At this the correspondent was openly incredulous. 'Do you mean this system has worked for ten years without needing to be repaired?' he asked, and all Russia shared his astonishment. The idea of factory machinery working that efficiently was hard to grasp. Almost everything needs mending frequently in the Soviet Union, and the word 'remont', denoting a cross between repairing, reconstruction or just patching up, has indelibly entered the vocabulary of every foreigner living in Moscow.

Every summer the hot water system in Soviet cities is switched off for at least three weeks while a 'prophylactic remont' is carried out to prepare for the long winter. The problem is that all such repairs take a long time. Workers lose interest halfway through, or are called out on some other priority. People wanting their flats repaired have to lay in a good stock of vodka as an incentive for workmen to turn up, and plumbers and electricians as a result appear to be permanently drunk. I remember when it was decided to install new lifts in one of the blocks of flats reserved for foreigners. A lot of expensive and delicate machinery was delivered to the yard outside and lay there for two wet autumn months, getting rained on each day. Eventually workmen came to install the new lifts, replacing the old clanging, hand-closed doors with swish cabins with automatic doors. But from that moment on the new lift failed, trapping at least one person in it each week until the workers could be persuaded to return for a 'remont'. In the same block the voltage was being altered once (old blocks still have 127 volts compared with the standard 220) by a man swaying acrobatically on a stepladder whose attempts to point the torch in the right direction were a little the worse for drink. After his task was done, the inhabitants found all the telephones had been connected to the telex lines and vice versa. Reuters was incommunicado and consequently there was little news out of Moscow for almost a day.

Most buildings are regularly given a 'capital remont', including even the Lenin mausoleum. Infuriatingly, cafés and museums often display large notices on the door, 'Closed for remont'. Piles of wood lying around usually indicate, at least in theory, that work is in progress. It is a good sign if women are walking about in what look like combat fatigues – they are the painters, camouflaged in splashed dungarees and hats. They operate with buckets and long-handled paint brooms, sloshing paint cheerfully on everything in sight, but at least they are more sober than their male counterparts. Their presence means the remont is almost over.

In the Soviet system even small repairs are state-run, and there are special 'remont' shops for shoes, watches, household goods and metal objects. Some, such as shoe repairers, provide good and cheap service. Metal repairers can handle spare keys or ski fixings, though are of little help in mending broken household goods. A lot of repairs – especially of cars – are done privately on the side, and very profitably, by mechanics during working hours. This is so widespread, and so costly in state time and materials, that there are now calls for licensed privately-run workshops to take over this function, as elsewhere in Eastern Europe. But until now the danger of ideological contamination has been deemed too great. If entrepreneurs started repairing umbrellas themselves, they might end up manufacturing and selling new ones, ideologists argue. This, of course, is already happening: privately-run underground workshops, stealing their materials from state supplies and run by fraudulently altering the records of the factories to which they are attached and by bribing the inspectors, have an enormous output of sought-after consumer goods, especially the smaller cheaper items. Such goods find their way on to the black market, but everyone acknowledges that without them ordinary people, as well as factories and offices, would find it hard to obtain many essential items.

The spirit of private enterprise throughout the Soviet Union, and especially in Georgia and Armenia, is remarkably vigorous still, despite all the obstacles placed in the way of individual initiative, and it is this spirit that is able to harness and channel energies which most Russians would not dream of devoting to ordinary legal work. But at the same time there are thousands of people who never work, despite the criminal charges and social disgrace hanging over 'parasites'.

Yuri Antonov was one such parasite. He lived in a small storeroom in his parents' house in Voronezh for over a year. About once a week he ventured furtively outside, took a few breaths of air and dashed back indoors, glancing round to see that no one had seen him. Every few months or so a policeman used to come to the house and call out for him, but his mother refused to let the policeman in without a warrant. The officer knew the son was hiding inside, but had no eye-witness proof from the neighbours. Antonov, a plumber in his early thirties, had not deserted from the army or done anything for which he could have been punished in the West. Indeed, he had not done anything for a year – and that was why he faced imprisonment as an idler. He refused to apply for the many plumbing jobs advertised in Voronezh, preferring to spend his time cooped up at home.

Under Soviet law a citizen may be legally instructed to look for work only if he has been idle without good cause for four consecutive months. He is then given a month to find a position, and after that is liable to arrest. Most workshy people find a job at the last moment. They register their employment with the police, begin at a factory and then a week later slip away without a word to anyone. Four more months pass, and if they are traced the process starts again.

People like Antonov are regarded as malingerers, anti-social elements who take advantage of the law to escape their obligations to work. And as the labour shortage worsens, so the campaign against them has intensified. Articles have portrayed idle young men as sick, filled with self-delusion and protected by indulgent wives or mothers. Vladimir Popov, for example, was known as the 'fish-farmer' to the local Voronezh police. A college drop-out, his only passion was breeding tropical fish. He stayed at home all day, tending his aquarium. Occasionally his mother used to sell the fish in the local pet market, but when challenged to produce her licence, quickly packed up her aquarium and turned herself into a park attendant. The father of Nikolai, a 'parasite' in Rostov-on-Don, told a reporter from a paper campaigning against the workshy that he did not know how he had raised such a son. 'Imagine, he'll do the odd job for a bottle of wine. But real labour to provide for himself, establish himself in life? No.' In another interview, Anatoly Litvinov was more sophisticated in justifying his idleness. He lived on his mother's pension and his wife's earnings. 'Someone has to stay and look after the house,' he argued. 'The government isn't a housekeeper, is it? Where is it said that the housekeeper must be a woman? Isn't this the age of equality?'

The authorities argue that parasitism is usually the fault of the family's indulgence. Nikolai's father, for example, used his influence to find his son a sought-after job in a factory when he finished his army service. But when harvest time came and the workers were sent into the fields to pick potatoes – as most Soviet factory employees are – Nikolai quit his job rather than dirty his hands. And his father agreed that he deserved a 'cleaner job' – which he never found.

In spite of the campaign to root out parasites, nobody wants to give work to the workshy. Factories are only too glad when poor and disruptive workers quietly disappear. Rather than report their absence, they allow their names to remain on the factory register, thus conveniently enabling the factory to draw state money for salaries, which are diverted straight into the management's pockets to be used for the inevitable bribes and pay-offs. The police also find the workshy an administrative nuisance. Most are armed with false medical certificates, forged documents giving them valid reasons to be unemployed, and phony addresses. Many are drifters, who have abandoned families and responsibilities and taken to drink. They hang around shops and warehouses and pick up a few roubles unloading lorries and goods. The money is generally spent on cheap wine. Often they are picked up for petty crime, or else, undernourished, fall ill and die young. Many end up in Siberia where, free from the all-seeing eye of the state, they move on from place to place.

Few Russians doubt that tighter labour discipline is to be the priority for Yuri Andropov and the post-Brezhnev regime. Already stricter annual guidelines have been set for factory directors, as more, rather than less, control from Moscow seems to be the preferred solution. Workers will not be allowed to quit their jobs so easily. Quality control will be more vigorously enforced – at present only the military sector, which enjoys the pick of all production and supplies, can reject with impunity any article not measuring up to its rigorous specifications. And there will be a new attempt to cut out fraud, bribery and reliance on the black market and unofficial connections to obtain supplies and get round bureaucratic obstacles. But can the new regime inspire a new enthusiasm for work? Without real incentives, and a willingness to bend orthodox ideology to fit the new conditions, as Lenin did when he introduced his New Economic Policy, that would seem impossible.

CHAPTER TWO

Women and Families

It is appropriate that Russians think of their country as a mother, for in few other countries do women play such a vital and predominant role. Throughout Russian history the mother has been the focus of the Russian family, and her image is that of a large, warm, strong woman, almost enveloping her family in her ample bosom. Russian women have traditionally been the backbone of the nation, bearing and rearing the younger generation, safeguarding and transmitting Russian values, culture and religion. They have also tended to do a disproportionate amount of work – toiling in the fields, digging roads, driving trams, working in heavy industry.

The Russian Revolution set out to change all that. It granted women full legal equality with men, and encouraged them to join in the task of building up a new society. Women were no longer to be slaves in the kitchen or underpaid workers in sweatshops. The early revolutionaries even wanted to liberate women from the duties of looking after children by setting up state crèches and nurseries, educating women and girls to encourage career ambitions and break down the traditional roles of men and women, together with their conservative outlook. In the 1920s there was much talk of free love. Divorce was made possible, no stigma was attached to illegitimacy, and the 'tyranny of the family' was to be smashed.

The experiment was Utopian, and like much else in the Revolution, quietly reversed by Stalin. Strictly enforced 'communist morality' replaced free love as the official ideal. The state could not afford to take over the job of being mother to every child, and after the appalling slaughter of the Second World War, motherhood became the sacred duty of every Russian woman.

But at the same time female labour became more and more vital in meeting the country's ambitious economic targets. Immediately after the war women had to fill millions of jobs left vacant by the lost generation of men killed in battle. Twenty years later the state launched a campaign to draw all women into full-time jobs in order to continue economic growth. And now the situation is such that women form over half the total Soviet labour force.

Every year, on March 8, the Soviet Union officially honours its women in a holiday that is meant to celebrate their liberation by the Revolution and acknowledge the vital role they have played in Soviet society ever since. While the winter snows are still on the ground, the country celebrates International Women's Day. There are tributes in the press, speeches in the Kremlin and flowers for the wives. *Pravda* publishes pictures of women doctors and teachers, articles about women's opportunities under socialism and comparisons with the benighted West, where legal equality is said to be far away. Valentina Tereshkova, the first woman astronaut and now chairman of the Soviet Women's Committee, sits on the podium beside the other Politburo leaders at a solemn Kremlin meeting where the minority – Soviet men – pay tribute to the majority – women. Every husband does his best to get hold of a carnation or tulip, flown up to the northern cities and sold at exorbitant prices – up to £4 a bloom – in the peasant markets by Georgians, Azerbaijanis and others from the south, to give his wife, mother, girlfriend or office colleague.

It is a happy holiday. It comes at the right time, when people are tired of the seemingly interminable winter and need a break before the final stretch of bad weather that comes before spring. In schools, every boy tries to bring a little present for the girl beside him, with an appropriately sentimental card congratulating Valia, Galia or Natasha on the occasion. At home, husbands are meant to give their wives a day off while they do all the cooking and domestic chores. It is a time for feasting and celebrating.

But in recent years Women's Day has also become an occasion when the Russians have begun to reflect rather painfully on whether the lot of women is really so happy. It is true that they now keep the wheels of industry turning. Virtually no factory could keep going without female labour, no hospital could function in a country where women constitute about 70 per cent of all doctors, and service industries would collapse without women hairdressers and waitresses, ticket-sellers and shop assistants. People are now wondering whether the price women have to pay for equal – or almost equal – opportunity at work is now too high. For there is no such equality at home. Soviet men are as chauvinist as any the world over. Women not only have a full day's work to do, but all the cooking, shopping and housework as well. Their lives are exhausting, and the demands impossible to satisfy. Fewer and fewer are willing or able to have more than one child.

Women's liberation does not exist in a country that insists it emancipated women long before the rest of the world. Feminist movements are regarded as dangerously subversive, and when three women from Leningrad banded together to agitate against the present situation a few years ago, they were quickly arrested. They are now in exile in the West. Nevertheless, women are beginning to demand real changes, and the campaign has been taken up by the press, which publishes their letters of frustration and near despair almost daily.

'I have two children,' a woman from Kishinyov wrote. 'I work as a senior engineer and my husband is also an engineer. I get back from work about seven o'clock in the evening and leave early in the morning, so that I am not at home practically all day, except for a few days off. There's no time or strength for a smile or a kind word. You get to bed after half the night and your head doesn't even touch the pillow before you're asleep. You get up in the morning a little bit earlier so as to be able just to look at yourself in the mirror for a moment before hurrying off to work.'

Russians are beginning to see that three striking sets of statistics, all detailed in the press, are inter-related: Women make up 51 per cent of the labour force, and 92 per cent of all working-age women either work or study; one in three of all marriages ends in divorce, and of all those married in 1977, a third had filed for divorce by the end of 1978; the birthrate in the western, industrialized part of the country has fallen to such a low point that in the Russian republic 56 per cent of all couples have only one child. Another 33 per cent have only two children and 6 per cent have three. That means that 89 per cent of all families in the largest and most populous republic have fewer children than the replacement rate.

The authorities have long been worried by this dramatic fall in the population in those areas where labour is most needed, but realize that only a comprehensive programme of social development will do anything to reverse the trend. It will have to be almost unlimited in scope, covering not only such things as better housing, higher family allowances, flexible working hours, but also more and better washing-machines, household gadgets, self-service shops, family counselling units, divorce, alcoholism, contraception and abortion – topics the Russians have until recently shied away from.

Most Russians would like more children and one of the tragedies of their lives today is the fact that it is impossible to have a big family: there is not enough room at home, not enough money and no chance of a good job. Anyone who took time off to raise children would be sure to lose her job. A typical case is that of Marina, an intelligent woman who worked as a research associate at an institute in a large city. She was happily married to a fellow scientist, already had one child, and took a step so unusual for urban women nowadays that no one could understand her: she decided to have a second baby. Her colleagues at work concluded that it was a 'whim' on her part, or even an 'aberration', and said any troubles she got into with her job would be her own fault.

In fact she wanted the second child so that her first child would become less spoiled and self-centred. But this, and only this, worked out as she had hoped. She took the first year off, as authorized, then put the child in a day-care centre and returned to work. The baby cried for three days and then became ill. Marina took sick leave and stayed at home to take care of the child. The next week the same thing happened, and again two weeks later. Eventually the doctors declared the baby too weak for the day-care centre, and Marina was told to find someone to stay at home to look after it.

Neither grandmother would help: one was unwell, and the other took the view 'I raised my children myself, and so can you.' So Marina and her husband put up help-wanted signs all over town offering a nurse-maid half the salary of a candidate of science, plus board. They found no takers, but received a 10-rouble fine for posting unauthorized advertisements. Then Marina went looking for a nursemaid among the old ladies sunning themselves on the park benches. The women smiled. They were on their way home to the countryside for the summer, where a well-grown garden would bring them a much better income than this young mother was offering, and would be more healthy and relaxing than looking after a crying baby.

So Marina left her job, and became a housewife. In some work a break of two or three years would not matter, but for Marina it was a severe blow. She was not able to keep abreast of developments in her field, was losing the foreign languages she had mastered, and, most importantly, her own research was at a standstill.

She ruined her career, but the newspaper that recounted her story congratulated her on getting her priorities right. It asked whether the tragedy was inevitable. What was needed, it said, was a different attitude by her colleagues and boss. There should also be more day centres for children unable to attend regular nurseries, with special schedules and staff. Could retired teachers not be persuaded to take part-time jobs as family helps, and could state agencies not make a register of such people? As for the old women who would not help, the paper noted with sadness that nowadays the traditional role of the grandmother was fast disappearing. They no longer lived with their adult children, and were no longer willing to help bring up grandchildren.

Strengthening and enlarging the family comes into direct conflict with the social and labour demands on the Soviet woman of today. Women's equality ends at 6.00 p.m. Housekeeping takes up four or five hours every day – far longer in the Soviet Union, with the lack of modern amenities and long queues in the shops, than in the West. One woman wrote to a paper to explain the problems: 'One morning I went out for milk with my little baby in a pram. In our town milk is sold from churns on the street beside the shop. There was a queue. I asked them to let me have milk for the baby without having to wait. Everyone called out "Why don't you get up earlier?" Have they forgotten how little sleep you get when you have a baby? I went away without the milk, and so in the evening my husband had to skip his classes and go and get some.'

She at least had a helpful husband. Most Soviet men prefer to drink or watch television. A professor found that in 61 per cent of families women did all the shopping, compared with 3 per cent in which men did; in 64 per cent they always prepared dinner (men 4 per cent); and in 64 per cent they did all the washing and ironing (men 2 per cent). In the remaining families household tasks were shared, with women and aged parents also helping, but the burden generally fell on women.

Housework takes so long because only 15 per cent is mechanized compared with 80 per cent in the United States. In the Soviet Union refrigerators, washing-machines and vacuum cleaners account for 60 per cent of all electrical appliances, against only 35 per cent in America. The result is that today's urban Russian women do not have time to cope with more than one child. As it is, one survey found the time working mothers could devote to their children was only one twelfth of the time they spent doing housework and one eighth of the time spent cooking meals.

But this is not the case all over the country. Down in Central Asia, in the traditional Muslim areas, large families are still the norm. In Tadzhikistan, a small republic of only three million, so many families have at least eight children that the authorities are hard pressed to provide enough flats, schools and jobs. For many years women with ten children or more have been awarded the title of 'heroine mothers'. They are entitled to special family allowances, large flats and even nurses and home help to cope with the brood. In the Slavic parts of the country, heroine mothers are extremely rare, but not so in Central Asia, or in the Transcaucasus where large families are also common.

Of course the conditions in these warmer climes are also more favourable. Children have more room to play outside, as most Tadzhiks and Uzbeks still live on farms and in the countryside. There is no harsh winter to imprison young ones indoors for half the year. Food is more plentiful, and the extended family system, with aunts, uncles, brothers, sisters and grandparents all living under one roof, or nearby, means that there is usually help at home to raise the children.

Deeply held traditional attitudes also govern the size of the family. Men in Georgia still believe that a large family is proof of their vigour and manliness. Uzbeks cling to the vestiges of traditional Islamic society, where it is not thought fitting for a woman to venture out of the home, and where children are seen as an honour to the family name and a guarantee of security in old age.

Above all, however, it is the fundamentally different attitudes to sex and relations between the sexes that lead to different patterns of family life. The sexual revolution has arrived in Russia and the Baltic republics, but not in Uzbekistan. And with it has come one of the most worrying features of family life in the Soviet Union as a whole: the soaring number of abortions. There are more abortions in Russian than in any other country in the world, at least three times as many as in the United States. On average, according to official statistics, every woman has six to eight abortions during her lifetime. And since most women in the populous Central Asian republics have none, this means that in the west and north many women have as many as fifteen. Soviet medical reports put the ratio of abortions to live births anywhere between 2:1 and 4:1.

During Stalin's time abortion was illegal. But, as in many countries, it was widely practised in insanitary conditions by poorly qualified back-street abortionists. And the high death rate so alarmed the authorities that Khrushchev legalized abortion. Since then it has established itself as the commonest form of birth control. Contraceptives are hard to obtain, especially in the countryside, are of poor quality and are unpopular. The pill is deeply distrusted for its side effects, and relatively few are imported from Eastern Europe. It is used mainly by women from the intelligensia, or those who have travelled abroad. As with so many things, supplies are erratic: and the consequences of suddenly being unable to obtain any more are, in this case, disastrous. Many women do use IUD contraception, but many more are put off by the unpleasantness of having it fitted in state polyclinics by doctors who are often brusque and unsympathetic. Male sheaths are cheap – 4 kopecks for a packet of two – but unpopular, and certainly lack the delicacy and sensitivity of those made in the West. They are popularly known as 'galoshes'.

It is above all the carefree attitude of most people, especially the young, towards contraception that leads to so many unwanted pregnancies. Free abortion in gynaecological clinics is routinely the answer. These clinics, found in all big towns, take women in for three days ('three nights in Sochi', the Black Sea resort, is usually the euphemism to explain such absences). Anyone producing a medical certificate from work is treated free; others have to pay a token fee. Abortions, using the suction method, are generally performed between the eighth and twelfth week of pregnancy; the law defines a foetus as reaching 'viability' at a weight of one kilogram (about two pounds).

The number of abortions can be judged by taking the statistics in Riga, the Latvian capital, where women make up a majority of the work force. It was found abortion was the sixth leading cause of temporary disability in the city's light industry factories. However, an all-out campaign has recently begun to stop women terminating their first pregnancies in view of the serious damage this has been found to cause to their health and the chance of their ever being able to complete any subsequent pregnancy.

In many cases these women are young: about 60 per cent of first pregnancy abortions occur among 19 to 26-year-olds, often unmarried students and workers living in hostels and communal flats who are unable to support a child. Soviet studies have detailed the hazards. A survey of 7,500 women in Byelorussia found that 20 per cent of women aborting their first pregnancies later suffered chronic inflammation of the sexual organs, and 8 per cent – 604 women – became infertile and were never able to bear children despite ten years of treatment. Another survey found that 36 per cent of young women became chronically ill after their first abortion, attributing this to the blow to their hormonal systems.

But social and economic pressures to have abortions are strong. In Riga, 40 per cent of women going to abortion clinics under the age of twenty are unmarried, and one third are students. Many married women regularly have abortions after the first child, because their flats are too cramped and the two parents' combined earnings are too low to afford a larger family.

Latvia, with one of the lowest birthrates in the country, is one of the republics that has done most to try to cut the abortion rate. It was a pioneer in sex education, something still almost unknown in the rest of the country's schools. In one experiment a team of doctors and social welfare counsellors visited local secondary schools, and gave advice on contraception, emphasizing especially the dangers of abortion.

Public discussion of the issue is increasing, and again Latvia has taken the lead. In 1980 a monthly scientific journal published an interview with a lecturer in the department of social hygiene at the Riga medical institute in which she was asked whether, in light of the campaign to increase the birthrate in Latvia, abortion should not be made illegal and contraceptives taken off the market. Her answer was an emphatic no. 'Legal abortions and the availability of contraceptives are essential for civilized family planning. When abortion is banned, the morbidity and mortality rates for young unmarried women rise sharply,' she said, adding: 'We should not be unconcerned about the consequences of abortion. Certain specific restrictions seem highly advisable, such as requiring medical and legal counselling for women who want to abort a first pregnancy. But our main effort should go into social measures.'

Since she gave that interview, measures have indeed been taken – measures that only five years ago were scorned as unnecessary in a country that refused to discuss in public sexual and social problems, partly because it maintained they did not exist, and partly because of the Victorian attitude to sex. For the Soviet Union is still very prudish. Official propaganda has long portrayed love and marriage in unrealistically glowing terms, as ideals to which all healthy young communists aspire. Reality, as everyone knows, is different, and indeed for many years Soviet novels have dwelt on the turmoil in contemporary life – some in language too strong for critics recently, who accused many modern writers of gratuitously introducing 'smutty scenes' and 'pornographic suggestions' in their works. Films have also taken up the theme with brutal frankness. But public attitudes have lagged behind. The sexual revolution in the West was long regarded with smugness and contempt, proof of the decadence of the capitalist system, and with a distaste which was largely based on traditional morality.

That revolution has now arrived in the Soviet Union, and it is no longer possible to ignore the consequences, though the authorities are – as ever – worried by a phenomenon neither wished nor controlled by the party. It is hard to judge levels of promiscuity today, but they would seem to be high, especially among young people in towns. The Russians have recently begun to study sexual behaviour scientifically, but an interesting survey of 500 men and women applying for marriage licences was published in 1982 which attempted to measure shifting attitudes to pre-marital sex in and around the provincial town of Chernovtsy. It found a relatively tolerant view: 38 per cent approved, compared with 58 per cent who disapproved – and the researchers found that the younger and better educated the respondents, the more likely they were to approve. Over half of all school leavers and graduates said sexual relations before marriage were right – giving pragmatic reasons such as the desire to test the relationship, the wish to get the maximum pleasure out of life, and 'physiological need'. Those who disapproved – not surprisingly, more women than men – also did so for practical rather than moral reasons, citing the fear of pregnancy and venereal disease. 'He might leave me', 'It's like a game – you don't know how it will end', 'I could get hurt', were common replies from women, while men added 'I · might be forced to marry her'. The researchers concluded that attitudes to sex were indeed changing, but said the 'liberalization' was often traceable to a mentality that saw sex as another consumer good to be enjoyed. 'This indicates a serious need to improve the effectiveness of upbringing among young people,' they said.

Changing sexual mores must be set against a great deal of public ignorance. Sexual indulgence has always been a feature of life in Russia, and has been regarded even in the villages with a certain tolerance. But Russians find the actual discussion of sex awkward and embarrassing. Of course there are thousands of very funny jokes about the subject, and Russian swearwords are often explicitly sexual. But I was amazed how often even young people would blush, if only initially, when the subject came up in normal conversation. Sex education was only introduced in some Moscow schools as an experiment in 1980, and even then there was considerable controversy and some parental opposition. Books on sex hardly exist, so great is the official fear of pornography, and those manuals that have been published contain information that can only be described as ludicrous. 'The ideal length of time for sexual intercourse is two minutes,' a man, of course – a learned doctor – opined in one booklet some years ago.

But sociologists and doctors recognize that this public silence at a time of changing morals can be extremely dangerous. *Komsomolskaya Pravda*, the youth newspaper, recounted a story that could have come straight from any agony column. Valera and Olga had a baby. She loved him, he loved another, but his duty towards the child forced him to stay with Olga. From time to time he managed to slip out and see Lera, his girlfriend, who adored him. Everyone was unhappy. Valera used to get drunk and hit Olga. Lera was beside herself with jealousy. Olga was withdrawn and embittered.

What made this human tragedy unusual was that it was going on in a remote town in Siberia. And not one of the protagonists was above the age of fourteen. Olga, a pupil at the local school, had been going out with Valera. No one had ever told them about sex, so it was not until the eighth month that she even realized she was pregnant. And when her illegitimate baby was born, there was a scandal. Olga's parents, overcome with shame, insisted she move out and live with Valera's parents – not because conditions were better there, but so that no one could say the baby did not have a father. By then Valera was going out with Lera. He used to come back late, angry and frustrated. Olga was worn out. She once went back to her home in tears after Valera hit her, but her father sent her straight back.

Teachers at the school thought it served Olga right. The stout, exasperated, middle-aged assistant head had no time for the 'would-be Romeo and Juliet'. They had disgraced the school, she told a reporter from the newspaper. Olga had to leave school. Prematurely old, surrounded by nappies in Valera's house, she told the reporter she had no intention of letting Valera enjoy himself. She had thought of leaving: but now she wanted him to pay for her 'shame'. Valera himself, like a sullen animal at bay, would say little. And Lera, who had sent the original letter to the newspaper with a plea for help, said simply that Olga had disgraced herself.

The story is not an isolated incident. In another school in another city there was a similar case: a schoolgirl had a baby. The doctor came to talk with the pupils, to tell them about the harm that early pregnancy causes, about the importance of treating one another with consideration, and so on. But he was not even allowed to set foot in the school. 'There's no reason for our children to know about such coarse and shameful things,' the teachers all declared. 'But how could they help but know?' the doctor said in amazement. 'Not only do they know about it, but they're doing it too.'

The article raised a storm of reaction. Predictably, readers from the Baltics sided fully with those advocating sex education. The reaction of workers in Kazakhstan, in Central Asia, was the opposite: 'We are totally opposed to such a way of bringing up children,' they wrote in a letter to the paper. 'To teach them about pregnancy and birth in schools only causes sniggering.' On this subject, as on many others, the party cannot lay down a single line where attitudes differ so widely according to the various nationalities.

Official attempts to strengthen the Soviet family go beyond simply starting sex education in schools. Special family counselling units are now being set up to combat the high rate of divorce, offer couples in trouble confidential help and advice. They face a formidable task. Russians get married very young, often on a whim, and many regard it as only a temporary alliance. Sometimes the main reason is to be able to get away from parents, to jump the queue for a flat of their own. Or else they simply want to be able to sleep together, but have no place to go. For many, marriage is a way round the regulations limiting immigration into the big cities. A person outside Moscow can move into the capital only if he or she is married to a Muscovite, and there is a thriving trade in marriages of convenience which entitle both parties to maintain their permit to live in Moscow even after divorce.

The state is trying to put back some sanctity into marriage. Couples have to wait at least two months after handing in their papers to the civil registry office, and are invited separately into the 'bride's room' and the 'groom's room' for a lecture on the concept of family life. Ceremony and solemnity are meant to characterize the Palaces of Weddings, where you can be married in greater style – though only if it is a first marriage. However, all too often the depressing conveyor-belt atmosphere means that the resident band, whose services cost a few roubles extra, is still playing the wedding march for one happy couple as the next walks in. Equally, couples filing for divorce are urged to reconsider, and the case is postponed to allow time for a reconciliation and referral to a family counselling unit.

These units now include a figure new to Soviet science – a 'sexologist', who is usually a doctor or psychiatrist specializing in sexual problems. I knew one in Moscow – a warm, cultured, outgoing woman. Her patients were those suffering from sexual complexes, neuroses or difficulties, and tended to come to her for lengthy sessions. The greatest difficulty, she said, was in winning their confidence and overcoming shyness. It was also important for her to remain detached, and so at her consultations in the polyclinic she always adopted a strictly clinical manner, wearing a white overall to emphasize the medical relationship. She once told a funny story that is bizarrely typical of the Soviet Union.

A man came to her to discuss his problem of flagellation. He could only achieve sexual satisfaction if he beat his partner with a new leather belt, especially the kind worn by soldiers. His difficulty was not that he felt awkward about this behaviour, or that he lacked partners. The problem was that the belt had to be a new one each time, and there were none to be had in the shops. After several sessions, she managed to bring him to the point where he was able to use the same belt on several occasions and still achieve satisfaction. She saved the poor man many a fruitless quest to the shops.

Despite all official help, the divorce rate remains very high. Couples often see little of each other: they work in separate places, and holidays do not coincide. Indeed, the idea of family holidays is relatively new, as the Soviet concept of a rest 'cure' means that the employees usually spend their summer leave at health resorts owned and run by their factories, in the company not of husbands and wives but colleagues from work. ('That's half the fun of it – having a naughty time away from your husband,' one woman once said to me.) Other pressures on newly married couples are also intense: they may have to live with in-laws while waiting for a flat, they have little money, and for many, brought up and spoiled as only children, it is the first time they have had to adapt to someone else's needs. And there is always that great destroyer, male alcoholism, hanging over virtually every couple.

Things are not easy for women after divorce. There is usually a small child to care for, and legal battles to obtain alimony from the husband who has walked out are long and often fruitless. The offspring can perhaps be cared for by a sympathetic *babushka*. But finding another husband willing to care for a stepchild is hard. Loneliness and despair are all too common among young divorcees.

The Baltic republics, more innovative in social questions, have taken the lead in promoting opportunities for the unmarried to meet each other. For some years a number of 'singles clubs' have existed where people can relax and chat over cups of tea or a game of chess – though the setting is a good deal starker than this cosy picture suggests. More recently a new experiment began: 'lonely hearts' columns in popular magazines where people can advertise for prospective marriage partners.

'Interesting brunette, engineer-physicist, wants to meet a person willing to start a new family. Anyone given to drink should not bother to telephone,' reads a typical advertisement in the Latvian paper *Rigas Balss*. Yelena B. from Kaliningrad announced in her advertisement: 'I would like to set up house with a single, well-to-do man. About myself: I am a friendly, tall brunette, size 48 clothes, energetic, a good housewife. I can cook well, have a secondary education, own a two-room flat and work in a sewing workshop. I have a son aged 8.' Andrei gave fewer details: 'Young man (aged 20) wants to get married. Please reply by letter.' Another young man was more specific in his demands: 'Man, (height 5 ft 7 ins, no children, solid character, non-drinker, non-smoker, well off, spends his free time in the countryside) wants to meet his future wife (no children, not older than 27), friendly, slim, hardworking, with a delicate character, preferably from the provinces.'

The paper was one of the first to run columns of this kind, and it was an immediate success – though some people in Latvia were shocked and criticised the idea. Another modest little monthly, *Family*, began a similar column a few years ago. Since then it has been swamped with letters pouring in each month from the divorced, the single and the lonely looking for partners. Many come from as far away as Georgia and Siberia, though the magazine does not circulate there. Only about half a dozen are published a month, and there is now a waiting list of at least a year to get a letter in.

In the conservative social atmosphere of the Soviet Union these ventures, approved at the highest levels by local party officials, are a real innovation. For 5 roubles – less than the cost of a bottle of vodka – readers can send in their advertisements, outlining their marketable points. Guaranteed full secrecy, they usually withhold their names and addresses, but give their age, profession, education, hobbies, interests and so on. For another 3 roubles readers can write to the magazine and get the addresses.

Most of the advertisements come from middle-aged women. They often do not mind what the man looks like, or what his job is, as long as he is kind, decent and loving. The men who advertise are more reticent about their age and personal details, but much more demanding of their prospective partners: they have to be able to sing, play chess, be educated and keep their natural beauty. Some men even dictate that the prospective bride's hair should be plaited.

Loneliness is a real problem for many Russian women, but less so for men – perhaps because they have more time for social contacts. Whereas a full-time job together with domestic work means that women, according to one survey, work an average of eighty hours a week, men put in only fifty hours. And men, it appears, are becoming less and less interested in marriage. This is not to the liking of Russian women, who still outnumber men by a larger proportion than anywhere else in the world, and there are growing complaints about the 'militant bachelor' – men who are rich, intelligent, accomplished, highly desirable prospects, but refuse to marry. They enjoy life in the cities, keep divorced women company, but have no intention of setting up a family, which many Russians regard as a man's essential function.

I know a young man who fits the picture of such a character drawn in a popular weekly newspaper. 'He is composed, businesslike, intelligent, capable, fashionable and always attractively dressed. He is good at cooking shish-kebab and an expert at brewing coffee. He is something of an athlete, a decent guitar player and a first-rate photographer. His flat is decorated with flair, and has certain details – a bearskin, a stuffed eagle, assorted sabres – that are guaranteed to spark the imagination of both male and female visitors. He has a stereo system and the latest records and books. He's a theatre-goer and is *au courant* with all sorts of things. He's ironic but outgoing, likeable and pleasant. He doesn't know the fatigue of young fathers who are kept awake at night by crying babies – his life is much easier and more elegant. He always has money to spare. He doesn't drink too much, and pays a great deal of attention to keeping physically fit.

'He is a thorough-going urbanite, a big-city product. It would be impossible for such a type to exist in the countryside, where a young man, as he grows up, begins to regard himself as the future head of a family. In him, the moral essence of manhood has been attenuated. He has even lost the instinct to propagate the species. Thus, he doesn't perform the natural social tasks man has deemed himself capable of from time immemorial. He has sterilized himself with the help of his own egoism.'

My friend would certainly reject criticism that he is egoistic by not marrying: only twenty-four, he is dedicated to pursuing his career in a field where he will clearly be successful. But he complains that already his mother and friends badger him about getting married, and cannot understand why he is still a bachelor at his age.

Another friend, in his forties, is already an outstanding artist – emotional, egoistic, vivacious, temperamental and extremely hard working. He is not married because he is a homosexual – and seems to lead a remarkably active sex life. Homosexuality is more widespread in Moscow, Leningrad and the large cities than the Soviet authorities will ever admit. It is also illegal. And during the Olympic Games, when thousands of police were patrolling the streets of Moscow in case of demonstrations or incidents and Red Square was thick with KGB agents, an Italian gay rights activist chained himself to a metal crush barrier in front of the Kremlin to draw attention to Soviet laws against homosexuality. He was, of course, arrested and promptly deported. And the Russians could not help a wry smile: they had expected all kinds of demonstrations on behalf of Jews, dissidents, political activists, minority races – but certainly not this one.

Article 121 of the Russian criminal code lays down a maximum penalty of five years' imprisonment for sexual relations between men, and eight years for relations involving minors. The law has not always been so strict. Indeed, after the Revolution the new government had little time to concern itself with sexual behaviour, and homosexuals benefitted from the generally tolerant atmosphere. But as Stalinism got a grip, the atmosphere changed, and by the 1930s homosexuality was considered anti-social, contrary to the ideals of communism and therefore illegal.

When the French writer and communist sympathizer, André Gide, who had earlier shocked French society by publishing a defence of homosexuality, visited the Soviet Union in the 1930s, he was told that such a bourgeois vice had been abolished and there were no longer any homosexuals in the country. His amazement and disbelief were important ingredients in undermining his faith in all else he saw and was told, leading to his famous renunciation of communism *Retour de L'URSS*.

The campaign against homosexuality was intensified after the Second World War when Stalin was intent on destroying the artistic community, then – as now – tolerant of homosexuals. Many were sent to labour camps, along with millions of other citizens. However in recent years official attitudes have softened. There is no longer any pretence that such a thing does not exist and the subject is a common talking point or theme for jokes, especially in student and intellectual circles. An administrative guideline in the 1970s laid down that routine prosecutions of consenting adults in private were to be dropped unless either party or relatives laid a public complaint.

Attitudes vary across the country: the Baltic states are more tolerant, whereas homosexuality is still strictly taboo in Central Asia. Armenia, however, has acquired a reputation for homosexuality and the theme crops up frequently in the many jokes told at the expense of Armenians. Tom Driberg, the late British MP, detailed from experience in his autobiography a number of well-known homosexual meeting places in Moscow, the square outside the Bolshoi Theatre probably being the best known. But the police keep a strict watch, entrapment is common and a number of arrests are made each year.

The statute against homosexuality is a convenient clause which has been used in recent years against dissidents and others who have fallen foul of the authorities. Two such cases have been taken up in the West: Viktoras Petkus, a Lithuanian who was sentenced in 1978, had a charge of homosexuality added to that of anti-Soviet propaganda; and Sergei Paradzhanov, a Georgian film director who was imprisoned in 1974, banned from film-making after his release and then re-arrested. Something of the official attitude came through in a Tass commentary responding to a French campaign on behalf of Paradzhanov:

'The shimmer of Paradzhanov's glory was darkened by circumstances which one would not like even to mention, particularly in the pages of the press.' Nonetheless, noting that he was convicted of sodomy, the agency added: 'By doing these things he placed himself outside art. In various states, laws have different attitudes to such deviations from norms, but nowhere, on the whole, are such inclinations encouraged. Our laws are humane and do not close the ways to the future for anyone. Of course, the peculiarities of Paradzhanov's personality do not make it easier for him to return to his former profession, the more so as it presupposes contacts with people.'

If the Russians were serious about the dangers of such 'peculiarities' they would have to dismiss a large number of dancers from the Bolshoi Ballet. There is naturally no gay rights lobby in the Soviet Union, nor any form of public pressure to change the existing laws, and blackmail is common. However Soviet medical opinion is quietly neutral and generally in line with that in the West on the subject nowadays.

The party knows it cannot get people to marry and have children by decree. It cannot even change the common attitude nowadays that there is nothing wrong in remaining childless. But it is fully aware that Russians, warmly sentimental about children, shamelessly spoil those they have, and in one-child families this encourages an egoistic outlook that ill fits in with the communist emphasis on the 'collective' and the distrust of individualism. Social workers frequently point to the importance of a stable family background in the fight against crime. And it is the attempt to encourage this that has led to recent measures to remove the obstacles to motherhood. In January 1981 sweeping new regulations came into force banning women from about 460 different occupations considered too physically demanding or unsuitable. These included mechanical and repair work, driving buses, trams or any vehicle with more than fourteen passengers, working in the chemical industry or on outdoor sites in very cold weather. Even before then women could not be employed in a number of heavy jobs. Since 1957, for example, no woman has been allowed to work underground as a miner. And the celebrated woman head of the Moscow metro, who began her career as a tunneller before the war, often points out that today's tunnellers are all men.

Unfortunately the effects will be felt only gradually: factories cannot spare their women workers, and even a year after the decree many buses are still being driven by women. But these regulations are also backed with incentives, both to women and to factories. A general rise in family allowances was announced at the end of 1981, together with an extension of maternity leave for women living in the northern parts of the country. Women who have worked not less than a year and full-time women students are now entitled to a year's paid leave with a monthly allowance of 35 roubles. Women in Siberia, the Far East and northern Russia, climatically harsh regions where salaries are higher, get 50 roubles. They are also now entitled to take an extra six months unpaid leave, until the child is eighteen months, with a guaranteed right to return to their former jobs. Working women with two or more children under twelve have been given an additional three days paid leave each year, and at the end of 1981 allowances for unmarried mothers went up from the old rate of 5 roubles a month to 20 roubles for each child under sixteen.

Not long ago an official publication estimated there were 9 million households headed by women. Because of their low income and poor social position, these families constitute one of the most poorly provided for groups in Soviet society, and an extra 15 roubles represents a real measure of assistance. All women also now receive a lump sum payment of 50 roubles for the first child and 100 roubles for the second and third. Significantly, payments for the fourth and subsequent children remain unchanged – which suggests the authorities are trying to get families with only one child – mainly in the Russian and Baltic republics – to have more while giving no incentive to mothers in Central Asia who have at least five. A population expert from the State Planning Committee once admitted in a surprisingly frank press conference that the effect was intentionally discriminatory. There was no point, he said, in trying to stimulate the birthrate in the south – 'That would be like trying to seed the clouds during a thunderstorm.'

Industry for its part is now being urged to make more part-time jobs available for working women. The press is full of stories of factories employing mainly women workers which have dramatically cut down their labour turnover and boosted output by introducing half-day shifts.

It is too early to see whether any of this will have much effect. But a lively debate is going on about what to do. One popular weekly magazine caused something of a scandal by openly advocating more illegitimate children. 'Motherhood at times brings more happiness (and at any rate no less) than marriage,' the writer said, 'especially if marriage is not accompanied by mutual love and happiness. I am convinced we should not be afraid of increasing the number of single mothers in the country. After all, she is not alone if she has a child, and two people already constitute a family.'

She was quickly shot down by others who pointed out that all children needed a stable and proper family environment. They deplored recent trends of cohabitation and unmarried motherhood, and said the attempts after the Revolution to abolish the family and bring up children in a larger, collective environment were futile as well as very expensive. One economist even worked out the cost nowadays of replacing mothers and housewives. It would mean employing 100 million state salaried workers at a cost of 150,000 million roubles (£120,000 m) a year.

So, ironically, the Russians are now searching for the old values of family and children. Today's official image is not that of the bulky woman swinging a hammer to build communism, but of a domesticated mother contentedly fulfilling herself by bringing up children at home. It is the state that now wants to get women off the shopfloor and back to the hearth, while the younger generation has taken over the ideals of the early revolutionaries – free love, the smashing of traditional patterns of life. Lamenting the casualness with which young people married and got divorced, a newspaper once reminded them of a good old Russian proverb: 'To know a person, you have to eat a *pood* (16 kilograms) of salt together.' Nowadays, it complained, people never gave each other time, but got divorced at the first mouthful of salt.

CHAPTER THREE

Health Care – Orthodox and Unorthodox

Russians are generally much concerned about their health. Life and the climate have always been harsh in Russia, and you had to be fit to survive. The older generation frequently complains that the young do not appreciate the privations they suffered during the war and in the harsh days afterwards. But good medical care, which the ideologists now insist is available to every citizen, is still a long way off. The rapid improvements in public health, the rise in life expectancy and the elimination of devastating epidemics from the rural areas were among the earliest and most spectacular achievements of the Revolution. But in the last decade the standards of medical care have not only ceased to rise, they have probably actually fallen. And the sorry state of Soviet medicine – in spite of some well publicised peaks – is one of the prime concerns of both the people and the government nowadays.

Russians still have a more fatalistic view of disease than people in the West. They are also natural victims for quacks. They are incurably superstitious, they have a strong and tested belief in the efficacy of herbal and folk medicine, and they are plagued by the constant shortages of up-to-date medication in the chemists' shops.

Most people have a deep-seated mistrust of tablets, a palpable fear of hospitals and a very negative attitude to doctors. Instead they have an enduring faith in the herbal concoctions their grandmothers brewed. Before summoning the medical assistance cars, with their white-coated doctors who travel from block to block, or queuing up at the local polyclinic, even city dwellers will first try out the age-old cures that once meant life or death to their peasant ancestors in their rural isolation.

Everyone has his own pet cure. Most involve vodka – to make compresses for sore throats and glands, to mix with honey to soothe a cough, or to rub on the chest and back to relieve stiffness and rheumatism. Young nettles or burdock soaked for a week in vodka in a cool, dark place are the popular remedies for sciatica. At private markets you can buy all manner of seeds, leaves, dried flowers, bark and roots needed for the various brews that will keep the family healthy in the long winter months. And when the inevitable cold comes, Russians drink quantities of tea with spoonfuls of jam, apply mustard plasters to their chests and chew berries, onions or garlic which are meant to keep the germs away as well as flushing out the kidneys and helping the heart and liver. They also tend to give Soviet buses and trains their distinctive aroma.

For years officialdom frowned on these unscientific panaceas, but so great is their popularity – and so essential were they during the years of Revolution, civil war, famine and shortage – that the tradition has never died. And now 'homoeopathic medicine' as the Russians call these herbal preparations, has been officially recognized and brought under the wing of the national health service. In 1977 the government ordered an increase in the production of medicinal plants. The All-union Herbs Research Institute has recognized as beneficial more than 220 species, and twenty-six specialized state farms cultivate forty rare varieties, including valerian, nightshade and foxglove.

But inevitably herbal medicine leads into fringe medicine, and here the field is wide open for quacks. Russia has a long tradition of untrained miracle workers of whom Rasputin was by no means the last. Tass news agency has carried stories about simple workers who are able to detail your medical history without touching your body, and the Academy of Medical Sciences has long been carrying out full-scale research into para-psychology, telepathy and bio-rhythms, a favourite topic of popular scientific journalism.

Many people believe fervently in these less orthodox forms of medicine – too many for the authorities' liking or for their own good. Ekaterina Dostoyevskaya, for example, is a quack whose patients include some of the top names in the world of music, literature and theatre. She works in secret, her address is known only to the initiated, but there is always a queue at her door in spite of her steep fees. She is said to have studied Tibetan medicine, and claims to be able to cure anything from cancer to the common cold. This is her method, as related by one of her patients: 'For three days an assistant gives you 12 pint enemas. During this time you fast and take salt. On the third day, you have to drink olive oil with lemon. Then four needles are inserted in the region of the liver. Afterwards you follow a strict diet. You have to bake bread yourself, using mineral water instead of ordinary water. There were several people in our group. All this gave my friend, who has chronic gastritis, a bad spell, and she had to be hospitalized. I myself lost five kilos, but I can't say I felt any better.'

One of the best known quacks is a former railway worker, Vitaly

Karavayev, who published an underground book of his cures. Well-thumbed *samizdat* copies circulate around Moscow, describing his theories of how to change a person's organism. He prescribes a diet consisting of two or three tins of tooth-powder or crushed eggshell, to which is added separated milk and fruit juices. Bread is allowed if soaked in a common medicinal liquid. You can use butter which you have first melted yourself, and you can also eat dates and dissolved sugar.

Official medical opinion has condemned Karavayev's ideas as misleading and causing serious biological complications, and a Moscow court officially warned him to stop dabbling in medicine. Immediately, according to an account in the papers, there was a storm of protest, and his patients began sending in petitions and complaints. One asserted that his discoveries were of 'immense economic importance', explaining that the government spent huge sums on health and medical research, whereas it could save a lot of money were everyone to follow Karavayev's cures, which did not cost anything.

Various other well-known quacks have been investigated by the Ministry of Health. Most have invented panaceas: one man, a mathematician by training, in partnership with his wife used to produce a medicine consisting of some Bulgarian preparation mixed with two pints of boiled milk. He maintained he had treated over 3,000 people before he was taken to court. Another, from Leningrad, used to work as a clerk for the state insurance company, but found it more profitable to dabble in medicine. She used to peddle a home-made elixir extracted from locally gathered herbs, and prescribed it for external and internal use. Ministry of Health scientists said the stuff was positively harmful, and an investigating committee examining five of the 'cured' patients found they were all in a serious state of health as a result of her treatment.

The details of these cases were published in an attempt to persuade Russians not to visit such folk heroes. But it seems to be a losing battle. As one highly educated woman asked me: 'What would you do if you were told you had an incurable disease?' She had gone to the best clinics in Moscow to cure a painful inflammation without success, until she followed the cure of an unqualified herbal practitioner.

Indeed Russians have long been fascinated by para-medicine, and by those possessing extraordinary healing powers. One woman in particular is now enjoying influential acclaim in Moscow, and numbers among her patients some of the top names in the Soviet establishment. She was rumoured to have treated President Brezhnev, though she always denied this. Her name is Dzhuna Davitashvili, a slender Assyrian from

Georgia in her mid thirties, with an angular face, long fingers, jet black hair and intense dark eyes. She dresses in black, heightening the almost witch-like effect, and is something of a self-publicist, handing out to enquirers signed photographs of herself which appear to show something like heat rays emanating from her fingertips. She is extremely rich – her flat is furnished with amazing luxury – and the chauffeur-driven Mercedes of her top clients, who include Nikolai Baibakov, the head of the State Planning Committee, and General Alexei Yepishev, the political head of the army, can be seen waiting discreetly in the street outside.

Rumours about Dzhuna's ability to produce burns on the skin without even touching it, to heal internal organs, remove ulcers, and to diagnose tumours and other disorders reached such a pitch that eventually the Sovet press began to write about her and a thorough investigation of her powers was carried out by the State Planning Committee's outpatient clinic – presumably thanks to the interest of the Committee's chief. Dzhuna, a medical school graduate, denies any magical powers: she says every living organism has a 'biofield' around it, and she can feel which organ is diseased by the different sensations these give her hands. Her healing sessions consist of 'therapeutic massage'.

In a famous report, one Soviet journalist interviewed her and testified that she was able to revive wilting roses by passing her hands over them, lift a cigarette pack by simply touching it with her fingers, and cure his headache by wafting her hands across his forehead. Scientific commentators asserted that she was no hoaxer, and even a round-table conference on her powers, where medical sceptics maintained it was all done by hypnosis, aroused enormous interest among ordinary people.

Unfortunately the normal medical services in the Soviet Union are, on the whole, poor. Even the comprehensive state health system – one of the first in the world as propagandists continually boast – now lags far behind its Western equivalents. The problems are those of a generally demoralized service: doctors, mainly women, are poorly paid, earning less than the average industrial wage, standards of hygiene are low, hospitals are impersonal, post-surgical care is very limited, medicines and medical equipment outdated and often unobtainable. But on top of this there is a crushing indifference, an absence of responsibility at all levels, and a lack of personal care and attention. Frequently the only way to get a doctor to attend to your case properly is to offer a substantial bribe, and public dissatisfaction, prompted by numerous scandalous cases of malpractice, became so loud that Brezhnev himself was obliged to single out corruption in the health service for particular attack during his speech to the party congress in 1981. Since then there have been blistering attacks in the press on sloppiness and low standards in the health service, and a number of high level debates on how things could be improved.

Medical training itself is reasonably good, and many third world students are studying in institutes all over the country. There are plenty of polyclinics, and the doctor/patient ratio is one of the best in the world. The Russians also take preventative medicine seriously, and most factories are equipped with surgeries, rest and recreation centres and a range of exotic prophylactic apparatus to effect treatment and cures for workers. Every year millions of people are sent away, largely at state expense, to sanatoria in the countryside or beside the Black Sea to recuperate from illness or to replenish their energies and improve their physical fitness. These centres, set in the woods or other picturesque surroundings, are more than just holiday homes. The Russians have adopted the old German idea of a 'cure', and the regime in the centres is strictly controlled: so many hours relaxing, so many hours exercising, so many hours in the baths or soaking up sunlight or undergoing medically approved treatments.

But throughout the health service poor organization often defeats the best of intentions. Nowhere is this more true than in the drug industry. How often are foreigners asked by Russian friends to bring back drugs for sick relatives, and how often does the press complain that cheap, effective Soviet drugs are simply unobtainable! Take the case of a researcher who discovered an efficient drug to stimulate growth and spent fifteen years trying to get it on the market. In spite of repeated clinical tests, scientific endorsement and an urgent demand from people with deficiencies in growth hormones, the drug was unavailable. Instead manufacturers were producing a less effective foreign product which first came on the market twenty-two years ago.

What is on sale in the shops or in special kiosks is so outdated or so general in its effects that few people buy the product. Packets of good pills are so valuable that they are sold at special foreign currency counters in tourist hotels. Doctors issue prescriptions even if the hospitals have no supplies, leaving it to the hapless patients to use their wits in trying to get hold of what they need. There are plenty of stories of dentists working without adequate supplies of anaesthetic, of polyclinics unable to supply a full course of treatment, of chronically sick people living from month to month, never sure whether their prescriptions can be renewed.

The drug industry suffers from none of the failings its Western counterpart is accused of: there is no risk of profit-taking at the expense of safety, no aggressive marketing of unnecessary drugs, no costly duplication of research laboratories. Instead, research, development, testing, approval, manufacture and promotion are organized as a public service. But the links between each stage are so weak that the time lag between research and retailing may be up to seven years. Responsibility for pharmaceuticals is divided between the Ministry of Health and the Ministry of Medication Industry. Everything used to come under a subdivision of the Ministry of Health, but because of poor results a separate ministry was created in 1967. The Health Ministry is still responsible for research, testing and licensing of new drugs. The new ministry deals with production and quality control. Most research is carried out in state laboratories, and if an effective product is discovered it is sent to the Ministry of Medication Industry which finds a suitable factory to try it out. Test batches go back to the Ministry of Health for clinical trials, and then, if approved, to another plant for mass production. A separate agency handles distribution and marketing, and quality control is the responsibility of an independent state inspectorate.

Theoretically each stage leads to the next with no waste or duplication. In practice the chain becomes a bureaucratic nightmare. The institutional separation means that each body operates according to its own terms with little concern for the total process. By the time the product gets to the chemists' shelves, it has often been rendered obsolete. Research institutes have no real leverage to press factories to put their results into production, and have little incentive to do so. As for the manufacturers, they cannot get back their initial production costs because of a rigid pricing system, and find it cheaper and easier to stick to the older and tested lines for which there is already a market.

The lack of advertising means that doctors are often unaware of what is available. Sometimes they prescribe drugs that have long been withdrawn from the market. Similarly, since brand-names play little part in the pharmaceutical industry, a factory manager is not too concerned about the name and reputation of his plant, and this breeds indifference.

The Russians have tried various remedies. The simplest is to import drugs. A large percentage of the newer and better products come from Eastern Europe, especially East Germany. Other drugs are made in such places as India in factories under licence from Western firms. Some drugs come directly from the West, but the limiting factor is cost and availability.

The Kremlin, of course, has its own clinic and all drugs are available to the country's leaders and those senior party members who are able to use this special facility. But the leadership has decided it is time for a big improvement in the health service as a whole. Perhaps the decision was hastened by some alarming statistics which show that as a nation the Russians are far from healthy, and things appear to be getting worse, not better. In the decade between 1970 and 1980 infant mortality rose and life expectancy fell. The gap between life expectancy for men and for women also widened. The infant mortality rate now stands at 30 per 1,000 compared with 24 per 1,000 in 1960. The figures have been influenced by the high birth rate in Central Asia, where the bulk of the population still lives in villages and where medical facilities are limited. But the fall in life expectancy, which reached a peak of 70 years in 1970, is largely the result of the aging of the population and especially also the result of alcoholism among men. One state official called this 'the most serious problem of our civilization' when he gave an unusually frank press conference on the subject.

Drunkenness now affects every aspect of life. It breaks up families, encourages crime and negates all efforts to increase industrial production. It is spreading rapidly, especially among young people, and chronic alcoholism is now said to threaten virtually the entire postwar generation. In spite of an unrelenting campaign against alcohol, stricter laws on the sale of drink, daily temperance propaganda in the press, and schools and on the factory floor, the Russians appear powerless against the waves of vodka and cheap wine now washing over the country. Alcoholism is literally killing the population.

In 1925 surveys showed that 11 per cent of workers were drunkards. Figures recently given by the State Anti-Alcohol Committee show that today some 37 per cent of male workers abuse alcohol. And the average drinking age has fallen sharply. The percentage of people who begin drinking under the age of eighteen has risen from 16 per cent in 1925 to around 93 per cent today. According to one press report, a fairly new city with a top priority construction project in it in the southern part of Russia found that each adult drank on average 50 litres of alcohol a year, more than twice the rate in France which is said to be the country suffering most from drunkenness. Excluding children and the negligible number of old people, it turned out that each working adult drank the equivalent of a bottle of spirits a day. 'What is more, this is not an isolated case,' the paper commented. 'Consumption is rising at a number of other priority construction projects.'

The cost to the country is enormous. Economists have calculated that about 1 per cent of all male workers in industry or on construction sites are absent from work every day because they are drunk. The problem is worst after weekends and holidays: on Mondays productivity is 12 to 15 per cent lower than on other working days. Among the serious consequences is the large number of industrial accidents and injuries. One sociologist wrote that in the Russian Republic 'more than half all fatal accidents in just one year involved people in states of inebriation. Drunkards caused a quarter of all industrial accidents. The number of accidents and injuries on days off and on holidays increases, and on pay-days doubles.'

The exact mortality rate due to drink has not been published, but the harmful effect on people's health has been widely discussed. Disease caused by alcohol abuse is now third only to cardiovascular disease and cancer in the Soviet Union. But perhaps the saddest effect is the high percentage of mentally retarded children born to alcoholics. As drinking increases among women, more and more children suffer. Researchers maintain that alcohol seriously damages the foetus and subsequent development of the child's personality. Furthermore, the children of alcoholic parents suffer from neglect at home, undernourishment and psychological disturbance as a result of drunken brawls between their parents, and many such children later become criminals.

Indeed, the effects of widespread drinking on family life are equally catastrophic: more than half of all divorces are directly attributable to drink, as well as a high proportion of domestic violence and household accidents. The increase in drinking among young people is especially worrying as it is closely linked with the rising crime rate. The papers detail case after case of grisly crimes originating in teenage drinking. In 1979 two youths, after drinking, broke into Moscow's zoo and stabbed and beat to death two rare kangaroos, to take an incident that provoked considerable outcry. New housing estates in provincial towns have been terrorized by drunken vandals who smash up cafés and cinemas, rob passers-by and attack old people. Drunkards have stolen cars and mown down pedestrians, knifed people after quarrels, badly injured policemen and gone on the rampage with an axe. In a typical month, 96 per cent of people convicted of hooliganism were intoxicated, as were 68 per cent convicted of aggravated murder, 67 per cent of the convicted rapists and 57 per cent of those inflicting bodily injury.

Special studies have been made of the situation in Georgia where wine is plentiful and cheap and there is a long tradition of heavy drinking. A university survey found that the number of alcoholics in this southern republic has risen by 150 per cent over the past fifteen years, and while the population, now 5 million, has increased by just over a fifth since 1940, the sale of alcoholic drinks has gone up four or five times in the same period. Two thirds of Georgian alcoholics lived in the cities, and the majority were from broken homes. Most had been treated for alcoholism but returned to drinking. The republic estimated annual production losses at 74 million roubles (£47 m). About 10 per cent of all car accidents were due to drink, and in one year police took licences from 12,000 people for drunken driving. In spite of all this, from 1972 to 1977 the number of drink shops increased from 50 to 57, while 220 extra grocery stores began selling drinks in the same period.

Why do Russians drink so much? People blame the cold weather, the Tsarist encouragement of vodka production before the Revolution, the hardships and sufferings of the war and civil war and public tolerance of drunkenness. But this does not explain the alarming increase in consumption since the war. The paradox is that at a time when the average citizen is better fed, housed and paid than ever before, his drinking has reached record levels. Several million people now suffer from alcohol psychoses or are confirmed alcoholics.

There are many factors driving people, especially the young, to drink. Old attitudes play an important part. Over the generations a cult of liquor has evolved in Russia, which has now spread to the non-Russian parts of the country as traditional Islamic temperance in the south has lost its hold. Alcohol is considered a nourishing food product, a stimulant to the appetite, a means of keeping warm, a source of strength, a way of relaxing and getting rid of mental tension and a source of good feeling. Prodigious drinking is associated with manliness, but society has always been lenient to those who cannot hold their liquor. And whereas Russians used to entertain guests with tea from the samovar, a host now cuts a better figure by producing a few bottles. In the mountains of Georgia, in the past, it was considered shameful for a young man to appear drunk in the presence of his elders, but now most people have forgotten these unwritten mores.

Ironically, increased prosperity has spurred greater drinking. After the Revolution and devastation of the Second World War, most people were barely able to afford food. Now they have more money than outlets to spend it on. The shortage of consumer goods leaves people with plenty of cash to spend on drink, and though vodka prices have more than doubled in the past twenty years, the price appears no barrier.

The rise in the standard of living and the fall in working hours have not been matched by an increase in leisure facilities, especially in the new housing estates that surround the big cities. So more and more people drink out of boredom. A questionnaire distributed among young workers in hostels in the Moscow region revealed that a third drank 'to raise their spirits', another third 'because their friends were drinking and they did not want to offend them by refusing', and the rest 'because they had nothing else to do'. Drinking out of boredom is especially common in towns. Many Russians are only first or second generation city-dwellers, and rapid urbanization has taken a heavy toll on traditional values. Lonely divorcees have only drink to console them. At the same time the lack of parental authority has led more and more young people to start drinking, often when both parents are out at work.

One alarming survey by the State Committee for Anti-alcohol Propaganda found that even children under seven were inured to alcohol. In one kindergarten 20 out of 27 children had drunk beer, 7 had tried wine and one had drunk vodka with his father.

Escapism is a strong motive for drinking, especially for those who drink simply in order to get drunk, as many Russians do. Life is still hard for ordinary people, especially women, who more and more are starting to drink. Doctors report that solitary women who are embarrassed by their alcoholism are slow to seek help.

But beyond all this lies a fundamental reason which deeply troubles the authorities and social workers alike and which has been touched on only obliquely in the press: Soviet society nowadays has lost many of its values. There is, said a writer in the atheist magazine *Science and Religion*, 'a spiritual emptiness' in the younger generation.

'The lack of inner values, the narrow outlook, the inability to live life (in the highest sense of the term) are what have given us that unpleasant phenomenon, hard drinking,' he wrote. 'The drunkards cannot be returned to a sober life without effort on their part. And ultimately the question comes down to the need to foster higher interests in each person.' But though the state argues that it provides a healthy moral atmosphere in schools and clubs for young people, it is the state itself, in its policy on the sale of alcohol, that bears most guilt for the present crisis.

Total production of vodka, beer and wine is never given, but the quantities are reliably believed to be colossal, and sales are extremely profitable to the state – as they were in the Tsar's day. In Georgia alone it was found that the cost of all economic and social losses caused by drink amounted to about 200 million roubles (£127 m) a year. Income from the sale of spirits alone – not counting the large sale of Georgian wine – came to 146 million roubles (£93 m) a year.

Many shops and restaurants do their best to sell as much vodka and fortified wine as possible in order to fulfil their annual sales targets. Restaurants, notoriously slow in serving food, quickly bring vodka to the table and are reluctant to serve cheaper drinks such as beer. Alcohol shops refuse to stock finer, drier wines because the coarser, more alcoholic 'portwine' is more profitable.

The early Bolsheviks seriously considered introducing prohibition to rid the young Soviet state of the scourge of drunkenness that was hindering their efforts to transform the country. They eventually discarded the idea as unenforceable. But many people engaged in the fight against alcoholism now regret that such a law was never enacted. As the campaign against drunkenness intensifies, prohibition is again being seriously considered.

Three broad approaches are used in the fight: persuasion, punishment and decree. Persuasion consists of a massive propaganda effort by the party, health workers, the press and local authorities to bring home to the population the damage caused by alcohol. Much is deliberately shocking. Television shows films of the burgeoning number of homes built to cope with the mentally retarded children of alcoholic parents. Disgusting scenes from sobering-up stations deliberately depict drunks in almost bestial depravity. The press gives details of the messy murders, the most grisly cases of assault and violence caused by drunks. Men are frightened with the prospect of madness or impotence, women with the breakup of families and the corruption of children by drink.

Persuasion is more subtle. Efforts are made to teach people to drink socially and in moderation. New cocktail lounges and restaurants have been opened with a light, attractive environment, serving light wines, beer and sandwiches, cocktails and soft drinks. Their fashionable exclusiveness is compared with the sordid drinking in dark entryways and the hangovers of the next morning.

The state has tried to boost the sale of beer and wine in an effort to cut down the consumption of vodka. More breweries have been built – several producing prestigious Czech beers – and shops are encouraged to stock the better Georgian and Armenian wines. In a clever move capitalizing on the obsession of youth with Western products and fashions, the Russians have allowed Pepsi-Cola to set up bottling plants in the Soviet Union, open street kiosks and even put up the familiar brand-name signs. It has become chic to ask for Pepsi or Fanta, the orange drink sold in the Soviet Union by Coca-Cola. Attempts are being made to get Russians to revive the old custom of entertaining guests with tea. The Ministry of Education has sent booklets to help teachers with temperance lectures.

Persuasion is backed with stiffer punishments for persistent drunkenness in an effort to reduce public tolerance of drunks. Ridicule has long been used to shame people into sobriety – drunks picked up by the police have cartoons drawn of their inebriation, which are then pinned up on street notice-boards. Drunkards are warned at their places of work about their behaviour and criticised at party meetings by workmates in informally constituted 'comrades' courts'.

It is now suggested that the coveted vouchers to holiday resorts should not be given to drunkards. Heavy drinkers may be expelled from the Komsomol, and it has been recommended that job references include a statement of drinking habits. The press has called for the fine on illegal home-distilling of vodka, now widely drunk in the countryside, to be increased to 1,000 roubles (£637). Restaurants that sell alcohol to minors will face stiffer penalties, and there are mounting calls for tougher action against drinking in factories, with hints that managers will be given a freer hand to sack drunken workers without having to find them another job. In the Ukraine, several mines run daily checks for inebriation among the miners as they report for work. Traffic police have also urged tougher penalties for drunken driving, which is already severely punished, and in recent years a number of people causing fatal accidents while drunk have been shot.

However only in recent years has a real attempt been made to tackle alcoholism on a social and economic basis. The state has sponsored serious research into the causes, and acted on key recommendations. One important measure is that restaurants will no longer be able to include alcohol sales in the fulfilment of their plans. Another decree provides for better treatment for alcoholics.

Kiev is one city that has done much in preventative treatment. The anti-addiction centre has set up a residential clinic in the countryside that can treat up to 700 people at a time. Alcoholics, all volunteers, are taught to relax without alcohol, and meet former patients and their families. Special buses take them to factories each day where they are given well-defined work schedules or taught a trade. The city also has two out-patient centres, including a hypnosis centre, where regular drunkards are invited to go for treatment. Courts can order compulsory attendance, and discipline is strict.

Kiev has found that more effective treatment can be offered in special fee-paying wings of local hospitals, where patients may admit themselves anonymously. In two years one such hospital treated about 2,000 people. Similar centres have been established elsewhere. Teetotal clubs have also been set up with some success. Members take oaths, wear badges, meet weekly in comfortable club-houses, provide entertainment and organize summer outings to which they may bring guests. The most drastic measure against drunkenness – prohibition – has already been tried in some cities, especially those with priority construction projects, but most Russians agree that national prohibition is simply not possible, so ingrained is the drinking habit.

Apart from cutting back drunkenness, the government has other schemes for improving people's health. An anti-smoking campaign has begun in earnest, and Soviet cigarettes now carry a warning as they do in the West. Smoking has been banned on all internal Aeroflot flights, and is not allowed in most public places. In theatres and concert halls it is permitted only in the front foyer and in the toilets, and in most office buildings special areas are set aside in the corridors. (It always struck me as strange to find large groups of men clustered around the lavatories of the Bolshoi, furiously puffing away before the bell rang. But it did have the advantage that they masked the pungent odour that invariably hangs over every Soviet toilet.)

Exercise is also the 'in' thing at present. In pre-war days every factory insisted on physical jerks for all workers at regular times of the day, and I have seen textile workers in Moldavia standing at their workbenches at 11.00 in the morning, waving their arms around rather half-heartedly in time to music from loudspeakers. But on the whole institutions are more concerned nowadays about fulfilling production plans. You can always follow the lissom couple who disport themselves every morning on television in time to the piano and the trainer's stern commands, if you wish to keep fit. However, most Russians are far from fit – too fat, pasty-faced and prone to colds and illnesses. If you go to the public steam baths, it really is a case of all flesh being revealed.

The generally stodgy diet does nothing to help, but many fashion-conscious women nowadays go to great lengths to overcome the national tendency to solid bulk. Dieting is another area where every quack has a different scheme, and Russians are forever swapping new diet ideas. The ultimate remedy, which is much in fashion, is total starvation:

women will take nothing but tea, and perhaps the odd apple, for days on end. I know one woman who could look very elegant after shedding several kilos. One Monday, after a week of rigorous starvation, she looked very depressed, explaining she had been to a funeral over the weekend. It turned out though that her distress was not caused by the death of a friend, but because at the gathering after the funeral the hostess had prepared *blini* – Russian pancakes. Temptation had so overcome her that she ate eighteen on the spot, thus ruining a complete week's dieting.

Jogging, like every Western fad, has also caught on: every evening and weekend thousands of people don track-suits and set off by the banks of the Moscow river or in the parks. The state is still not satisfied with the level of physical fitness, however. Military chiefs complain that young people are way below the mark when they are drafted for national service. And so a decree was issued in 1981 ordering a thorough reorganization of the country's sports policies so that less time and money was spent training top athletes and more on getting ordinary people into shape. 'Regular exercise has an important influence on the productivity of industrial enterprises, helps reduce loss of working time, strengthens labour discipline and cuts down on labour turnover,' it said.

There are areas of excellence in Soviet medicine: eye surgery receives a lot of money and attention, and much pioneering work has been done in this field. Unusual publicity has been given at home and abroad to Professor Svyatoslav Fyodorov, director of the Institute of Eye Micro-surgery, who in 1974 pioneered a technique of correcting near-sightedness by micro-incisions on the cornea, which on healing contract and alter the curvature. It sounds a risky operation, but Professor Fyodorov has travelled around the world to promote his technique and invited a delegation of American eye-surgeons to a seminar on his work. He has one of the best equipped hospitals in the Soviet Union, and the results are impressive. A Norwegian journalist, watching an operation, asked if his own myopia could be treated. He went around with rather pink sore eyes for several weeks – he said it felt as though he had sand in them all the time – but after that he was able permanently to discard his thick dark-rimmed glasses. The professor has carried out well over 3,000 operations and given many press conferences overseas. Britain runs a programme of co-operation in eye-surgery with the Russians, and a number of British children have travelled to Moscow for specialist treatment.

The Russians are also investing a lot of money in facilities for

hyperbaric medicine – the carrying out of operations in an atmosphere
of intensified oxygen pressure – and have hosted international conferences on this. In another field, a well-known paediatrician has developed a novel technique of underwater childbirth. And in one experiment in 'spelaeotherapy' in the town of Perm a hospital ward has been set
up at the bottom of a potash salt mine, and every night patients are taken
750 feet below ground to spend twelve hours in a cave microclimate to
cure bronchial asthma and other allergies.

These are the publicised peaks. Unfortunately, however, in spite of
sophisticated eye surgery, ordinary spectacles are very difficult to obtain.
And in other fields the general medicine available to the ordinary citizen
is less than impressive. I once visited a hospital where sportsmen and
athletes who break bones are treated – supposedly a rather special ward.
But although the nursing staff were friendly, the standard of hygiene in
the ward was poor, and most of the patients had food brought in for them
by relatives. A fellow journalist who went to hospital once was admitted
to the normal wing of the Botkin, the Moscow hospital to which all
diplomats are referred, and facilities there were rudimentary. As he was
being taken up on a stretcher to the ward, the lift got stuck, which did not
inspire confidence. The second time he was admitted, he was taken to
the special wing for foreigners, where standards were much higher, with
a private room, television and better food.

The ambulance service is staffed by qualified doctors, but ambulances are frequently grounded by a shortage of petrol or spare parts. In
addition unscrupulous drivers use them to make money on the side as
taxis. (A colleague was once surprised when his translator returned so
quickly from a visit to the Bank for Foreign Trade, where he had sent
her. 'Oh I was lucky,' she said, 'I caught an ambulance.' And the wife of
another colleague who was late for her ballet class managed to get there
on time by hitching a lift in an ambulance which happily stopped for
her.) But all too often ambulances can take over an hour to respond to an
emergency call – and I have seldom seen one hurrying through the city
traffic.

Outside the big cities the medical services are indeed primitive. Few
doctors want to work in the villages, though many are obliged to spend
their first two years after training in these isolated communities. In most
villages there is only a 'medical point', a simple first aid hut staffed by
semi-qualified para-medics under the old *feldscher* system. The seriously ill have to be taken far away to regional hospitals and polyclinics.
Health care for the aged has also been frequently criticised in the press,

and the disabled have so few facilities, mostly spending their lives virtually incarcerated in special institutions, that their case has been taken up by a number of dissident groups which are agitating for better conditions. The handicapped are kept well out of the public eye: apart from a few war veterans, it is rare that you see a mentally retarded person or indeed anyone in a wheelchair in public places in the Soviet Union.

Some aspects of medicine appear very old-fashioned to Westerners. The standard treatment for heart attacks is lengthy confinement to bed, and enforced immobility for weeks after the attack: quite the reverse of Western thinking nowadays, which insists on exercise and therapy as swiftly as possible. 'Cupping' is still used, drawing impurities to the surface of the body by placing heated cups on the skin. And in many maternity hospitals swaddling is still the rule. Fathers are not allowed to see their newborn or visit their wives for at least ten days – and of course there is no question of their being present at the birth. Many Russian women cite their unpleasant experiences during childbirth as a principal reason for not wanting any more children.

But in other areas the Russians are close to practices used in the West. Mental health perhaps is one (I am not referring to the horrific practice of committing dissidents to psychiatric hospitals and forcibly treating them with mind-altering drugs). Freud is still officially taboo, his works are not published and the role of psychoanalysis is disputed. But the role of society in promoting mental health, and the causes for breakdown are more and more being recognized, especially in the big cities. In 1981 the Russians began their own version of the 'Samaritans' – a confidential telephone service for people in despair. In Moscow groups of volunteers and psychologists man the lines twenty-four hours a day, and do their best to refer callers to the city's fifteen regional mental health clinics, where patients can seek help anonymously. Similar services are operating in Riga and Dnepropetrosvsk, Kharkov and Tomsk.

Russians find it hard to understand that Westerners can be so nonchalant about their health. They are especially surprised that the West puts so little store by prophylactic medicine, for this is taken very seriously by everyone. One friend was for ever trying to get me to eat the right berries and herbs, to drink special home-brewed tea and eat all the other things he was convinced were essential if one was to ward off the regular bouts of flu that struck people down every spring and autumn.

Keeping warm is an obsession. Woe to the naive foreigner who ventures outside in winter without a hat: he will be nagged and lectured by a dozen passing *babushki*, made to feel that he is half naked and irresponsibly toying with his health. We knew a solid and simple woman who was convinced that opening the *fortuchka*, the little vent in every double window, was an invitation in winter to instant pneumonia, and who would fuss and cluck unceasingly if she detected the slightest draught in the overheated room. And it is worse where children are concerned. No matter how warmly you wrap up your children in winter, you can be sure they will appear criminally underclothed to some good soul: an extra hat, another pair of leggings, a thicker coat are urged on the child. And only when the little mite is so padded out that he is almost immobile and waddles around like a woollen ball will the *babushki* feel they have taken enough precautions against the cold.

I sometimes resented these busybodies, and once tried to argue it out with an old woman who complained I had not dressed my young son properly. It was no use: she looked bemused at my talk of fresh air and exercise, did not understand that light down clothing was actually warmer than heavy padded coats, and went away shaking her head and asserting that 'With us, it is different. We don't do things like that.' And so in the end I cowed before them, and began to feel guilty if I sneaked outside even for a few minutes without my fur hat until it was at least mid-April and I felt secure in seeing other Russians discard their fur hats (though they usually then wore light summer hats).

Perhaps Russians are natural hypochondriacs, or perhaps the older generation has not yet got used to a state health service. In any case, most people go, whenever possible, to a doctor or dentist who operates unofficially – and illegally – in private practice. Only this way, they believe, can their ailments be properly diagnosed and attended to. It is certainly true that as the complaints about the state system mount and the instances of sloppiness and malpractice appear to increase, so the recourse to alternatives – private practice, herbal medicine and quacks – has grown. A friend used to go regularly to an excellent Jewish dentist, who had set up a complete clinic in his own flat. He showed me the professional bridging work the man had done on his teeth, including some intricate gold work, and wondered what he would do in the future. For the dentist had been granted permission to emigrate. And nothing would persuade my friend to entrust his teeth to the state's care.

A campaign to improve medical services is now under way. Whether it can have much effect on the alarming mortality statistics and the apparent drop in standards of public health over the past decade without the expenditure of vast sums to strengthen the infrastructure and ancillary services remains to be seen.

CHAPTER FOUR

Leisure: The Timeless Approach to Life

When Russians enjoy themselves, they do so to the limit. Casting aside the protective mask of formality or indifference they wear at work or in the street, they throw themselves into their pleasures with gusto. No party is complete without singing, dancing, quantities to eat and drink, tears, laughter and an almost sensuous indulgence in argument, discussion and the baring of innermost feelings. Hospitality is overwhelming: the guest is expected to stay for hours, to use the house as though it were his own, to let his hair down in spontaneous displays of affection. The Russians are wary of formal entertaining, of anything that smacks of protocol and the surveillance of the outside world. They enjoy being themselves, behaving spontaneously in the warmth of each other's company.

Leisure and free time are precious, and opportunities must be seized when they arise. The working week is still long, and the occasions limited when families and friends are all able to be together. Society provides little organized entertainment: apart from activities for children in the Pioneers' palaces and the clubs run by factories and places of work, there is no leisure industry as such in the Soviet Union. And Russians therefore depend more on each other for entertainment than do most people in the West. They enjoy the basic pleasures of life: eating and drinking, getting out of the towns into the woods and countryside, singing, talking or simply lying in the sun or beside a warm stove in winter doing nothing.

Russians are sociable people and spend their free time in the company of others. The collective consciousness, strongly reinforced by the ideological approval of the *kollektiv* and distrust of individualism, throws Russians together not only at work, in shared flats and in the crowded cities, but also determines the pattern of Soviet leisure: organized excursions, groups and clubs for enthusiasts of chess, philately, music, sport and drama, rest-homes and sanatoria where millions of workers join their colleagues from work for the annual holiday in the sun.

There is nothing a Russian likes better than getting together with friends and relatives for a good meal. Public holidays are always a good excuse: New Year, International Women's Day on March 8, May Day, and the revolutionary celebrations of November 7. But apart from New Year, which has all the trappings of the Western Christmas, these state holidays seem too official to most people. It is more personal, more satisfying, to throw a party on a whim, or in celebration of a traditional event such as a birthday, a name-day (according to Russian Orthodox tradition each saint after whom most people are named has a designated day of celebration), a house-warming or Old New Year, which now falls on January 13.

Birthdays are especially popular. The Russians organize lavish parties, and everyone brings a present. There are always toasts, and virtually every guest makes a flowery speech. Of course there is vodka, wine and Soviet 'champagne', a rather sweet but, to my taste, delicious sparkling wine that is drunk in enormous quantities and produced on special occasions. The table groans with whatever food the enterprising host or hostess can procure. For starters, or *zakuski*, there may be red or black caviar, still a favourite delicacy though hard to find nowadays and expensive, smoked salmon, tuna fish, pickled tomatoes, cold sturgeon in aspic, assorted salads with strongly tasting herbs and greens from the south, freshly baked pastry pies with meat or cabbage inside, pickled gherkins, cheese and an infinite variety of mushrooms, invariably gathered and bottled by the host and a source of special pride.

All this is just for starters, something to accompany the vodka that is downed by the glassful in one great gulp after every toast. Dinner itself begins with soup such as borsch, the typical red beetroot soup, or clear broth or perhaps a fish *solyanka* soup or, in summer, a chilled soup of vegetables or meat in a stock made of *kvas*, a kind of beer made from fermented bread. And then there might be fish in cheese sauce, or mushrooms in individual pots baked in sour cream; and after that the main course – chicken or filet or beef strogonoff with potatoes, carrots and whatever greens can be found in the private peasant markets. Dessert may be fruit compot, ice-cream, sweet dumplings filled with fruit or a home-made cake. By this time you have been sitting many hours and drunk and laughed a good deal, and everyone has been pressed to eat more than he or she can, to make a speech and to regale the guests with some good story or anecdote.

Sadly the present food shortages mean that it takes a lot of ingenuity to find all the ingredients for such a feast. But for a special gathering

Russians spare no expense or effort to get enough to make their table a proud sight.

Russians eat at almost any time of the day. I could never get used to the sight or smell of other hotel guests tucking into meat and vegetables for breakfast, or finding I was expected to sit down for a hearty meal with vodka and wine at 11.00 a.m. Big meals in Russian homes take all day to prepare, and often begin at around 4.30 in the afternoon, lasting – on and off with breaks while people smoke or stroll about – until at least 10.00 at night. By that time the table has become the focal point for talk, and the subsequent discussion can go on for hours, as glasses are refilled and the room becomes a fog of smoke. Guests depart as the last buses go, or when they can get lifts in cars, or when they are ready to haggle in the street with a private motorist acting as an unofficial taxi. The last guest is usually still there at 2.00 in the morning, and many have no hesitation in dossing down for the night where they are.

No one stands on ceremony. Of course a party is an excuse to dress up, show off fashionable clothes; but there are no such things as black tie dinners in Moscow (except among the foreign diplomatic community), and jeans are just as smart as the best suit and, provided they have the right Western label, a great deal more chic.

There are some old-fashioned courtesies. Russians never arrive as guests empty-handed, and come with flowers or chocolates for the hostess, a bottle of wine, vase or some appropriate gift for the house. Many men still insist on the gallantry of bowing and kissing a lady's hand. And toasting and speechifying have an etiquette all to themselves. But the setting is never formal. Russian flats are too cramped or too untidy, and guests squeeze round the table as best they can, sitting on an assortment of different shaped chairs, elbowing each other, sharing the room with the dog or children who stay up late and are always fussed over by parents and guests alike.

Most people hanker after a little more ceremony and sense of occasion – though probably would not like it and would feel intimidated. Russians are acutely self-conscious when foreigners first come to their homes, apologizing or joking about the small rooms, and seem to expect the foreigner to be used to something grander. But tact and good humour on both sides can melt this barrier, and soon the foreigner will be drawn into the talk and drinking as though he were a long-standing friend (though in his presence even drunken Russians are careful not to let slip remarks that could raise eyebrows among the other guests).

Often parties are impromptu. Friends unexpectedly descend on someone who has a birthday, bearing food and drink, records and gifts, and whatever plans he had for the evening disappear in the jollity. Someone who sees friends at the theatre or meets old acquaintances unexpectedly invariably invites them all home, dashes off to get whatever food and drink can still be bought at that late hour and spreads out the cloth on the table. In a short time there is a meal and a celebration.

Nowhere is feasting and drinking more ingrained in the national culture than in Georgia. And, being Georgia, everything is on a more lavish scale, more showy, exuberant, costly than elsewhere in the Soviet Union. I vividly remember a baptism party in Tbilisi. With typical Georgian hospitality my wife and I were invited because we were friends of friends, although we ourselves knew neither the baby boy, his parents or relations. The table, laden with fresh summer produce, seemed to stretch for ever along the upstairs balcony of a picturesque wooden pre-revolutionary house in the city centre. At the head of the table sat the *tamada* – the toastmaster – whose job it was to cap all the speeches with a toast. We were drinking fresh white wine, which tasted at first like lemonade but whose lethal kick was only apparent some time later. Two large rams' horns were passed from guest to guest, full of wine, which could not be set down before being drained. As a foreigner I was expected to make a witty speech – rather difficult after several hornfuls of wine, when my Russian was still rudimentary and all the other guests were speaking Georgian. I hardly remember how the evening ended.

The toastmaster is a key figure not only in Georgia, but in all Russia, especially at weddings. And in a move to restore some old-fashioned dignity to these ceremonies, as well as cut down excessive drinking, the Soviet authorities are discreetly trying to breed a new generation of toastmasters whose apparently contradictory task is to keep most of the guests reasonably sober.

A few years ago a special faculty to train toastmasters was opened in – of all unlikely places – the National University of Atheism in the Estonian capital Tallinn, and was promptly inundated with applications. Local factories begged the university to enrol their candidates who could then officiate at new factory banqueting halls. Letters poured in from as far away as Irkutsk in Siberia asking whether would-be toast-masters could follow the course by correspondence. Instruction consisted of lectures on how to plan receptions, organize speeches, amuse guests and – most importantly – see that everyone was so busy singing, dancing, eating and playing games that there was no time for downing too many glasses of vodka or champagne.

The revival of this traditional figure has been prompted by growing concern over the rowdiness of many weddings nowadays. The press has called them 'elaborate displays of wealth', where all the talk is of how much the dresses cost and what the presents are worth. At the other extreme, weddings are too casual – the briefest meetings on station platforms or at airports where a few friends toast the couple with quick sips of champagne before they set off on their honeymoon.

Most Russians would like a proper wedding, but are put off by the difficulties of booking a reception room, making the arrangements and getting tickets for the honeymoon. The press has reported cases of couples who were obliged to join hiking tours for their honeymoon as it was the only kind of holiday available.

Drunkenness at weddings is certainly a problem nowadays. But not only wedding guests suffer from a tide of vodka. A meal out in a restaurant usually ends with several of the guests having to be carried out and escorted home. By comparison with other nations, Russians do not eat out often: it is expensive, the choice is limited and the menu uniform. Moscow is not a city of little cafés and corner restaurants, and the quick-service 'dining-rooms', as the buffets are called, are nowhere to go for pleasure. The food is greasy, often cold, and you eat standing up at high tables.

An evening meal out in the Soviet Union is a serious business. The first problem is deciding where to go – the best restaurants are invariably full, and advance booking is essential. Moscow connoisseurs have their favourites: the Aragvi for Georgian cuisine, the Uzbekistan for Turkish-style kebabs, the Peking for Chinese-style food, the Berlin, Prague and Central Restaurants for Russian food, the Arbat and a restaurant in the Intourist hotel for a floor show and so on. Some of the best are on the outskirts of Moscow, beside the river or in the woods, where carved wooden decoration gives a more traditional and intimate atmosphere.

It is best to go with a group. Soviet restaurants seem happiest with groups, whereas individuals are usually left sitting forlornly in a corner for hours before being served. The first challenge comes when you arrive. How do you get in? The door is usually locked, with a large group of hungry people standing stoically in a queue. You have to negotiate your way past the suspicious doorman, using the diplomatic skills outlined earlier. But if these still fail to convince him you have a bona fide booking, the best way is usually a five-rouble note slipped hastily into his open palm, or a packet of foreign cigarettes.

If you regularly patronize a restaurant you can sometimes avoid this procedure. An American acquaintance was entertained in the Berlin restaurant, and was brought in round the back through the kitchens. The manageress seated him amongst senior Soviet officials. Next time he went there he again went in through the kitchens – and noticed the other diners did so also. Going to the main street door to investigate, he found it locked, with a cardboard notice stuck in the window. On one side it said 'closed'. On the back was written 'No free places'. It was turned from one side to the other according to the time of day.

Service is maddeningly slow but Russians rarely complain. They go out to celebrate, and that means taking time and having plenty to drink between courses. Placing an order is a matter of pot luck. The menu is large, but only dishes with prices marked beside them are on, and not always those. On designated days, as part of the economy campaign, many restaurants observe a fish day and do not serve any meat.

The best restaurants in hotels frequented by Western tourists have orchestras in the evenings. The repertoire generally includes Western pop music, deafeningly over-amplified, and appears to be the same in every hotel. Dancing is *de rigueur*. If the men are too preoccupied with the vodka, as they often are, the women dance together. Foreign men are just as likely to be approached by buxom blondes as vice-versa.

The quality of food in all restaurants leaves much to be desired. The main problem is that it is served luke-warm. The waiters earn the same salary no matter how many people they serve. They have little enthusiasm for the job and no proper training (except in the big Intourist hotels). They tend to regard the idea of service as undignified and degrading, and food can wait twenty minutes in the kitchens before the waiters bother to collect it. Not surprisingly, Russians leave large amounts of food on their plates, but this has more to do with over-ordering and the status of showing that you are wealthy enough not to need to eat every morsel than with the cuisine itself.

Few restaurants attempt gourmet cooking. The tradition has almost been extinguished by revolution, famine, war and ideological disapproval of frivolous eating. But demand, fuelled by public grumbling, is growing. Some new restaurants, smaller than the cavernous eating halls that were favoured in Khrushchev's day, are attempting to build up individual reputations. And in the Baltic republics intimate restaurants have been opened in historic buildings in city centres, where there is something of a family atmosphere. Indeed, so successful has this proved that there is talk of licensing privately run 'family restaurants' all over the country. In Georgia most restaurants, serving better food than in the north, are virtually – though not officially – privately run already.

The best food is to be had in places not open to the general public: clubs belonging to the Union of Actors or Journalists, Writers and so on. Genuine foreign cuisine is a rarity. The head chef at the Intourist hotel does know how to prepare haggis, as groups of Scots fly to Moscow every January, bearing dozens of uncooked haggis with them, to celebrate Burns night at the hotel with members of the Soviet Burns society (who, I suspect, are sometimes there just for the free whisky). The Peking hotel does boast Chinese food, but it is not what it was. In the days when Russia and China were linked in comradely unity, the hotel was built as a monument to friendship. The restaurant ceiling was hand-painted in extravagantly beautiful Chinese style. Chinese cooks prepared the dishes with Chinese ingredients. But after the ideological break they all left. Soviet chefs now attempt to cook the same dishes using Soviet contents. And nowadays 'chicken trepang' is something all to itself. I once asked for it. 'You won't eat it,' the waiter replied. 'Why not?' I asked. 'It's disgusting,' he answered flatly. And he was right.

There are sporadic attempts to set up foreign restaurants in Moscow. There were long negotiations with a well-known American hamburger chain before the Olympics, but they foundered on Soviet insistence that Soviet meat, not considered by the Americans to be up to standard, be used in the hamburgers. Since then a Japanese restaurant – catering only to foreigners and accepting only convertible currency – has opened, and for two brief weeks in 1982 a so-called genuine Italian restaurant opened as an experiment. All the food was imported from Italy, and there was almost a crisis when the truck bringing it ran out of petrol in the Ukraine and could only be refuelled by having a truck sent all the way from Moscow to its aid. However, this did not deter some determined pasta lovers from setting up a real pizza parlour a few months later, which naturally became overnight the 'in' place to go.

The influx of tourists has had some effect in improving standards in the big cities. The main hotels in Moscow and Leningrad have had to introduce self-service restaurants, as tour groups spent so long waiting for breakfast that they missed the treasures of the Hermitage. Nowadays most hotels have set meals laid out ready for the tourists. I remember a blazing row that ensued in Samarkand when a colleague sat down and ate a breakfast apparently intended for a member of a tourist group. He was roundly chastised by the restaurant manager, the waitress, the

American tour guide and the unfortunate tourist who then had to go without breakfast.

Still, the Russians themselves consider things have a long way to go. A survey in Georgia found that 87 per cent of those who went to restaurants did not like the quality of the food, 90 per cent said it was too expensive, 83 per cent criticised the service, and 87 per cent did not like the atmosphere. Similar surveys in Moscow have shown similar results.

Finding a place in a restaurant is doubly difficult on public holidays, and especially at New Year, the big secular holiday that has replaced Christmas in the Soviet Union. New Year is a time for parties, family gatherings and drinking. Nowadays it has all the trappings of the Western Christmas. Several huge trees are put up in the city centres, decorated with coloured lights, glittering balls and imitation presents hanging from the boughs. A giant tree, still smelling strongly of the forest, stands inside the Palace of Congresses inside the Kremlin, admired by the thousands who stream in every evening to watch the Bolshoi Ballet perform there. Throughout Moscow, officials boast, about 50,000 trees go up in shops, offices and on street squares.

In Russia, as elsewhere, the Christmas tree tradition has been borrowed from Germany, but by now it is firmly established. Every home tries to get a tree, and for the ten days before New Year people mill around the markets where trucks deposit about 700,000 small pines from the state plantations. In the evenings you see people hurrying down the metro escalators clutching their prizes tied up with string. There are still not enough trees to satisfy demand – a third of all buyers go away empty-handed or have to make do with plastic ones. And those lucky enough to get hold of a *yolka*, as the traditional shaped tree is called, queue at least two hours, and often up to eight according to one newspaper survey, many doing so in working hours.

Every year some entrepreneurs sneak off into the forests to poach trees. The fine has now been increased to 100 roubles (about £63), but the papers annually report such cases as that of the man who chopped down a tree in the avenue outside his flat – for which he had to pay an extra 45 roubles replanting costs – or the man in Siberia who was sent to jail for three years for cutting down a rare cedar. The authorities estimate the annual damage inflicted by illegal cutting at 120,000 roubles.

New Year is the time for Grandfather Frost, the Soviet Santa Claus. He comes naturally in boots, a red fur-trimmed costume and a flowing white beard, and nowadays he is as commercialized in Russia as in the West. Down in Kirghizia, where snow rarely settles and Grandfather

Frost is as far removed from Central Asian customs as Muslim customs are from Moscow, the men in beards and boots nevertheless have a busy time. As everywhere in the country, they use the occasion to promote feelings of public gratitude to the state and party, opening shops and cinemas, and presenting the lucky owners in the big towns with keys to flats, holding sessions in the palaces of culture and entertaining children.

In Moscow Grandfather Frost does his stint at the main toy shop Detsky Mir ('Children's World') just across the road from the headquarters of the KGB. But he also has a plan to fulfil – and there are sometimes complaints that he only spends forty-five minutes a day in the shop. On New Year's Eve thousands of Grandfather Frosts – selected after a tough examination by a special commission, according to *Pravda* – take part in Moscow's 'Dial-a-Santa' service. For a fee of 5 roubles one will appear at your door, fill up his sack with the presents you quickly hand him, and then delight the children by delivering their toys. The only hazard is hospitality – after a glass of something warming at each of the first ten flats, Grandfather Frost tends to radiate something more than seasonal jollity. It needs the icy eye of 'Sneguruchka', the Snow Maiden, who usually accompanies him dressed as a maiden in comely white, to keep things in control.

The toy shops do a brisk trade before the holiday, and by New Year's Eve almost all the shelves are bare. The best toys are East German – well-made electric trains, stuffed animals, jigsaws, construction kits and so on. The worst, by a long chalk, are locally made Soviet toys, which have an uncanny ability to fall to pieces in five minutes or simply do not work at all. Toy trucks cut your fingers with their sharp edges, wheels fall off the plastic tractors and even the imitation machine-guns – a great favourite despite official propaganda which maintains that unseemly war toys are sold only in the West – are considerably shorter lasting than the real thing. A friend once saw a mother complaining that the radio-controlled toy tank she had bought for her son did not work. The shop assistant took another. That too would not move, so she threw it in the corner, and took another. That also ended up in the corner. She took another and then another, until about the twelfth worked and the corner was full of useless toys. 'Let's hope the real ones work better,' some wag remarked who had watched the sorry scene.

The press has often criticized the poor standard of toys. The problem is that there is no single ministry of toy-making. Toys are made by 950 factories working under a dozen different ministries. Despite exhortations for more Meccano-type construction kits, tool sets, model lathes and toys to instil a love of industry and work, anything produced is snapped up by adults who cannot get hold of real tools and make do with toy versions. The papers once recounted how one ministry decided on its own initiative to invent a toy suitable for handicapped children. It devised a rattle for deaf children that flashed a light instead of making a noise. When the All-Russian Society for the Deaf received a sample, it sent out a letter to let parents know about it. Not one person ordered the flashing rattle.

The New Year break is a favourite time for winter sportsmen and outdoor skaters. Many people go into the woods cross-country skiing, or ice-fishing on the frozen lakes. Hardy swimmers known as 'seals' brave sub-zero temperatures, cut a hole in the ice and plunge in. Children can go on special troika rides at Moscow's Permanent Exhibition of Economic Achievements. There, for a fee, they can whirl through the snow in a sleigh pulled by three steaming horses and pretend the old days live on.

Russians are hardy, outdoor people, and for many the greatest pleasure is being outside, close to nature in winter and summer. Nothing typifies the Russian character better than the national passion for mushrooming. When the summer comes and the sun lights up the damp woods, people in their thousands flock out with baskets and sharp knives to go mushroom hunting. Enthusiasts set off in the small hours in hired buses, and many make a weekend of it, taking the late night suburban trains into the villages on Fridays. They take a short nap in the stations – the hardier venturing to camp in the woods – and at first light they begin.

To go mushrooming you need sharp eyes, waterproof boots, old clothes and a stout stick. Experts know the best ground for the various fungi – spongy and damp for some, and a little drier and near birch trees for some of the tastiest. You need the stick to poke at the fallen leaves, as some of the commonest fungi look just like yellow leaves. Or if you lift up the branches of small pines you can find a variety of mushrooms sprouting in the sheltered gloom.

There are up to forty varieties of edible mushrooms commonly found around Moscow. Generally considered the best are the *belyie* – white ones – but also common are *chernushki* – black ones – and *lishichki* (little foxes). Others have picturesque names like 'Under the Aspens', 'Under the Birches', 'Little Pigs', 'Caesar's Mushroom', and a popular sort called *opyata*, meaning 'Round the Tree Trunks'. Mushrooming is hard work. You wander from glade to glade, poking, bending, picking and scrabbling through the trees. In some places there are little colonies of bright red button-shaped mushrooms; in others you find a large, gnarled-looking, yellowish-brown one standing on its own or half hidden under the soil.

In the excitement of the chase you can go on for hours and get completely lost. People go in groups and call to each other now and then so as not to get parted. Or else they call over their friends to work a particularly productive patch or to view a giant mushroom (newspapers regularly report the finding of mushrooms several feet across). Of course, not everything is edible. As a rough rule anything with a thin stem is an inedible toadstool. The Russians call these *poganki*, from the old world *pogani* meaning foul. Some toadstools are well-known in Britain – the bright red one with white spots, called in Russia 'fly poison' (fly agaric in English), or the temptingly smooth white ones (avenging angels in English) so similar to common field mushrooms.

Most *gribniki*, as mushroom hunters are called, know the difference between good and bad, but unfortunately not all. Every year there are cases of poisoning, sometimes fatal. Hospitals prepare for a rush of cases when the season starts in early summer. For people's guidance many booklets and pamphlets are published on the attributes and characteristics of fungi. Children learn about them at school. Large illustrations are put up beside market stalls where huge heaps are on display, all shapes and colours, waiting to be bottled, preserved, salted, fried, baked or eaten raw by those who have not had time to gather their own.

At the end of the day the *gribniki* sort out their baskets of fungi, rejecting the bad or very dirty. The laborious task of cleaning them properly begins at home. It is usually work reserved for women, while the men discuss their finds, like anglers boasting about a good catch. Russians love mushrooming because they feel they have enjoyed nature to the full. But this enjoyment is only complete when it involves suffering. When Russians walk, ski, fish or go mushrooming, they go on for ten or twelve hours until it hurts; otherwise they feel the day has not been properly exhausting. The reward is warmth at home later, or several glasses of vodka with pickled mushrooms from an earlier crop, or a visit to the steam baths to relax.

Even in the cities older enthusiasts can be found mushrooming on the grass medians that separate the dual carriageways, or in the little parks between Moscow's boulevards. Russians do not lose their mushrooming instinct when abroad. If you get up early enough, you can sometimes see Soviet diplomats hunting for mushrooms in London's parks, amazed that such delicacies are neglected by the natives.

Russians have an almost mystical belief in the value of fresh summer air. For six months of winter they seal themselves off from the freezing world outside, swaddling themselves in layers of padded clothing. They nail shut the windows and seal every crack with strips of sticky paper, heat up their buildings to an extraordinary degree and live in a fetid fug from November till May. By spring everyone is pale and coughing, and most have had several bouts of flu. When summer comes at last, the one thought is to get outside, fill the lungs with country air, get back to the rural roots that still bind even city dwellers so closely to the land.

Those who have money, position and influence usually have dachas – country cottages which have sometimes remained in the family for generations. Nestling in woods or near rivers, these slightly shabby painted wooden structures look like stage sets for a Chekhov play. Those belonging to writers, artists and intellectuals are virtually unchanged inside. The Revolution, instead of abolishing these country seats for the privileged, simply made them communal. Many of the best dachas, formerly belonging to the nobility, are now owned by factories, newspapers and trade unions which let their members use them in turn. But it is still everyone's dream to have his own dacha, and all round the big cities hundreds of privately owned cottages, some no more than two-room huts, are clustered in woods and fields. The lucky owners pack up on Friday nights, take the suburban train to the outskirts of Moscow or Leningrad and relax on their country plots all weekend. Some even commute daily from their dachas throughout the summer. On the hills around Tbilisi, the Georgian capital, the dachas are minor palaces – all marble and stone and sumptuously decorated. The wealthy are still building their retreats. 'It's our millionaires' row,' remarked a local official who took me on a tour of the area.

Recently the state has tried to entice people back to the land by giving grants to build modest dachas on condition they cultivate the surrounding land and put in a stint in the communal orchards. These 'orchard cultivation co-operatives' are so popular that there is a waiting list to join.

The British embassy, like other western embassies, has a dacha, rented from the state in prime dacha land where the Bolshoi Ballet, Soviet ministries and other top bodies have their retreats. It is a cosy, rather dilapidated, rambling wooden house near the Moscow River. It has a big room for parties, several bedrooms, a sitting-room with an open wood fireplace, deep old sofas and piles of well-thumbed magazines. Long ago the heating stoves, built into the walls, used to work, but now they are sealed up and radiators keep it snug when the snow piles up outside.

Only a fraction of Moscow's 8 million people can get out to dachas. And when it is hot and sultry, as it often is in summer, many just go to the nearby lakes, reservoirs and rivers. A favourite place is Seryebroni Bor ('Silver Wood') on the Moscow River. Only about thirty minutes from the city centre by trolleybus, it is quiet, green, fresh, and a world away from the rush and squash of the city. It is just beyond the diplomatic dachas, so Russians have to leave their cars far away and take a bus down to the river. Foreigners, of course, ignore the 'No entry' sign and drive down to the beach.

There *is* a beach, and a seaside atmosphere, although it is 400 miles to the nearest coast. On a Saturday afternoon Silver Wood is crowded with ordinary people enjoying themselves. They sit around on wooden benches playing cards, drinking beer, and munching dried fish wrapped in old copies of *Pravda*. Someone has usually brought a transistor, tuned to Radio Moscow's 'World Service' – not because he wants to practise his English, but because it is the best way to hear the latest Russian or even Western pop music. (Taxi drivers who speak no word of English usually have a stream of impeccably American English from this service pouring out of their radio.) Here and there a cassette recorder is playing the Bee Gees. Someone sporting a black market T-shirt with 'Pop City Music' printed on it strolls past.

Families are tucking into sardines or boiled eggs bought from the pavilion, a dilapidated wooden hut that is open only about ten weekends a year – though not during the lunch hour – and sells lemonade, beer, assorted snacks and those peculiarly Russian cigarettes (*papyrosi*) with an inch of strong, sweet tobacco at the end of three inches of hollow cardboard tubing. Corpulent grandmothers with no inhibitions entrust their voluminous bodies to garish and outsize bikinis and manufacture triangular paper hats from old copies of *Pravda*. (This organ of the Communist party appears to have a hundred more useful functions than purveying the daily party line). They fuss over little children, who also wear floppy hats. As soon as it is warm enough to remove the woollen bonnets that envelop children all winter, the grandmothers insist on a sunhat in case of sunstroke.

Some romantic young couples lie speechless and supine in the sun. Many more take part in organized games of volleyball, punching the ball around in a group with a lot of laughter and shouting. There is always a match going on at the two old table tennis tables near the entrance to the beach enclosure. A group of fifteen-year-olds are horsing around, burying each other in sand and trying to smoke illicit cigarettes undetected.

In mid-summer you can hire rowing boats for 47 kopecks (30p) an hour, but police launches cruise up and down and a stentorian voice bellows through the megaphone at any citizens who row their boats beyond the marker buoys. Now and then an enormous barge, laden with coal or pig iron, is tugged along in the direction of the city. My young son and I and a Russian friend once hired a boat during the Falklands crisis. We rowed about in circles very ineptly for a while, almost being run down by a large pleasure steamer, and then attempted to steer back to the bank. The man in charge must have heard us speaking English, for he shouted out as we approached: 'Falklands Islands, over here!'

Naturally there are rules: no Russian place of enjoyment is complete without instructions on how to enjoy yourselves. 'Citizens!' say the placards, with appropriate cartoons, 'observe the following rules! Don't jump into the water from ice, benches, car tyres or floating objects. Don't swim too far from the bank or overestimate your strength. Don't let children play unsupervised. Don't play around in an unsober state. Don't swim near oncoming boats. Don't remove the life belts from the stands . . .' and so on. No one takes much notice of these eminently sensible regulations – that is the way with all rules in the Soviet Union.

The families and groups of friends stay till dusk when they queue for the trolleybuses home. By evening the place is usually deserted. In the distance can be seen two of Stalin's gothic wedding cakes, markers of the city skyline. Nearby is an old church with gleaming cupolas. On the opposite bank thick trees hide what must be a more exclusive area closed to the public. Under the silver birch trees behind the beach, people wander down the paths, while old women in headscarves gossip on benches in clearings.

Despite their love of the open air, Russians have little interest in gardening – unless it is for profit. Most city dwellers do not have a garden, and the communal gardens in the courtyards of apartment blocks are a pathetic sight: a few straggling flowers are planted in the early spring, but they are quickly forgotten as they are surrounded by weeds. Dacha gardens are not tended and trimmed as the English would have them. For the Russians, nature is meant to be enjoyed *au naturel*, and the ideal garden is one that most closely resembles a jungle. Grass should be a meadow, thick and lush, flowers should ramble wild and trees should have that forlorn, untamed look that features in every painting of the Russian landscape.

This outlook is convenient in a country where a lawnmower is almost unknown and where the idea of disciplined work with a trowel in your free time seems idiotic. You have to go to Estonia to find more Teutonic order and tidiness. But the unkempt look is not so suitable for the big parks. Here gardening has been refined to a semi-industrial art. A planting brigade goes out in spring and huge beds appear to bloom overnight. I have watched a street-washing lorry water all the flowers outside the hotel in Yalta with admirable economy of time and labour. The driver directed a high-pressure hose on to each tub, and within ten seconds it was inundated, with spatterings of mud and flowers on the ground as evidence of speedy delivery.

Growing for profit is a different matter, however. With the increasing shortage of fresh fruit and vegetables, more and more city-dwellers are turning – with official encouragement – to the cultivation of private plots. Books on kitchen gardening are in demand, and translations of Western manuals on running your allotment are even circulating in *samizdat* copies. At the markets peasants sell home-collected seeds in little newspaper cones with gaudy handpainted cards beside each pile illustrating sumptuous marrows or succulent tomatoes. I know of one man who set up a hothouse in his flat. He filled an entire room with trays and earthbeds, and in spring was able to offer tulip bulbs and vegetable seedlings at prices that quickly made him very rich.

Flowers are easily the most profitable thing to grow, and inhabitants of the sunny south, especially Georgians, used to book up all the seats on Aeroflot every spring and fly north with suitcases of flowers (though this has recently fallen under official disapproval). The demand is insatiable – flowers are essential not only for weddings and banquets, but to greet delegations at stations and airports, to throw on stage at your favourite theatre or ballet star, present to your teacher on the first day of school and to take round to friends in hospital or entertaining at dinner. Roses and gladioli sell for a minimum of 3 roubles (£2) a bloom. There is a well-known joke about the flower trade; an airliner from Georgia to Moscow was hijacked and ordered to fly to Paris. Suddenly two passengers sprang up, overpowered the hijackers and told the pilot to continue to Moscow. On landing the Georgians were fêted with a heroes' welcome, but a friend took them aside and asked why they had done it when they could otherwise have been in Paris. 'But,' replied one Georgian, 'what are we going to do with 2,000 daffodils in Paris?'

The one area where urban Russians excel is indoor gardening. Potted plants have become voguish, with huge palms adorning hotels and private homes. One of the best displays I remember used to be in the cashier's office of the Moscow customs house. I was pleased to discover the cashier's penchant, and once took her a particularly nice plant when I knew a consignment of mine arriving from Finland bore a rather steep duty. She was delighted, and with rare and infuriating Soviet rectitude accepted the gift and charged me the full duty.

The Russians know the English as keen gardeners. But English people are also celebrated as dog-lovers, and the typical Englishman in Soviet films and popular imagination always has one or two dogs in his home. Nowadays the description applies equally to the average Muscovite. A mania for dogs, cats, birds and pets of all kinds is gripping the country. Almost every household boasts some four-legged creature.

Dogs are especially fashionable. At any time of the day or night you can see young men exercising their dogs in the parks or pensioners walking them in the yards beside each block of flats. As you go up the staircase in almost every block you can hear barking and yapping coming through the usual black, supposedly soundproof padding on people's front doors. All breeds can be found: poodles, terriers, wolfhounds, Alsatians, St Bernards, collies and English sheepdogs. Especially popular, in spite of a natural and somewhat embarrassing disadvantage in the winter snow, is the dachshund. Indeed at the moment the dachshund is in short supply. Ten years ago there were plenty to be had. Now you have to wait years if you apply for one at a recognized kennel club.

A dog has become a prestige symbol, a sign of money and good taste which can be trotted out daily to be shown to the neighbours. It is a far cry from the postwar years when most Russians could hardly feed themselves, or from the terrible 900-day siege of Leningrad during the war when dogs were eaten to keep a starving population alive. The bigger the dog, the greater the prestige, and people will go to inordinate lengths to acquire the right status symbol. I know of a couple who live in Yakutsk, in eastern Siberia, where the winter temperature can fall to minus 50 degrees, who travelled 4,000 miles to Moscow to collect a huge Afghan hound which they took back to share their one-room flat together with a child and mother-in-law.

A good pedigree dog can be quite expensive – up to 100 roubles – and breeders make a fortune. The Moscow pet market is one of the most fascinating places to visit. Every Saturday and Sunday it is thronged with pigeon-fanciers, fish-breeders, peasants from the countryside with rabbits, hamsters, canaries, coypu and other creatures for sale. A huge crowd jostles and pushes round the stalls, prodding, peering, filling up old pickle jars with brightly coloured miniature fish or spooning out birdseed from a sack into newspaper cones.

Dogs are not officially meant to be sold in the market, but there are plenty around. Usually their owners hang about the entrance, carrying large baskets covered with a blanket from which you occasionally see a wet, black nostril poking out. Big dogs sit on the ground under the trees, looking rather forlorn, especially in midwinter when only a bit of straw or old newspaper is put down for them on the snow. Many sellers, on the lookout in case they are moved on by the police for trading without a licence, keep their puppies tucked inside their jackets. As you walk past they flash open their coats, with a furtive 'psst' like dirty postcard sellers, to reveal a trembling, furry face.

All dogs should be officially registered with the local veterinary authorities and are given a number or address tag which they have to wear on their collars at all times. They are inoculated against rabies and the owners are told to look after them. Most Russians are fanatically proud of their dogs and eagerly take part in the shows and competitions organized for kennel club members. The winning dogs are awarded certificates and medals, and sometimes their owners take them for Sunday walks with all their medals and ribbons strapped to the animals' chests.

There is a sad side to the present explosion in the canine population. More and more people buy dogs out of caprice and do not look after them, turning them loose when they tire of them or move into a new flat, and the number of strays has increased alarmingly. In 1981 the press began a vigorous anti-dog campaign aimed at preparing people for the introduction of a dog licence of up to 200 roubles, a colossal sum which would have meant millions of dogs having to be destroyed. *Pravda* said the state spent 1,500 million roubles a year in subsidies on meat eaten only by dogs. A draft law was prepared enabling local authorities to ban the keeping of dogs in flats near kindergartens, and spoke of the diseases spread by dogs. But news of this leaked out, and such was the outcry, especially from pensioners, that the draft never became law.

Even attempts by municipal dog-catchers to round up strays have been hampered by angry citizens attacking them, smashing their vans and screaming abuse. But the strays are now a real danger in some cities. One pack made its home among the scenery and discarded props of the main Moscow film studios. Becoming hungry, they attacked people working there and killed four black swans which were the studio's pride. When they were finally put down there was such an outcry that the local authorities had to set up a special inquiry.

Another campaign began recently to suppress the latest fad: exotic pets. Many people have started keeping wild animals in their flats – monkeys, foxes, badgers, snakes and even lions. There was a tragic case in Baku of a family whose lion killed the child and then attacked the mother, and this was given great prominence in the press as a warning.

The Russians do not have organized greyhound racing, as in England, but they do have a strictly limited form of another Western sport, horse racing. I once went to the Moscow hippodrome to see what it is like. Built in 1955, the hippodrome is an extraordinary edifice looking like an imitation classical Greek building. The cream-coloured façade is topped with a spire and surrounded by statues of prancing horses. The entrance is through a marbled hall with a vaulted ceiling, and the two-tier grandstand is all columns with decorated capitals, painted ceilings, plaster frescoes of horses in Elysium.

In this classless society there are three classes of seating. For 30 kopecks you can go to the main stand with its wooden seats and high railings. For the top price you can go into the emptier, smarter section with its elaborate covered stand, stained glass windows (again of horses) and decorative canopies. Inside, the betting hall looks like a railway waiting-room, with women bookies (the word in Russian is *bukmaker*) sitting behind a wire grille. It is all a bit shabby, worn down by countless people and too little maintenance. And the attempt at grandeur is at odds with the eager, jostling, smoking, garlic-smelling crowd.

Racing begins at 1.00 on Sunday afternoons. The first thing to do is to queue up for a programme. The twenty-page booklet lists all the horses for each race, their age, parentage, times and placings in previous outings to give an idea of form, and the names of the jockeys and their colours.

Actually they are not really jockeys because on most days the events are trotting races, with the riders being pulled along in two-wheeled buggies. The flat racing season opens in the middle of summer, and on one grand day there is the equivalent of the Grand National, the Derby and Ascot all rolled into one. But usually on the three racing days – Wednesday and Saturday evenings and Sundays – it is trotting.

I arrived too late to get a programme, but persuaded one of the plump and friendly bookies to give me hers. She explained the betting: you have to pick the winning two horses. There is no place or show option, and the basic stake is a rouble. You get a cardboard ticket with the choice scribbled on. Of course all betting is on the totalizator system – there are no private bookmakers, at least not officially. In theory the odds are worked out before each race and the payouts vary accordingly. But there was no way of finding out the odds, and people say the winnings are suspiciously uniform and never more than a few roubles.

All types go to the races: actors, artists, rugged workers in rough clothes, the smart and fashionable sporting anoraks and T-shirts with familiar Western emblems on them, war veterans in their Sunday best with medals on their chest, leather-jacketed youths, swarthy mustachioed faces from the south, a few old women and the occasional blonde bombshell.

In the depths beneath the stands are more betting booths, beer bars, a smell of shashlik and the lavatories. Loudspeakers play oompah music. There is a happy, relaxed atmosphere. Even the police lounge against the fence and chat with the spectators.

For the 3.00 race I bet on a horse with the unlikely name of Cardiff. He had a promising lineage – born of Ideal and Culture. I wagered that Kashma would come in second. A bell rang three minutes before the race. Already a tanker truck, of the kind used for washing the streets, had been round the course spraying the dusty track. In the in-field was a large banner proclaiming 'Glory to work', a large illuminated indicator that did not work, a few heaps of sand and two clocks, one stopped at 12.00 and the other at 2.00. The finishing post – *finish* in Russian – was opposite the most expensive part of the stand.

The horses and buggies lined up beside a truck carrying a gate that stretched out across the track. The truck led them trotting down to the start, and then sped on ahead, drawing in the folding gate like wings and turning off the course as the horses raced on round. People cheered their favourites. Cardiff was meant to be number one, but there seemed to be three other horses also marked number one, which was confusing. The commentator seemed more laconic than his Western equivalents, but Cardiff was clearly in the lead. In the smart stands the enthusiasts were looking through binoculars. A few were squinting down telescopes.

They trotted round once, and Cardiff won. I pushed back through the throng to my friendly bookie to claim some money. She explained I had not understood the system: Kashma came in fourth instead of second as I had wagered. 'But I wish you'd won,' she said kindly, as she took my money for the next race. They went round again, the riders in their coloured plastic helmets and striped jackets, the horses stepping high with a few laggards breaking into an illegal gallop as the jockeys restrained them (a notice in the programme announced that there would be no payouts on any horse that galloped). Unfortunately Dialogue and Kamchatka, my next choices, came in second and third instead of first and second. My betting ticket joined the thousands of others littering the ground.

Russians have a passion for gambling. Perhaps that is why it is so carefully controlled. There have been scandals from time to time that the jockeys fix the races. I know of one man who used to put large sums with illegal private bookmakers (who operate with a few winks and nods). He even gave in his party membership card and his internal passport as guarantees when his request for credit was denied. In the end he literally laid his suit on a horse then and there in mid-winter, caught pneumonia and died.

From time to time the authorities have twinges of conscience that horse racing is not really suitable for good communists. There was considerable debate over the building of the hippodrome to replace an earlier one that was burnt down. In the early seventies the press waged a long but fruitless campaign against racing. And there are still invectives against gambling. But the state makes millions of roubles out of the legal outlets, especially from the many and various national lotteries.

Buying a lottery ticket from a street kiosk and scanning the papers for the winning number is a national pastime which, in the absence of football pools and off-track betting, occupies a central position in many people's lives. The main lottery is held every six weeks, and is called, rather prosaically, 'Money and Things Lottery'. A ticket costs 30 kopecks, and the prizes include cars, carpets, motor cycles, refrigerators, cameras, vacuum cleaners and so on. Or the winner can choose the equivalent in money.

In the draw in the Russian Republic's lottery (each republic runs its own) about 12,000 consumer items are offered in prizes, and some 5 million money prizes totalling about 10 million roubles – a considerable sum and a good indicator of the popularity of this form of gambling.

One of the most popular lotteries is called Sportlotto. There are two kinds, the commoner being the regular weekly draw on Wednesdays. The system is rather like bingo: at a cost of 30 kopecks entrants have to cross out six numbers on a card of forty-nine numbers, and the completed section is sent in and the competitor keeps a copy. The winning numbers are published in the press and announced, like football pools, in a ten minute television programme on Wednesday evenings. Sportlotto kiosks can be found in all the main streets, plastered with details of the winning prizes and slogans wishing all entrants good luck. Metro stations often have tables outside (inside in winter) where tickets are sold. The lottery has little connection with sport, though one version substitutes the names of sports for numbers and the competitor again has to pick the winning combination. There are also at least half a dozen other specialized draws. The art lottery, for example, offers pictures, vases, carpets and such objects as prizes, and tickets are sold mainly in art shops. There is no choice of prizes: it is just bad luck if the winner does not like his picture or sculpture.

The gaming instinct is manifest not only in gambling but in the Russian enthusiasm for sport of all kind. Even more than in the West, sport is the opiate of the Soviet masses. Football matches draw capacity crowds, and fans follow their clubs with fanatical devotion. When Tbilisi won the national cup one year, there were unprecedented scenes in the Georgian capital as thousands upon thousands of people poured into the streets, dancing, cheering and creating such a commotion that the authorities, ever nervous of spontaneous demonstrations, were on the point of intervening to break up the huge gatherings. During football matches, the police take no chances with rowdyism. The sale of alcohol is forbidden and throughout the game a steel cordon of soldiers rings the pitch, facing outwards up at the crowd.

Ice-hockey is however the real national game, and emotions run high during all matches. Brezhnev himself was a keen fan, and even when his health did not permit him to carry out state ceremonial functions, he was occasionally spotted at matches. When the Soviet national team plays the Canadians or the Americans, the streets are deserted as everyone makes for the nearest television set. Indeed so sure are the authorities of the popularity of hockey and football that the party has interrupted sports programmes when it has an announcement it wants seen by the largest possible audience – such as denials of rumours that food prices are to rise.

Almost everyone follows some kind of sport. In winter improvised rinks in courtyards are crowded with youths practising ice-hockey shots, and supporters' clubs are often the central focus of young people's lives. The initials and emblems of different clubs are daubed on walls and staircases, and youth gangs are formed on the basis of team loyalties. Sport is the instant topic of conversation with foreigners, the only part of the evening television news people watch. Sports stars in the limelight are allowed a certain amount of personal publicity – something rigorously denied most public figures.

Like the Americans, the Russians play to win, and pressure on clubs and sports stars to succeed are enormous – so much so that regular cases of corruption are uncovered. Partisanship is intense, and never more so than when a national team is playing another country. The communist party plays skillfully on this emotion, appealing to deep-seated patriotism, using sport to cement national feeling and portraying success as the result of ideological rectitude and the communist way of life. The Kremlin clearly had every intention of exploiting the 1980 Olympics to the full for their propaganda value, and was therefore that much more chagrined by the American-led boycott.

In such an atmosphere the penalties for failure, especially on a national level, are severe: instant public oblivion and an almost total silence in the media. But success, especially if it has an ideological overtone, brings stardom. Perhaps no one better demonstrates this than Anatoly Karpov, three times world chess champion. A brilliant, cold, slight man with prominent cheek bones and a high-pitched voice, he has willingly played the role required of him in a sport where the Russians have long dominated the world stage. He has effusively praised former President Brezhnev, the party and the Soviet system, and demonstrated an icy dignity in the bitter personal feud with Viktor Korchnoi while managing to imply disdain for the defector's politics. He received in return the Order of Lenin, the highest civilian award, is chairman of the Soviet Peace Fund, lives in considerable luxury and is frequently in the public eye. He has even been featured on a Soviet postage stamp – a rare honour for a living person.

Using his position, Karpov does much to encourage chess in the Soviet Union. The game is in little danger of losing its appeal however. Russians play chess at almost every opportunity – in trains, in corners of public parks set aside for enthusiasts, in clubs and palaces of culture, on picnics and at the seaside, and of course at home. Chess newspapers and journals have a vast circulation, millions take part in national tournaments and every opportunity is given to those showing particular promise at a young age. Because of the prestige a string of Soviet successes has brought them, the Russians take the game with a patriotic earnestness and determination that suggests it is viewed as more than just a hobby: it is a fundamental part of the Soviet way of life.

In chess, as in every worthy freetime activity, the authorities see it their job to promote and organize, claim credit for successes and direct people's energies into edifying pursuits. But often it is all to no avail. For millions of people have no interest in any of these constructive activites. To them leisure means doing nothing – absolutely nothing. Western Europeans, particularly those conditioned by the Protestant work ethic and the feelings of guilt that idleness arouses, find it hard to understand how Russians can be so happy doing so little. But they are. Soviet society has much that is Oriental about it and, like Oriental people, Russians can sit for hours watching the world go by, or waiting for a fish to bite, or simply sleeping. They complain they have enough to do at work, where the constant urgings-on, the exhortations for greater heroic toil, go against the Russians' timeless approach to life; they feel, and believe, they are worn out after a day's work – and often are. What nicer than simply resting at home, or in the sun, or anywhere. It is an attitude that leads activists to despair about ever getting the country to bestir itself. But I sometimes had a sneaking feeling that it was not so bad after all.

CHAPTER FIVE

The Arts

In few countries do the arts occupy such a vital and exposed position as they do in Russia. Not only do ordinary people look to the arts for answers to questions that cannot be raised elsewhere, but the authorities have a strong belief in the power of the written word and the painted image to persuade the masses. The public want books, films and paintings to say what they dare not say, to bring colour and diversity to their monochrome lives, whereas the party wants to enlist writers and painters as persuasive and acceptable propagandists for the Soviet system.

Artists are caught in the middle. And the conflict within and around them is often bitter and confusing. Few countries have such a record of suppressing their most original and talented intellectuals. And yet in few countries do these people have such a following and wield such influence. The role of the artist in Russia, both before and since the Revolution, is unenviable: he is expected to speak out, to lead society and give voice where others keep silent. But both honesty and compromise are denounced, in different quarters by different people. And the pressures for both are enormous.

In such a polarized atmosphere, it is the extremists who stand out. Russia has always produced the lonely, brave, uncompromising titans, people whose courage in saying the awkward things, challenging official positions, flouting the advice of friends has sharpened their observations, toughened their prose. It has also produced sycophants by the score – people who have disguised a lack of talent by subservience and compromise, which lined their pockets and allowed them to sleep easy.

But there are also those who do not fit either category – the talented writer, loyal at heart, who wants to criticise but realizes that silence is often more sensible and the rebel who is all bravado but a second-rate artist. These people have tended to be overlooked at home and abroad. But they are overwhelmingly the majority.

All Soviet artists have a self-consciousness verging on egoism about their position that is rarely found in the West. They define themselves as 'artists' and 'intellectuals' in a way that would seem arrogant to the British or Americans, who tend to be suspicious of self-proclaimed prophets and self-trumpeted virtues. Partly this is because they have to hold officially defined positions if they want to be published or exhibited. They have to be members of state-controlled unions, with regular salaries, meetings and work quotas, and this somehow puts the job of 'artist' on a level with 'doctor' or 'lawyer'. More importantly, in Russia the artist has always been *de facto* a member of a social group uniquely Russian – the intelligentsia.

The party and the census enumerators define the intelligentsia as meaning anyone who earns a living from mental rather than manual labour – an ideologically acceptable way of talking about the professional classes. But most people understand the term in a narrower sense. They mean a group of educated people who are well-read, cosmopolitan, intellectually alert, creative and intense, standing apart from both the masses and the rulers. The intelligentsia is tightly knit, élitist in its views, often intolerant of others' views though tolerant of unconventional life-styles, disdainful of the ignorance and passivity of the 'people' and generally alienated from the political establishment. Some party members can be considered members of the intelligentsia; but there is a long history of conflict and suspicion between the two sides.

Virtually every Soviet artist is by definition *engagé*. There is no such thing as art for art's sake in Russia. Poets are not people who work in offices and ministries and quietly write in their free time: they are full-time poets who earn their living as such. Artists tend to believe the roles expected of them, and believe they have a mission as the voices of their generation. Meeting Soviet artists can be exhilarating because of their eagerness to communicate their ideas, find out what is happening beyond the frontiers, pursue a subject to the limits regardless of time or consequences. It can also be exhausting: they want to preach and are often dogmatic, they crave serious, thoughtful attention but are easily wounded by criticism, they are possessive and demanding of time and friendship, and they believe their struggles and achievements must be of great interest to the rest of the world.

In some cases they are right: the world is fascinated by the treatment of the arts in the Soviet Union, because often this is the only clue to the prevailing political mood and hidden struggles within the party. The trial of Yuri Daniel and Andrei Sinyavsky, two dissident writers, in 1966 was of crucial importance. It came at a time when there were moves to rehabilitate Stalin, and was the first real indication that the new Brezhnev–Kosygin leadership was determined to put an end to the erratic liberalism of the Khrushchev era. At the end of his reign Brezhnev again stated the importance of Soviet artists toeing the party line, telling the 1981 party congress that they should do more to 'strengthen the intellectual foundations of the socialist way of life'. It was all very well, he said, for writers to produce works that made people sit up and think, and it was quite right they should show what he called 'civic passion' and 'irreconcilability to shortcomings'. He approvingly quoted the poet Mayakovsky's wish that the State Planning Committee 'sweat in debates, setting yearly tasks for me'.

However, ideological poverty or a departure from clear-cut 'class assessments' of historical events and personalities were not to be tolerated, and Soviet critics and artists' unions had to 'correct' those who were carried away in one direction or another. Brezhnev added: 'It goes without saying that they should take an active, principled stand in cases when works appear that discredit our Soviet reality. On this point we should be firm. The party was not and can never be indifferent to the ideological orientation of our art.'

The message has been stated even more bluntly since Brezhnev's death. As part of his crack-down on all forms of dissent and laxity, Andropov has made it quite clear he wants writers and playwrights to stop dabbling with questionable ideas, to drop the candid criticisms of daily life that have been given voice on the stage and in print and to do more to support the party in getting the country back to work and back to a 'healthy' frame of mind.

This does not mean there is going to be a wholesale return to the rigid limitations of 'socialist realism' as it was propounded in Stalin's day. Times have changed, and what was unacceptable thirty years ago is now taken for granted. But that is only because what was once considered avant-garde has become the normal manner of expression in art forms throughout the world. The party, ever mistrustful of innovations whose effects it cannot gauge, has still not reconciled itself to anything genuinely experimental in today's terms.

Nowhere is this more evident than in the Bolshoi Ballet. This magnificent company, over 200 years old, and one of the jewels in the Soviet cultural crown, is suffering like much of the country from stagnation and stifling conservatism. It has stuck rigidly to its classical repertoire, but has not produced much that is exciting for some years. Unrest has been simmering, and a series of defections in 1979, in particular that of Alexander Godunov, threw the spotlight on the internal feuding and problems of the company – a spotlight particularly unwelcome to the authorities who take considerable pride in the Bolshoi and see it as an important means of enhancing the Soviet image and creating goodwill towards their country overseas.

Going to the ballet is nevertheless still a thrilling experience – though one which, sadly, is increasingly rare for ordinary Russians as more and more seats are reserved for tourists paying hard currency, are booked long in advance by those who have strings to pull, or are taken by government ministries buying up an entire evening's performance for their own officials.

The Bolshoi performs in its own famous theatre, or in the massive 6,000 seat glass and concrete Palace of Congresses in the heart of the Kremlin. The Bolshoi Theatre is more impressive, with its Greek portico and eight columns surmounted by a bronze chariot and prancing horses, a stone's throw from Red Square. At around 3 roubles tickets are cheap – if you can lay hands on them – and a crowd of hopefuls invariably mills around the entrance before each performance. 'Any spare tickets?' they ask, as you fight your way to the door.

Inside, all is red plush and gilt, with intricate plasterwork and vast chandeliers. Tier upon tier curve round the edges of the open auditorium, rising up to levels from which you can scarcely see the stage. All traces of the theatre's Tsarist past have been removed: the Soviet emblem has been carefully blended in with the tracery and emblazoned on the curtains.

The orchestra still wears black ties, and some of the audience still dress up in smart gowns. A sense of tradition and occasion fills the air in that hush while the conductor, illuminated only by the music-stand light, lifts his baton and waits. As anywhere in the world, no two performances are the same. Sometimes the mood is electric, especially if the best dancers are on form, or when for example Maris Liepa, a legendary male star now in his forties, gave a performance in a role he is unlikely to dance again, or when Ekaterina Maximova, one of the principal ballerinas, returned to the stage after a long illness. Sometimes things go badly: the stars are listless and convey a weariness with roles they have danced dozens of times and can expect to dance dozens of times again in the future. The corps de ballet is sometimes ragged and the conductor erratic.

The audience invariably senses the mood. Many of them have found a channel through which to obtain tickets, and come often, knowing the dancers by their first names. They whisper that Katya is not at her best, or Volodiya's Mercutio is overshadowing Slava's Romeo. If the applause is too perfunctory, the cheerleaders, two or three thick-set young men who take up position on the steps at the side, force a second curtain call. And everyone in the theatre awaits the reaction of the 'ninth pillar', as she is known – a giant of a woman with a huge, heavy face and powerful hands who has attended virtually every performance for the past thirty years and who can make or break a dancer – as he or she well knows – by her booming applause or derisive hissing.

Everyone seems to have friends in the audience: they wave across to each other and swirl down together in the intervals to the buffet where they queue for champagne, bread and caviar and macaroons, or stroll into the foyer, already thick with cigarette smoke. After the final curtain there are always flowers for the stars, brought on by the usherettes, solid middle-aged women in blue suits. The clapping – always rhythmic if the audience is impressed – and whistles of 'Bravo' go on for a long time. Dozens of small bunches of cellophane-wrapped carnations are hurled at the stars, raining down on the stage from the gods and elegantly acknowledged with a bow and a smile.

But as the dancers leave the side entrance of the great classical building, their make-up wiped off, wearing jeans and T-shirts or high boots and thick coats in winter, they leave the glamour of the stage for ordinary Soviet life. For a short time they are still the stars, surrounded by eager autograph hunters, friends and fans who press round with embraces to congratulate them. And then most of them take the bus or metro to their flats in the city. It is often thought all dancers lead privileged lives, but it is not so. Of course the big names come almost as near to celebrity status as the system will allow: a theatre car will take them home if they have not come in their Volvos or whatever other foreign car they have been able to buy from earnings on overseas tours. Maya Plisetskaya, the ageing but splendidly graceful prima ballerina, was, at the age of fifty-six when I last saw her in 1982, still magnificent in the roles her composer husband Rodion Shchedrin wrote for her in *Anna Karenina* and *The Seagull*. Her lifestyle is regal: her apartment is beautifully furnished, her costumes created by Pierre Cardin, she can pick her partners, her tours, what she will do and whom she will see. She commands respect, awe and affection from her colleagues – not least because she unfailingly goes to the daily repetition sessions, has a sharp sense of humour, an absolute professionalism and is not above using some of the rich Russian vocabulary of swear-words.

But what of the ordinary members of the corps de ballet? The pay is not good: there are two scales, soloists and others, and several grades in each. The management periodically reviews the dancers' achievements, and recommends them for a higher grade. But a 25-year-old ballerina earns about 160 roubles – less than the average national wage. And it is no mean achievement to get into the ballet. The Bolshoi runs its own training school, taking children who already show outstanding promise. The criteria are ruthlessly exacting: at the age of seven the children must already show the required musical talent, and must have a bone structure, height, weight and the physical characteristics that promise the right kind of body for the tough demands of dancing.

The reward is the coveted chance to join one of the world's most prestigious companies, one that never lacks for funds, never has the uncertainty of having to struggle for state support. Not all the dancers come from the Bolshoi's own training school however: several are taken on from the good provincial companies in Minsk, Novosibirsk, Tallinn and especially from Perm, the industrial town in the Urals which has made a name for itself in ballet ever since the Kirov company was evacuated there from Leningrad during the war. Nadezhda Pavlova, a petite, vivacious ballerina and winner of the Grand Prix at the Moscow ballet competition, was trained at Perm. She and her husband, Slava Gordeyev, now form one of the leading partnerships of the company.

Gordeyev joined the company at the age of nineteen in 1968. He has danced most of the leading roles, and has an unrivalled virtuosity and experience. But he freely admitted that it was hard to stay on top. 'There are always others coming along. You have to dance so that your performance is unlike anyone else's, offers something special. I don't want people seeing my name and being unable to remember who I am.' Only age could make a difference – as he and every dancer have found. 'I am already thirty-two,' he said with a sigh when I spoke to him. He did not feel age creeping up, though as he said: 'I could go on dancing another twenty-five years. But the audience could not watch.'

Like other top dancers, he has travelled a lot – to Western Europe, three times in America, twice in Australia, and of course on tours of the Soviet Union. He remembers London only vaguely from a brief visit in 1968. 'The theatre was rather big and cold. I think it was in a place called Wimbledon, rather far from the centre.'

The tours are often tiring, and sometimes there is a performance every day – a change from the situation at home where many good dancers complain they are able to dance only about three times a month, so large is the company and so restricted the repertoire. Every dancer looks forward to the tours – there are usually about two a year – as much for the chance to see the world usually closed to them as to perform for a different public. But even dancers are allowed abroad only after stringent vetting for political loyalty and reliability. An overseas tour is used as a reward, and well-known dancers who fall out with the company's management or with its party executive can be dropped from a tour at the last moment. They may also be found unsuitable because they have no family to leave behind in the Soviet Union while they are abroad, or because they have mixed too much with foreigners in Moscow ('You are too Western in your attitudes,' one young man was told when he was informed he would not be included on the tour of Italy. 'And why don't you get married?')

Those who make it are of course chaperoned by security officials whose job is to ensure there are no embarrassments (meaning defections). But they still have a rare opportunity to see Paris, Rome or Mexico and to go shopping. The limitation is the very small amount of foreign currency any Soviet citizen is allowed to spend abroad, which makes shopping extraordinarily frustrating. 'I remember walking all round the shops in Paris just trying things on,' one dancer told me. Many try to save money by not spending any on food while overseas. They eat vast breakfasts and other refreshments that are provided free and get through the day on bread and cheese or whatever they have brought with them from home. But one ballet troupe that went to the United States some years ago had a sad experience. The American customs, following the food and health regulations, confiscated all the tinned provisions they had brought to see them through the tour. For a while they tried living on breakfasts and water until some began to faint during rehearsals and had to squander their carefully calculated clothing fund in the restaurants. Only the stars who make private, under-the-table arrangements with the Western impresarios sponsoring the tours are able to earn enough Western currency to buy cars and other luxuries.

The authorities are ever fearful of political 'incidents' on such tours. There have been times when demonstrators have interrupted performances, awkward moments when dancers have been the unwitting targets of political protests, as happened during the 1979 tour of America. But the greater embarrassment is defection, which represents a grave loss of face for the Soviet leadership. In fact, in the case of the Bolshoi at least, the 1979 defections in the United States, followed by the loss of a distinguished ballet teacher Sulamif Messerer and her son Mikhail in

Japan the following February, had less to do with politics than with the bitter feuding that had been going on within the company over artistic policies and personalities.

At the centre of much of the strife, which has continued intermittently since then, is Yuri Grigorovich, the brilliant, austere, autocratic chief choreographer and artistic director of the Bolshoi. Accusations against the talented former dancer have ranged from favouritism and petty blacklisting of promising dancers he disliked to the more fundamental ones that despite his many triumphs he was becoming tired, had not produced a good ballet for some years and was squandering the company's formidable talents with a lack of innovation. His staging of *Romeo and Juliet* evoked bitter criticism – echoed by Italian critics when the company took it to Rome in 1982. Five leading dancers, headed by Maya Plisetskaya, demanded that the old version be retained, and there have been some bitter open confrontations at meetings of the company.

Grigorovich, however, has his defenders – those who value his early work, especially his much acclaimed 1968 version of Khachaturian's *Spartacus*, still the most popular ballet with Moscow audiences. The Soviet cultural authorities who dislike any challenge to established leadership, artistic or otherwise, have also given him full support. The controversy over his direction flared up again in 1981 with the publication of a seemingly innocuous book on the history of classical ballet by a respected ballet scholar. The book paid ample tribute to Grigorovich's stewardship of the Bolshoi, but suggested his later work had been dull and that by contrast with Western choreographers such as Béjart and Balanchine, Grigorovich was no longer innovative: a wounding accusation.

The criticisms were contained in only a few short sentences, but the matter was blown up by the over-reaction of the authorities. Grigorovich complained bitterly to the party's Central Committee, a furious attack on the book was published in the press, and the editor of the edition was reprimanded. Many critics thought the response out of proportion to the criticisms, with which they agreed. But in the rather brittle atmosphere everything in the Bolshoi has become highly politicized, and any suggestion of change brings a sharp reaction from entrenched conservative interests.

The ballet may be the most prestigious of the Soviet arts. It commands enormous respect and serious attention from vast numbers of people, unlike the rather precious status of ballet in the West. But the most dynamic of the Soviet arts at present, without doubt, is the theatre, which is enjoying a remarkable boom. It is almost impossible to find a free seat in any Moscow theatre nowadays, and it takes considerable ingenuity and pull to lay hands on a ticket to the Taganka, the relatively avant-garde theatre where plays stretch the limits of official approval, or to a rock-opera or even to a good production of Shakespeare.

A young generation of imaginative actors and innovative directors has made the theatre the real touchstone of current concerns and attitudes. And not only in the capital do productions play to full houses: theatres in Georgia and Estonia vigorously uphold local language and culture and have established reputations beyond their small republics – the Rustaveli Theatre from Tbilisi has played Brecht in Berlin, Shakespeare in London to enthusiastic critical acclaim, though not a soul in the audience probably understood Georgian.

It is not simply that theatres are warm, comfortable and cheap and one of the few public diversions on long winter nights; nor that they are fashionable places to be seen where it is now modish to dress up in your furs or Levis and display your jewels; nor simply that all the would-be intellectuals gather to find out what their friends and rivals are up to. As well as all this, there is a genuine intellectual curiosity among Soviet youth and a public thirst for discussion of real issues free from propaganda, which was increasingly possible in the Soviet theatre in the twilight years of Brezhnev's reign.

Theatres have responded to this demand. Of course there are the obligatory plays on the life of Lenin and other worthy themes. But even in this much ploughed field, directors recently have presented plays which are surprisingly full of touchy nuances and pointed political morals. One such play, *Thus we shall be victorious*, dealing with the last year of Lenin's life, had to go to politburo level before it was finally approved. When it opened at the Moscow Arts Theatre in spring 1982, Brezhnev and virtually all the members of the politburo went along to see it.

There are also plays that stir controversy, satirizing bureaucrats, depicting the wheeling and dealing of daily life, loneliness in big cities, family problems, village values. Some only just scrape past the censor; the late Yuri Trifonov's chilling *House on the Embankment* is a document of betrayal and cowardice during the Stalin purges. And as neighbours in the house in the play – based on a real block of flats still standing beside the Moscow River not far from the British Embassy – denounced each other, I wondered what kind of frisson ran through the white-haired citizens in the audience, who had themselves perhaps spoken the same words forty-five years earlier.

Controversial plays are the hallmark of Yuri Lyubimov, the liberal director of the Taganka who has periodically been locked in struggle with the authorities – most recently over his attempt to stage the life of the controversial balladier Vladimir Vysotsky. In 1983 the authorities also vetoed his production of *Boris Godunov*, although a trial performance was publicly given in December 1982. But the Taganka is small and acts as an authorized safety valve. In the bigger theatres playwrights and directors resort to nuances to express forbidden judgements; and in keeping with long Russian tradition even Gogol, Bulgakov and other classics are staged to make devastating comments on society today. Of course the censors are fully aware of the implications, wisely ignored by the critics. I wondered, for instance, whether the cardinal's role in the staging of Musset's *Lorenzaccio* by the Sovremennik Theatre was really intended as a portrait of Suslov, the iron ideologue of the politburo.

Almost all theatres are repertory. Sometimes eight productions run concurrently, and this makes for extremely long runs. If you missed *Richard III* at the Vakhtangova five years ago, you can take heart: it will still be running in another five. This sometimes leads to restlessness among the actors and directors themselves, who cannot try anything new while people are still clamouring to see what is running.

Productions are lavish as state funds are plentiful, and stage design is sometimes strikingly modern. Many of the best Soviet artists find a freedom in theatre design not readily granted to the more ideologically restricted arts of painting and sculpture.

Perhaps some of the best drama is found in the thriving unofficial – but not underground – experimental and youth theatres that play in clubs, Pioneer Palaces and converted basements in blocks of flats. Students in jeans and sweaters pour in, always more than capacity, and sit cross-legged around the small stage. It gives the performance intimacy and intensity, thought it does create an alarming fire-risk. The aim is to break down the gap between actors and audience, to do away with theatricality and the paraphernalia of props and sets, and to use the theatre very much as a medium for the exchange of ideas, for communication between the director and the audience. Critics have often praised some of the productions, and have called on the larger theatres to learn from the freshness of these experiments.

Youth theatre has been especially innovative and stimulating. A

studio theatre at Young Pioneer Palace in one Moscow borough put on
Romeo and Juliet using thirteen- and fourteen-year-old schoolchildren,
relying on their improvisation, intuitive sense of naturalness and freedom and present-day rhythms. A different actor and actress pair played
Romeo and Juliet on each successive 'day' in the four-day time span of
the play in an attempt to reflect their rapid maturation as the play
proceeds. The production was quickly acclaimed and the director,
Vyacheslav Spesivtsev, widely praised. He has done much with youth
groups, and his experiments are closely related to the theatre of the early
post-revolutionary years, with its vast carnivals, processions and productions staged on huge indoor sites. The audience is always engaged as
fully-fledged participants in the productions; in one play – about the
staging of *Romeo and Juliet* – for example, instead of sitting in one place,
the audience spends most of the time walking about the studio theatre,
witnessing rehearsals, discussions and arguments among the members
of the theatre. At any one moment a member of the audience does not
know whether he is standing next to a fellow spectator or an actor in the
play.

Much of the zeal of youth theatre is a direct result of the emphasis the
cultural authorities put on drama for children. In this field the Russians
have an example to set the world. According to a decree issued more
than sixty years ago every theatre is obliged to put on a performance for
children once a week, with more during the school holidays. Even the
Bolshoi does its bit with ballets for children on Saturday and Sunday
mornings, preceded by lectures about the company and the art of ballet.
Throughout the country some fifty children's theatres have been
established, and in Moscow there are several permanent companies,
including a children's musical theatre. The actors are closely involved in
teaching and lecturing about drama, and children are often invited to
help stage the shows.

One of the favourites with children is the Moscow Puppet Theatre,
founded in 1931 by Sergei Obraztsov, a formidable figure now in his
eighties who was still the director fifty years later. Though ostensibly for
children, the theatre now enjoys a world reputation, attracts many adults
and tourists and has made many tours overseas. The puppets, standing
about two feet high and controlled by rods from below, are uncannily
lifelike. The repertoire includes the usual pantomime stories such as
Puss in Boots, but has been broadened to include romantic tragedies,
vaudeville, special shows such as that staged for the Moscow Olympics
and such sophisticated parodies as *Unusual Concert*, a spoof of a poor

variety show that contains not a little sharp political satire. So successful is the Moscow Puppet Theatre that others have sprung up all over the country. There are now some 110 companies performing in thirty different languages (a mark of the influence of the Soviet presence in Afghanistan is that one has even been founded in Kabul).

Theatre in general enjoys a remarkable freedom to experiment and to cut through propaganda stereotypes. Alas, this is not true of other art forms. Painting especially is bound by the strictures of socialist realism, the need to express an optimistic message and inspire people with the triumphs of progress. But Soviet artists are too good to be so limited, too intelligent to confine themselves to the mediocre. Some use the framework of 'official' art so skilfully that they are able to achieve an intensity and personal commitment that defies any categorization; others turn out routine stuff to fulfil their plan but paint dozens of other works which they know will never be publicly exhibited but which they keep piled up in their studios to show to friends in hope of public recognition one day.

Not all modern painting is now taboo, nor is every abstract work beyond the pale. It is what one sculptor once described to me as the 'Three Ss' that upset the authorities: *stranoe*, *strashnoe* and *sexualnoe* – strange, frightening and sexual. Such works are considered morbid, perverse, upsetting to the comforting image of order and complacent self-assurance which marks official intellectual society. Pure abstraction offers no such challenge, and indeed is virtually accepted. So too are religious themes, unless provocatively over-emphasized. But unfortunately many artists believe that it is more important to challenge official restrictions by harping on such themes than it is to explore what can be done within the limits.

I was much struck by this when I visited two exhibitions that happened to be on in Moscow at the same time: one official and one semi-official. The latter was held at Malaya Gruzinskaya, the centre that has been permitted to exist in the basement of a fourteen-storey block of flats ever since an attempt to stage an open-air exhibition of unofficial works was broken up by police with water cannons in 1974, amid much adverse publicity in the West and subsequent official embarrassment.

It is an odd place for art exhibitions. A hand-written notice on the ground-floor door directs to the entrance round the corner. Inside you buy a ticket from a makeshift office and make your way down the concrete stairs and along a narrow corridor into the basement, where a uniformed policeman stands at the door. Not only is there a literally underground feel to the place: none of the paintings are accepted for display elsewhere.

It was the fourth public showing of works by twenty avant-garde artists since the centre was sanctioned. The themes were clearly 'unofficial' – openly religious works, surrealist and super-realist treatment of traditional Russian themes, symbolic representations of good and evil, a few abstract compositions. None would have excited much interest in London or Paris. Many appeared narrow and derivative: Salvador Dali had clearly struck a responsive chord. The public, still in coats and scarves, was pushing and jostling around three small rooms, hoping for something daring, something to give them a feel they were where the new wave was having its first impact.

Before the exhibition watchdogs from the Ministry of Culture removed several paintings by one strictly religious artist, Vitaly Linitsky, saying they were religious propaganda, which the law allowed only in the churches. The paintings showed pussywillows, an emotive religious symbol in Russia, and candles against an industrial background. Linitsky protested that five paintings of the Crucifixion by another artist, Vladislav Provotorov, were allowed to stay. 'They just show a myth,' the officials retorted. 'We don't want any new icons like yours.'

The Daliesque crucifixion paintings aroused much comment among the audience – young people in sweaters and anoraks, middle-aged women carrying shopping-bags, even the occasional army officer in uniform. One picture showed Christ horizontal against a blue-black sky, the huge, wounded soles of his feet pointing out at the viewer. Another showed Christ being whipped by bald and evil old men, and another of the Resurrection had him holding up huge, bloodied palms. Provotorov was one of the leaders of the unofficial group. At the first exhibition in 1978 he was equally startling with three large canvasses of tortured, decaying flesh, one of them entitled *Inquisition*.

Many of the paintings consciously referred to famous pictures: a painting of Calvary showed a mountain made up of Bosch-like symbols – an ear, shells, a knife, a church. *The Generation of Shepherds* had a landscape peopled by lizards and evil-looking reptiles. One artist, making fun of the famous painting of Venus at her toilette, showed a rather ordinary, haggard woman looking at her reflection in the mirror, while a devil, not a cherub, gazed down from a nearby picture. There were twists on themes by El Greco and the legend of the birth of Venus – in this case a saccharine-sweet girl enclosed in a glass bell-jar sitting beside a manhole cover on an ordinary Moscow backstreet.

Many paintings impressed with their immense attention to detail. The crystal brilliance of super-realism seemed to be much in vogue, but there were also soft-focus views of ethereal onion-domes of Russian Orthodox Churches and brilliant purple and maroon domes seen as geometric cloud patterns in the sky. Subjective themes such as loneliness probably also kept many of the works out of the state's official displays.

A number of the artists themselves were at the showing. A large book of comments was filled with appreciation: 'Well done! Each exhibition is better and more complete,' one woman wrote. Others went into detailed discussion of what they had seen as though they were writing a professional review.

The other exhibition that was on at the same time could not have been more official. Entitled 'We are Building Communism', it opened at the Central Exhibition Hall, a stone's throw from the Kremlin, to coincide with the 1981 party congress. It was surprisingly rewarding. There were of course the ritual political obeisances: a giant bust of Lenin in front of a red flag as soon as you walked into the long, low hall, once used to stable the imperial horses. Oil portraits of Brezhnev and posters with appropriate slogans about peace and international friendship dominated one corner of the building. But tucked away in the maze of dividing walls were paintings that seemed to me to deviate as far from socialist realism as any at Malaya Gruzinskaya. The themes were entirely proper: oil-rigs in the frozen Siberian wastes, spacemen in their quaint uniforms, workers casting the millionth ton of pig-iron, pioneers building the new Trans-Siberian railway, peasants in Central Asia parading around the old Islamic monuments of Samarkand in celebration of Soviet power.

But the artists, most of them in their early thirties, had used what were clearly safe subjects to convey their own, sometimes disturbing vision. Three young construction workers in the Far East had a bored and blank gaze as they looked across the empty Siberian landscape. A tiny figure on a camel riding across the desert was dwarfed by a huge, cold, unreal nuclear establishment with its three giant globes, one of which seemed to burn with a steely flame. A portrait of three Latvian architects had an uncanny feel of the secret police knocking at the door at midnight: one, dressed in bright casual clothes, stood indoors, while on the threshold stood two sinister figures, wearing raincoats and painted entirely in grey.

Such attempts to use the limitations of the subject go on all the time. I was equally struck by some of the works shown in the Central Exhibition

Hall – usually known as the 'Manezh' – in 1980 for the cultural exhibitions that accompanied the Olympics. 'Sport, the Ambassador of Peace' was the title, and all the paintings had sporting themes. But what a difference in the output of the young artists, mostly under thirty, from the suffocating socialist realism of a 1935 painting, also on display, entitled 'S. M. Kirov takes a sports parade'! The works were refreshingly varied – weird, stylized, modernist, sensual, humorous, corny, some like pop art, others with sly references to famous Picasso pictures, most using the theme not to glorify Soviet sport but to express very individual emotions. The one quality that was striking and so conspicuously absent from the output of Stalin's day was humour.

The avant-garde in Russia is self-consciously aware of its exposed position. Sometimes, alas, it plays on the reputation of taking risks, and there are quite a few second-rate artists whose main interest is making a good deal of money out of their pictures from illegal cash transactions – for Western currency only, of course – with resident foreigners in Moscow. Indeed some have been notorious in employing their friends and wives to tout their wares around journalists and diplomats, closely watched as ever by the KGB. One artist told me a story of a reception held in the Kremlin shortly before Brezhnev's death for members of the official Artists' Union at which this subject came up. One painter noticed the tall, white-haired figure of Yuri Andropov, then chairman of the KGB and known for his intellectual tastes, standing talking in a corner. He went up and asked him whether it was right that unofficial painters were making a fortune trading on their quasi-dissident status selling their canvasses to Westerners whereas he and fellow loyal members of the union had no such rewards.

In his typical dry, ironic manner, Andropov looked down at his glass and answered, with a perfectly straight face: 'Ah, but you have the love of the motherland instead.'

To some extent the phony avant-garde, if I may so call it, has had the ground cut from under it by an event whose importance is hard to over-estimate. This was the long-awaited 'Moscow–Paris 1900–1930' exhibition, comprising more than 2,500 paintings, sketches, theatrical and costume designs, architectural plans, sculptures and posters from the richest flowering of Russia's revolutionary avant-garde. For the first time it publicly displayed the dazzling heritage of revolutionary art that had been locked away for more than fifty years in the vaults of Soviet museums. It rehabilitated the standing and reputations of such artists as Chagall, Malevich, Kandinsky, Tatlin and Yuon.

The exhibition, which ran throughout the summer of 1981 and drew vast crowds, had a profound influence throughout the country, for at a stroke it made respectable the remarkable flowering of Russian art that was gradually strangled as Stalinism got a grip on Soviet intellectual life. In recent years there had been a quiet but steady rediscovery of names who have increasingly been recognized elsewhere in the world as the leading figures in modern art movements. But it was not possible to hang paintings so long suppressed in Soviet galleries without raising awkward questions about why they had not been seen before. It was also strongly suspected by Russian artists that the Soviet art establishment had no interest in letting the world see what had been achieved sixty years ago, for their own cautious steps towards modernism would straightaway seem insignficant and derivative by comparison. Yet the exhibition was able to overcome the taboos and political difficulties simply by its size, importance and by the fact that it was held in conjunction with the Pompidou Centre in Paris. And rehabilitation, when it came, was sweet: Leonid Brezhnev, no known lover of modern art, went on a symbolic visit to the Pushkin gallery to look at works he had never previously expressed interest in. 'It was the best thing he ever did for us,' an artist remarked to me at the time.

I came to know several artists in Moscow. They all led lives that were almost caricatures of the Bohemian image: their studios were at the top of winding stairs in attics above the blocks of flats, or in basements among heating pipes and the general rubble usually strewn about the courtyards of blocks of flats. Everything in the studios was higgledy-piggledy, with half-completed canvasses lying around, bottles of wine and vodka on the floor, dusty old broken sofas and chairs, plates of half-caten meals, books, prints, tubes of paint and numerous other objects scattered on tables and chairs. Their main complaint was not their studios, in which they felt comfortably at home, or the restricted outlets for their work, or even the ideological framework of Soviet art, which most found quite normal. The real drawback was the lack of materials – the shortage of good paint, brushes, lacquer, art paper and so on. They often had to rely on what they could scrounge or borrow, on the good offices of friends travelling to East Germany or to the West. Sometimes I became rather cross at the assumption, shared by so many Russians who get to know foreigners, that my suitcase was bottomless and my time sufficient to scour the shops in London on visits to England to bring them all the things they needed for the next six months. But again, on reflection, it was understandable, and certainly worthier to ask for sable brushes or fixative than for jeans and T-shirts.

If artists are expected to paint to order, to convey the right message in their works, how much truer is this of writers. Literature has always been the most exposed intellectual activity in Russia, and the most influential. And it is on Soviet writers that the heaviest decisions lie – how far to go in expressing social criticism, how much to compromise – and from whom the most is expected. The attempts to defy censorship and the penalties paid by non-conformists have been well documented. Solzhenitsyn, after all, is almost a household name amongst the Western reading public, and the tribulations of Boris Pasternak are still as embarrassing to Soviet intellectuals as they are well known to Western readers of *Dr Zhivago*. In recent years it has been writers especially who have most felt the calls on creative artists to support the party line, to show that indefinable quality of *partinost* or 'party spirit' in their works. And those who did not were forced into emigration – Kopelev, Voinovich, Aksyonov – or consigned their output to their desk drawers.

But powerful writers still flourish and publish and attract an enormous following. One of the most remarkable is Chinghiz Aitmatov, a Kirghiz writer from Central Asia, who writes sometimes in Russian but also in his native language (though he is as forceful and passionate in translation). His strength lies in the unusual combination of a contemporary outlook and a sensitivity to his Oriental background, to the ways and traditions of this otherwise intellectually undeveloped part of the Soviet Union. He is much valued by the authorities as a representative of non-Russian culture, winning the Lenin prize for literature at the age of thirty-five. Indeed, he is a deputy to the Supreme Soviet. But he skilfully uses his good standing to powerful effect. His last major novel, published in November 1981 by *Novy Mir*, the main literary journal, is an extraordinary science fiction work that manages at the same time to be a sharp depiction of attitudes in Central Asia and a telling indictment of Stalinism.

Other writers include the powerful group known as the 'village writers', who number among them the late Fyodor Abramov and Valentin Rasputin (a name that evokes the same smile among Russians as it does among foreigners). They write much about the values and changes in small village communities, and their tone is often far from that of the bland optimism in progress that is meant to uplift Soviet readers.

Unfortunately I neither spoke Russian well enough nor had the time to read the large output of the many good writers in the Soviet Union. But ordinary Russians followed their work and doings with passion and devotion. They took it as a matter of personal concern if writers went against what they considered their true convictions, or fell into disfavour. One well-known poet once showed me a whole drawer full of letters from a young woman who wrote to him almost daily – without ever having met him – taking his poetry as a personal communication with her. My own teacher of Russian, a woman of great sensitivity and culture, found in some works of literature a satisfaction that was vividly real, and she ably transmitted her excitement at the latest work by Aitmatov or her intensely felt love of the Russian classics. To her, literature was the real world, the medium through which she viewed ordinary daily life.

Perhaps it is only in Russia that poets can fill an entire football stadium. Andrei Voznesensky, once one of the angry young men of the Khrushchev days and still a man who has never been far from controversy, gave me an amazing photograph of 80,000 people banked up all around the stadium listening to his readings. His mass following is all the more surprising in view of his abstruse metaphors, complex imagery and intellectual challenge. A disciple of Pasternak, he is an arresting, lyrical poet whose works have been translated into a dozen languages. His latest collection of poetry was published in an edition of 200,000 and sold out almost immediately.

The role of the public poet in Soviet society has its disadvantages: Voznesensky, for example, is a rather private person – though by no means oblivious to the uses of publicity – happiest when alone in the woods of his country cottage near Moscow. But he is instantly recognized on the street – perhaps because he has several times appeared for over an hour on prime time television. And he has come under intense political pressure to express the correct political message, to write less about his feelings and more about the message of the party. Thanks to some well-timed silences, he remains one of the few writers still in official favour who has made very few compromises.

He has tried to remain an individual. 'Only an individual expressing his individuality can give anything to the ordinary person. You believe in yourself if you know millions are waiting for your voice. I cannot give people any answers. But I can put the questions, suggest ways of looking at things, help people to be brave and analyse their feelings.'

His poetry reflects the changing concerns of Soviet society. As an outspoken and often wild young man, who once blew his entire foreign royalties on a reckless week's spree in Rome, he mirrored the hopes and naivety of the post-Stalin thaw. Now he says he is more 'classical', but at the same time has taken up new and typical obsessions: the search for the mystical in a cynical and disillusioned age, interest in the occult and extra-sensory forces. He has also turned increasingly to pop music. He wrote the words for 'Drum', a song that remained a hit for many months in 1980. A year later he turned one of his longer narrative poems into what could be called Moscow's first rock opera, a noisy, eclectic production that had strong hints of Western musicals such as *Hair* and *Jesus Christ Superstar* but which was a revolution on the Soviet stage and was always fully booked. Voznesensky was amused at one poetry reading after that to find all the questions were about his next pop song. He says he writes pop lyrics for a joke – but a joke he now takes half seriously, believing that pop music, the mass culture of today, can lead people to more profound poetry.

Voznesensky came under official disapproval in 1979 when he lent support to an attempt – brutally suppressed – by a group of distinguished writers to publish an anthology of uncensored material. He was reprimanded and banned from travel for two years. Others were expelled from the Union of Writers, and one, Vasily Aksyonov, was subsequently forced to emigrate. Voznesensky is back on the board of the Union of Writers, and made a successful tour of Britain and Ireland reading his poetry in 1981.

Voznesensky retreats to his beloved Georgia to write, but usually lives on the ground floor of a dacha in the village of Peredelkino, about twelve miles south of Moscow. This village is perhaps one of the most famous in all Russia, for it is the official writers' colony, and many distinguished men of letters have made their home there. Boris Pasternak lived for many years amid its cultured peace. He is buried in the cemetery that stretches down from the ancient village church, itself an architectural monument (though, surprisingly, still also a working church). Every year on May 30, the anniversary of his death in 1960, people still gather at the grave beside the three pine trees on the edge of the cemetery to pay homage to a man generally considered one of Russia's finest poets, whose disgrace following the furore over *Dr Zhivago* still rankles among the intelligentsia. Indeed on any ordinary weekend you can find the odd couple sitting on the wooden seat in front of the simple stone slab. It is a place of constant pilgrimage.

Such tributes to Pasternak are far from unique: Russia honours it literary heroes with posthumous respect that is widespread among ordinary working people. In Vaganskovskoye cemetery in Moscow another poet is buried, a tiger of a man, emotional, unstable, a heavy

drinker, who committed suicide more than fifty years ago – Sergei
Yesenin, known in Russia for his passionate poetry and in the West as
Isadora Duncan's lover. His grave is also a place of pilgrimage. There
are always fresh flowers, always crowds. On a typical Sunday when I
went there, a man in a grey raincoat stood near the monument, took off
his hat and recited some of Yesenin's poems. Everyone clapped.
Another elderly man with sunken face and close-cropped hair then gave
a quavering rendering of a long poem. To both men Yesenin was a living
presence, his words had shaped their emotions.

Though both Pasternak and Yesenin lived mainly in the capital and
were quintessentially Russian, it is a mistake to think of Moscow as the
only centre of culture in the country. Indeed it is surprising that in a
centralized society where virtually all political and economic power, all
main decisions and all important personalities are found in Moscow, so
many of the most interesting developments in the arts are now found in
the provinces. Cultural life in Estonia, Georgia, Armenia and even
Siberia is in many respects more dynamic and innovative than in
Moscow and Leningrad, the traditional centres. Plays, novels and
paintings are being produced whose political daring would never be
accepted in the capital. The success of the Rustaveli Theatre production
of Shakespeare's *Richard III* at the Edinburgh Festival and in London
established the reputations of Ramaz Chkhikvadze, the actor, and
Robert Sturua, the director, in the West. But there are altogether some
twenty-five theatres in the mountain republic, and each includes
Shakespeare in its repertoire. Georgia has won a reputation for innovation in stage design and art, and Georgian designers dominated an
exhibition of theatre art in Moscow I saw in 1979. Estonia also has a
lively theatrical tradition with some outspoken young playwrights. Both
its ballet and symphony orchestra are judged among the best in the
country – though are little known outside as Gosconcert, the monopoly
concert tour agency, invariably gives out the plum invitations to those
who are close at hand in Moscow to pull strings.

Opera flourishes in the provinces too. The seaport of Odessa in the
Ukraine still retains something of its former cosmopolitan flavour, and
its ornate late-Victorian opera house can stage productions that rival
those of Vienna. In Kiev, the Ukrainian capital, there is a vast palace of
culture, whose theatres are as experimental as any in Leningrad, staging
such things as rock ballets to the music of Pink Floyd.

Even Muslim Central Asia is seeking a vigorous revival of traditional
architecture, decoration and music. Film-making is an enormous and

successful industry in most of the southern republics, and many a talented actor has made a national reputation for himself.

The best-known writers too live outside the capital – Valentin Rasputin in far-away Siberia, Chinghiz Aitmatov in Central Asia.

There are several reasons why the arts do well in the provinces. In many cases they continue the traditions of old and proud cultures that are quite separate from the Russian tradition – in Georgia, Armenia and the Baltic republics, for example. People support the arts partly out of nationalist and linguistic sentiment. Secondly the arts are far less politicised outside Moscow. Ideology still permeates all productions perforce, but there is more room for quiet experiment outside the political spotlight. Finally, it is often a matter of local pride to make money available for local film studios, opera and theatre companies and concert halls. Novosibirsk, for example, is extremely proud of its opera house and ballet company and does not stint money. Unlike the situation in the West, standards can thus survive even if the audiences are not always there. (And I have sat through some good productions in half empty cavernous halls.)

Above all, however, both in the provinces and in the metropolis, the arts are officially considered something worthwhile. Culture is deemed to be good for the masses, and the masses respond with a somewhat old-fashioned respect for culture. All schoolchildren are taught Pushkin and Tolstoy, encouraged to honour Russian writers and musicians. And this attitude sticks. And though the number of people who would really prefer to swill beer and watch television to sitting through an opera is potentially as large as in the West, there is no dictatorship of the philistines, no lowering of standards to achieve commercial success. The achievements of Soviet artists are not disparaged out of boorishness, belittled by the incomprehending masses. It is true that in the depths of rural Russia there is precious little time or regard for high culture. And steelworkers are more likely to talk about football than poetry. But in the public domain there is no democracy of taste. People are offered what is considered worthy and elevating. If they do not like the fare, bad luck.

The attacks on Soviet culture are much more likely to come from the intelligentsia, from self-appointed critics who denounce this artist for shallowness or insincerity, that writer for triviality and that musician for political obsequiousness. Or the attacks come from the party, which is ever convinced that without strict monitoring and rigid discipline, Soviet artists will lapse into what they call subjectivity and individuality, apolitical or pessimistic criticism which does not encourage love of the party and acceptance of the system. The task of the officially organized unions of artists, writers and musicians is not to promote their members' interests, but to ensure their members stay in line. Perhaps in no field has this deadening influence been clearer than in music, where Tikhon Khrennikov, the elderly, pudgy head of the Union of Composers appointed by Stalin over thirty years ago and still imbued with the spirit of those days, has ruled with an ideological rigidity that has left Soviet music far behind other art forms. Small wonder that in face of repeated exhortations to display class consciousness, to denounce modern music as an enemy of communism, many composers have become stale and weary.

Nevertheless, the likes of Khrennikov, with his calls on his members for vigilance in the sharpening ideological struggle, do not hold absolute sway. There are many more sensitive and sensible figures in the intellectual establishment who are steadily trying to widen the framework of what is permissible. And though – or perhaps because – it is a constant struggle for good artists to give public voice to their most honest feelings and reactions, there is enough good stuff being produced to merit acclaim and influence at home and greater attention overseas.

CHAPTER SIX

Patriotism and Propaganda

Politics is an inescapable fact of life in the Soviet Union. From the big cities to the smallest dusty village of Central Asia, the communist message is daily drummed in: on the radio, in the press, in huge red and white banners and illustrated slogans, in public speeches, rallies, trade union meetings, political education sessions, in books, films, schools and children's camps. The message is always the same: the 'monolithic' party is the repository of the nation's wisdom, the vanguard that will lead the country to prosperity while moulding a new Soviet man – selfless, idealistic, self-disciplined and courageous. The leadership, being the quintessence of party authority, can do no wrong – though individuals may come and go – and should be accorded respect and obedience. The workers are the masters of the state, but the workers need guidance, and must therefore heed the injunctions the party draws up at its five-yearly congresses: 'Raise the quality of production!' 'Make the economy economical!'

Propaganda is the first thing that strikes any visitor to the Soviet Union. 'Glory to the Communist Party of the Soviet Union', the banners proclaim. 'Glory to work', 'May the deeds of Great Lenin live for ever', 'Forward to Communism'. The slogans are fixed on rooftops, painted on walls, pasted on billboards together with pictures of new factories, dams and space rockets and graphs of statistics going ever onwards and upwards.

Giant portraits of Lenin striding purposefully forward in his boots, greatcoat and peaked cap beam down from the blank sides of buildings. At major traffic intersections and between dual carriageways, solemn portraits of Brezhnev – at least, until his death – used to show him delivering his speech at the last party congress or waving cheerfully to the masses. There were pithy quotations of his exhorting the workers to greater efforts, or pledging to do his utmost for world peace. His features were touched up to make him look younger, more serenely wise. Down in Central Asia his eyes appeared to be subtly narrowed and his face flattened to give him an almost Asian appearance. They disappeared within weeks of his death. Andropov, who shuns publicity, has refused to sanction any pictures of himself in Brezhnev's place.

Russians scarcely notice these slogans any more. They are part of the city landscape. In 1981 the ubiquitous 'We shall fulfil the decisions of the XXV party congress' needed only the hasty addition of a Roman I to last another five years. And in Mayakovsky Square a giant slogan exhorts citizens to 'turn Moscow into a model communist city'. Above the rickety old generating stations along the Moscow River that belch forth beautiful clouds of pinkish steam on winter days there is the inevitable Lenin quotation that 'Communism equals Soviet power plus the electrification of the whole country'. (Given Soviet envy of the shops where foreigners can buy things unavailable to the ordinary Russian for hard currency certificates, a cynical joke defines communism as 'Soviet power plus the certification of the whole country'.)

The slogans never change: 'Workers of the world, unite!' 'Communism will overcome!' proclaim the banners unfurled each May Day and at the November Revolutionary parades. The wording has an old-fashioned ring to it, recalling the heady days when the Bolsheviks had to galvanize the illiterate masses with the battle-cries of the new order. Indeed, the banners and the slogans, the little red flags that flutter from trolleybuses every May Day, the stentorian exhortations have become part of a ritual. What was spontaneous in 1917 and 1918, a response to the turbulence and exigencies of the time, has, like so much in Soviet ideology, been set in an unbreakable mould, hallowed by repetition. As with religious ritual, any alteration in practice and creed would now appear a significant challenge to the legacy.

So the slogans remain. And twice every year, in preparation for the Red Square parades, the party issues a list of slogans. Some are the general assertions about the victory of communism. But others are more specific, and trip less easily off the tongue: 'Toilers in agriculture! Strengthen the fodder basis of animal husbandry! Raise the production and sale to the State of meat, milk, eggs, wool and other products.' Unlike the clichés intoned through loudspeakers and echoed, with appropriate cheers, by the masses shuffling across the Red Square cobbles, these longer slogans, though supposedly suitable for chanting by enthusiastic demonstrators, are never actually spoken. They are published in the papers and serve as pithy summaries of policies the party will urge on the country for the next six months until the next parade.

The order is important. As in everything, the Russians have a hierarchical view: if a slogan slips down the charts by comparison with last year, it means that this aspect of policy is less urgent than it was. If an altogether new one appears, it reflects a new domestic concern or changed international situation. The general order however is always the same, and follows that adopted by all Soviet media in presenting the news: party affairs first, followed by slogans dealing with the Soviet government and institutions, workers and trade unions, the armed forces, industry, agriculture, science, the arts and sport.

Most Russians look at these exhortations and affirmations of loyalty to the party with hardly a second glance. But the party committee in every small village, if it is conscientious, will make sure that they are understood by the workers for whom they are intended. For these party committees are the inheritors of something else spawned by the Revolution – the 'agitation centres' which were used to win over hearts and minds. In the early days 'agitprop' (agitation and propaganda) was vital to the revolutionary effort, and many leading artists were enlisted to produce bold, modernistic posters that raised propaganda to the level of proletarian art. Propaganda had positive connotations, and still does in a country that regards information as a vital weapon in the unceasing struggle to establish complete acceptance of the communist party's supremacy. Access to, and control of, information is carefully regulated on a 'need-to-know' basis. To be well informed in Soviet society is a privilege, not a right.

I was always struck by how much Russians knew about things, especially life in the West, in spite of formidable obstacles. For even everyday information is hard to come by. There is, for example, no readily available telephone book listing private subscribers, and books listing official organizations are published only in very limited editions every five years or so. You can dial 09 for directory inquiries, but the service is almost always engaged, and if you want the number of someone with a name as common as Ivanov or Kuznetsov you will not be served. (There are some 150,000 people in Moscow called Ivanov, and 10,000 of them have the first two names of Ivan Ivanovich.) The alternative is to go to an inquiry kiosk, where for 2 kopecks you can be given a phone number – though not of a foreigner, an embassy or any other organization considered inappropriate. These kiosks give out other details that are equally difficult to discover: opening times of museums, addresses, directions, day-to-day matters taken for granted in the West.

Getting information on the workings of Soviet society from books is not easy: many factual references are not published – including accurate street maps of Soviet cities – and official statistics are restricted in scope. Indeed statistics that do not point up a favourable trend have become harder to obtain over the years. When infant mortality started to rise, the regular statistical tables suddenly ceased. Oil production and other sensitive economic indicators have been blurred by combining the information with other general production statistics. And after a poor harvest, in 1981, the third in a row, the total figure was simply not announced in the autumn.

The age-old worry about security explains much of this secrecy, but Russians also think it is unnecessary to tell those lower down what is going on or why. Aeroflot does not explain to passengers when and why flights are delayed. Shop assistants can never say when this or that product will be available. No one seems to know why this particular road is closed, what purpose a new building will serve or who is responsible for a decision. It is thought unusual and suspicious that anyone should concern himself with details of something that he has no professional need to know. A foreign journalist who once rang up the Moscow meteorological office for a comment on the summer's weather was told to write a letter explaining his reasons for wanting to know. There is the famous story of the opening session of talks with the Americans on strategic arms limitation some years ago. The Americans were puzzled to find that the civilians in the Soviet delegation, which included a deputy foreign minister, knew less about Soviet strategic potential than they did. Later General Nikolai Ogarkov, a deputy defence minister, took the Americans aside and rebuked them for revealing to the Soviet civilian negotiators matters the military considered their own pre-serve.

A Soviet press conference, especially on matters of state policy, is breath-taking for what is not revealed. Generalities refer to this or that party decision, or to the recent speeches of Soviet leaders. But if a foreign journalist (Russians do not ask embarrassing questions) wants to know exactly how, why and how many, he is usually given an evasive answer or a friendly wag of the finger with a joke about wanting to know everything. Revealingly, a Soviet interview with a well-known liberal American columnist whose views were respected in Moscow began with the flattering remark, 'We know you are a very important figure because you are very well informed.'

Perhaps because real factual information is so hard to find do ordinary people value it. Russians devour knowledge with the same ravenous impatience that they devour food. Any foreigner who succeeds in striking up a casual conversation is bombarded with questions: Is it true that in the West there are 18 million unemployed? How much does a teacher earn each month? How much do cars cost? Do all Americans clean their teeth five times a day? (That last, true question was asked by visitors at a travelling American agricultural exhibition.) Often Russians want to check whether information given to them by the official media is true. Most people know full well that much of what they read in the papers, especially on foreign affairs, is distorted and important issues ignored. But they cannot gauge the extent of the distortion, for unlike home affairs there is not the stark reality of experience to compare with the glowing official picture.

Nevertheless, Russians are great newspaper readers. The press is taken far more seriously in the Soviet Union than in the West. Not only are journalists political figures in their own right, but much more care is taken with the choice and presentation of material so that the message properly reflects the thinking of the Soviet leadership. As a result, *Pravda*, the official organ of the communist party, can boast that it is the most quoted paper in the world. It certainly has the biggest circulation (apart from the Chinese *People's Daily*) with some 10,700,000 printed each day and an estimated readership of 50 million. The world knows *Pravda* only from its official pronouncements laying out Soviet policy or denouncing the latest actions in Washington. The image is of turgid official prose, stupendously dull, and this is often the case. But it is not the whole picture. Stories of embezzlement, fraud, muggings and hold-ups, investigations into ministerial cover-ups and attempts to falsify the figures, challenges to ministers to tell consumers the truth – all this is the stuff of Western journalism. It is also the daily fare of *Pravda*, *Izvestia* and *Sovietskaya Rossia*.

Contrary to common perceptions in the West, the Soviet press is one of the most campaigning, hard-hitting and effective in the world. The headlines may be smaller, the lay-out more staid, and the pictures less revealing of human flesh, but Soviet papers are just as committed to getting their message across, setting the world to rights and entertaining their readers. The difference is that the message is not just the editor's musings, but the party line. Within that framework, however, Soviet editors like nothing better than to unearth a racket or name the guilty men in this or that office or factory. Of course, they have to have clearance first, and this depends on what the party wants publicising.

The large number of crime stories appearing nowadays are printed not to shock or entertain but as a warning. Once the party has decided that a sector of the economy is not pulling its weight, or public concern should be aroused over drunkenness, hooliganism or corruption, woe betide the offending factory when the *Pravda* journalist starts snooping around. He has the power to inspect any official documents for his investigations: police records, economic plans, factory accounts. He is not afraid to take on the government itself – provided the party has given the go-ahead. *Literaturnaya Gazeta* once produced a memorable satire. A reader wanted to know why several holiday trains that were already rather slow had been reclassified as expresses in the new timetables, yet took several hours longer to reach their destinations. The paper requested an interview with the minister of railways (who was sacked a few years later, incidentally). As it later disclosed, it tried to get an answer for six months – telephoning, writing and sending telegrams to his office. Eventually the paper printed all the pertinent questions, but left blank spaces for the minister's answers, saying he had had long enough to make up his mind about them.

Literaturnaya Gazeta, the intellectuals' favourite paper, occupies a special place in Soviet society. Although officially the organ of the Soviet Union of Writers, this weekly has become the main forum in which social issues are discussed, often with remarkable frankness, and where subjects normally taboo are touched on. It gets away with this by taking a very tough line on ideology and foreign policy. But more than any other newspaper it sounds out and reports on public opinion on domestic issues, acting as an important safety valve.

The party is always calling on the press to be more energetic in rooting out shortcomings, more critical, less uniform. Dozens of daily papers are published in Moscow and hundreds in the provinces, but instead of differing in their level of sophistication – quality or popular – they cater instead for different organizations: the trade unions, the Komsomol, the army, Soviet industry and so on. But even these distinctions are rather artificial. All papers carry identical texts, pictures and lay-outs when reporting party functions or official announcements. They invariably have very similar foreign news sections, and many stories on social themes could just as well be in one paper or another. Most papers are only four pages. *Pravda* and *Izvestia* have six, and on Mondays, when other papers are not published, *Pravda* has eight. Without advertisements, a lot can be fitted in the limited space. And though papers cost only a few kopecks, they are still pasted up on pavement display boards, as they were after the Revolution. Old people still stop and read them as they shuffle off to the shops.

The Russians are only now catching up with the age of the electronic media, for official thinking has long regarded the press as the most important, certainly the most authoritative, medium. This reflects perhaps the age-old attitude that only what is written down is official, a record that can be quoted in evidence. Indeed, *Pravda* is notorious for its attempts to alter the record, to fit the facts into the desired mould. This is especially true of pictures. Photographs of the Soviet leaders are frequently switched or altered to show them in a better light. The line-up of the politburo atop the Lenin mausoleum during the November parade is usually a photo-montage from stock shots, carefully arranged so that they all look approximately the same height. (The tall, gaunt figure of Mikhail Suslov had to be cut down by at least a foot.) Sometimes there are mistakes: a Moscow evening paper once forgot to include Andrei Kirilenko, although he clearly appeared in every other paper, leading Kremlinologists to speculate furiously about possible feuds between Kirilenko and Viktor Grishin, the Moscow party boss. I myself was once the victim of a photograph purge. When Michael Foot and Denis Healey came to Moscow and met Brezhnev in 1981, British journalists were allowed into the room for the first two minutes, as is customary, to record the opening of the talks. All the papers subsequently published the normal photograph of Brezhnev talking to the visitors across a green baize table, with journalists hovering in the background. But *Pravda* believed the room was too cluttered, and eliminated at least two of Brezhnev's aides sitting beside him and a dozen figures in the background, myself included, filling in the gaps with carefully painted-in continuations of the walls. By chance, a colleague remarked on this to a Soviet photographer. 'Oh *Pravda*'s always doing that,' he said. 'There was a bit of a scandal last week when the Kampucheans were here. They rubbed out one of the delegation from the official picture, thinking he was just an interpreter. He turned out to be the foreign minister.'

Another official recalled the embarrassing moment in 1955 when Chancellor Konrad Adenauer arrived in Moscow on an important visit. *Pravda* had the official picture of the airport meeting, but thought it undignified that while Adenauer wore a neat trilby, Khrushchev was bare-headed. The picture was sent along to the art department to be touched up, and it was only when it was published that anyone noticed that Khrushchev indeed was now wearing a similar trilby, while in his hand by his side he held another hat.

It is harder to fake things on television, though Soviet producers and cameramen are skilled at avoiding unflattering shots of Soviet leaders, and in his last few years were quick at cutting, when Brezhnev, tired and ill, had difficulty negotiating the stairs. Television was sorely tested during the Olympic Games, when it showed the opening ceremony but contrived, with careful editing, to mask the fact that many Western sportsmen refused to take part in the parade.

Television as a mass entertainer is fairly new in the Soviet Union, but it has already established a firm grip on the population, and is provoking arguments that have a familiar ring in the West: it is spoiling family life, keeping children up too late, not giving people what they want to see, has too many repeats, does not offer a choice. More and more Russians now switch on when they come home from work and leave the set on until they go to bed. Addiction is common not only in towns, but also in the countryside, where television sets, relatively cheap and plentiful in line with the party's realization that television has propaganda potential, provide the only relief from suffocating boredom. What do people want to see? Principally, sport. Ice-hockey and football are the most popular, and there is plenty of both. If an important ice-hockey match is running overtime it has been known for even the sacrosanct nine o'clock evening news programme to begin late. Figure-skating is also popular, and Soviet triumphs at international championships are keenly appreciated. Commentators – like those the world over – are far from impartial: 'Here come ours! A fine pair – look how well they're doing, just watch that movement!' 'Ours' by definition must do well. It seems sometimes that the prestige of the entire Soviet system hangs on a win by the Soviet competitors.

Like the early BBC, Soviet television broadcasts what is deemed worthy and edifying (as well as politically instructive). That means occasional excellent programmes of ballet, opera, orchestral music and poetry readings. Yevgeny Yevtushenko and Andrei Voznesensky can still command an hour or more of prime time reading their poetry. (There was rather a row once when Sergei Lapin, the director of Soviet broadcasting, took offence at Yevtushenko's remark that much of the stuff on television was rubbish, and abruptly cancelled his performance, but the quarrel was patched up.) High culture has to make token obeisance to the achievements of the various Soviet republics, and so there is also a great deal of folk troupes, national dancing and local choirs.

The Second World War and the Civil War are still standard fare. Civil

War films are the equivalent of westerns: Reds versus Whites, with quite a few people biting the dust, heroic Red volunteers and evil White commanders and no possible doubt about the outcome. The Second World War is treated more meaningfully though just as bloodily. And naturally several lavish television series have been based on Brezhnev's memoirs of his wartime exploits and supervision of the Virgin Lands scheme in Kazakhstan afterwards. Mr Yuri Andropov has so far been more modest about his achievements.

Brezhnev several times said television was too dull, and his words, unlike Yevtushenko's, were taken to heart. The criticism is mainly directed at the news and current affairs programmes; but while ideologues complain there are not enough party or atheistic propaganda programmes, most people think there are too many already. 'I always know when the evening news comes on,' one woman told me, 'as all the toilets in our block start flushing, doors bang and people move about.' News programmes with commentaries, analysis and studio discussion of current issues have been started to liven things up, but of course there is never any real argument.

Strengthening the ideological content was a declared aim of a fourth channel, introduced in 1982. It was to make programmes 'showing the Soviet way of life and asserting communist values,' Mr Lapin announced, adding: 'Be it a programme on socialist emulation, on the five-year plan or a concert of political songs, television is called upon to promote the ideological and civic education of working people.' Plays especially were to portray the correct outlook. The hero 'typically demonstrates social activity, singlemindedness and a sense of responsibility, not only to those matters entrusted to him, but in everything that affects him as a Soviet citizen and lord of his country.'

The viewing public cares little for such stuff. They prefer the outstanding nature programmes, especially those about wildlife abroad. Or the quiz programmes where experts are handed strange objects which they have to identify and talk about. Increasingly, despite Mr Lapin, television is producing police thrillers, fast-moving and slickly made films about Soviet militiamen tracking down some convincingly real crooks. Detective series with a touch of socialist realism – that is, realism about life under socialism – are fairly new and very popular. Previously, crime stories had to be set in improbably depicted capitalist countries or in the far-off days before the Revolution, lest they be thought to glorify crime. And good foreign films, with even the occasional series of historical dramas from the West, can command audiences of tens of millions.

Some pearls are still uniquely Russian – daily early morning exercises with the archetypal healthy young couple running on the spot and doing press-ups to old-fashioned piano music, while the earnest instructor bids the viewer do likewise; the occasional anti-alcohol sessions, when experts in white coats sit in a studio gloating over the horrific effects of drink while a psychologist who seems to be trained in televisual hypnosis urges you to save your health and kick the habit; and the annual hairdressing competition where the winners stand beside their creations, while the models sit demurely on stage showing off the most outlandish entanglements atop their heads, looking for all the world like entries at Crufts. It is, perhaps, the nearest Soviet thing to the Miss World contest.

Apart from two Moscow television channels which broadcast all over the country, each republic has its own channel where programmes are usually in the local language. And though television is state-run, there are, surprisingly, advertisements – shown in occasional blocks of half an hour. They depict all the latest and smartest consumer goods available in principle (though by no means always in practice), while attempts are made to raise consumer consciousness by setting out what the indignant citizen should do if sold defective shoes. The ads are really no more than state boasting, and have an ironic counter-effect. The general reaction is either 'I'll believe it when I see it in the shops', or 'It can't be worth buying if they need to advertise it to get rid of it'.

Soviet television, like any Soviet institution, tries hard not to build up any individual personality, though inevitably some news commentators come over better than others. The radio is more suited to the anonymous announcement, the disembodied voice of the party. I once met that voice – perhaps the most famous voice in the Soviet Union. It belongs to the man who has delivered all the important announcements for the past forty-five years – the voice that told the Soviet people they were at war, and four bloody years later announced the victory over Nazi Germany. It introduced the speeches of Stalin, and broke the news of his death. It chronicled the rise and fall of Malenkov and Khrushchev and the era of Brezhnev. For millions of Russians, Yuri Levitan is the voice of history.

He has been broadcasting for over fifty years, and became Moscow radio's principal announcer. He used to give the commentaries, year in year out, at the Red Square parades, and it was his vibrant rising crescendo that called out the slogans and intoned the 'oorahs'. Levitan, a Jew as his name makes clear, is a courteous man of personal modesty and charm, the ultimate self-effacing servant of the party, of which he has been a member since 1941. He never comments on the news broadcasts, nor voices his own opinions on the many twists and turns of policy he has witnessed. He was born in the ancient town of Vladimir, the son of a tailor, and wanted to become an opera singer, but in 1931 after his father's death won a competition for a radio announcer in Moscow. In spite of a strong provincial accent, his rich baritone voice made him the obvious winner, and he began broadcasting the next year at the age of eighteen.

Levitan told me about the hardest and most bitter broadcast of his life: the declaration of war on 22 June 1941. 'It was about 6.00 o'clock on a sunny morning,' he said. 'An alarming voice on the phone ordered me quickly to the radio station. I sensed something terrible had happened – people in my profession listen not only to the words but also to the intonation. I rushed to the studio. Faces were sad, women were crying. There were calls from our correspondents saying the Germans were bombing Kiev, and Kaunas was on fire. A call from the Kremlin said an important government announcement would be made. First Molotov (then prime minister) spoke. Then I read the announcement. It was repeated five times, each hour. I was unusually nervous, and after each phrase paused to take breath. I had to clench my fists. In my voice was wrath and indignation, but there was also belief in victory.'

As the war continued, the Germans repeatedly tried to destroy the broadcasting station. Levitan is said to have headed the list of people Hitler ordered to be hanged when Moscow was captured. Bombs fell all around the studio and the broadcasters worked in the dark with only their torches to read the text. The mood was very different when he read the announcement of victory at 2.00 a.m. on VE Day, as people danced in the streets. During the war he introduced all Stalin's broadcasts from an improvised studio in the Kremlin. 'I was told not to give advice to Stalin, as I did to other broadcasters, and merely to answer his questions briefly. He asked me whether he should broadcast sitting or standing. I suggested standing, and told him to speak in a normal voice.' Ten years later he announced to a stunned country that Stalin was dead. And a few years after that he broadcast denunciations of the 'cult of personality'.

Nowadays Levitan does not meet Soviet leaders. President Brezhnev's rare broadcasts were all prerecorded. But the sound of his voice, presaging some momentous announcement, still sends shivers down most Russian spines. Levitan smiles modestly at this faceless fame, and recalls how a policeman once stopped him for speeding, and refused to believe the name on his driving licence. It was only when he began speaking in his powerful, surging voice that the shaken policeman quickly handed him back his licence, saluted and waved him on.

It is not only when they hear Levitan's voice, however, that the Russians remember the war. The Great Patriotic War, as the four year struggle with Germany is called, was the greatest challenge the regime ever had to face, and one of the bloodiest periods in Russian history. Soviet historians say altogether 20 million Russians perished. In the Ukraine alone 28,000 villages were destroyed. And the Soviet authorities are determined that no one shall forget. To a visitor it seems the war has only just ended: in every town there arc memorials to the dead, eternal flames guarded with solemn reverence by schoolchildren, in their Pioneers' uniforms and bearing real guns. In 1978, thirty-three years after the German surrender, Minsk was awarded the banner of a hero city for its wartime resistance. New memorial complexes are constructed every year. Statues to young partisans stand in city squares and schoolchildren regularly visit the museums where all the horrors of the conflict are displayed. The war is the theme of almost every leader's speech, and every year new memoirs are published by wartime commanders, sold in special bookshops dealing in the literature of the war. Even now at least half a dozen elderly people are shot each year for war crimes or collaboration with the Nazis.

For the older generation, the war is a fearful memory that still provokes deep emotions, and the younger generation has grown up with the trauma of the war hanging over every household. The first thing every foreign visitor is told by party members and grandmothers alike is: 'Let there be no more war,' and the toast at every official dinner is always 'to peace'. Few Westerners, unused to the sharpness of wartime memory, can go away unmoved. I once visited the cemetery on the outskirts of Leningrad where more than a million dead are buried, victims of battle and starvation during the 900 day blockade, on a December day so cold that the freezing numbness reminded tearful old women of the bitter winter of 1941. The rosebeds covering the mass graves were blanketed with thick snow. In the evening sky huge, silent clouds of steam rose mournfully from the city factories as from all sides of the memorial complex clichéd but cuttingly sad dirges played to the frozen desert.

There is something so vast, so profoundly felt in the Russian war memorials that the sentiment is not cloying nor the emotions artificial. The little Byelorussian village of Khatyn is one of the most moving. The punitive SS battalion called 'The Black Death' came there on a freezing March morning in 1943. They herded all the inhabitants, 149 people including 75 children, into a barn, doused it with petrol and set it alight. Machine guns were trained on to the inferno to shoot anyone who escaped. The village was then looted, set alight and abandoned. But one man was not in Khatyn at the time. When Joseph Kaminski returned he found his young son still alive among the charred bodies. He picked him up – and the boy died in his father's arms.

Today a harrowing bronze statue of Kaminski carrying his dying son and staring in blank horror straight ahead stands at the entrance to Khatyn. But no one lives in the village any more, although over 15 million people have visited it in the last twelve years. Khatyn has been rebuilt as a memorial to its dead, and to the dead of 185 other villages that were similarly destroyed during the three-year German occupation. Where each house stood, four cement beams now represent the first row of the wooden log constructions and a rebuilt chimney stack with a bell in it marks each site. The stacks bear plaques with the names of families who lived there. Once every 30 seconds the bells of all the houses ring out together to the forest around. Byelorussia lost one in every four people during the war. At Khatyn – not to be confused with Katyn, where Polish officers were massacred by Stalin – three birch trees have been planted in a square. Where the fourth should grow, burns the eternal flame. A concrete representation of a concentration camp wall runs down one side of the village. Behind bars in niches of varying sizes are the names of the large or small camps where people were killed or children bled to death to provide blood for the German army.

These painful memories have been kept alive in countless films, shown regularly on television, including the impressive Soviet–American documentary series *The Unknown War*, when Stalin reappeared on Soviet screens for the first time in many years. Since 1945 however, genuine emotions of the war have been exploited to justify a range of Soviet policies, including vigilance in all dealings with the West, a hard line towards West Germany and the question of German reunification, high defence spending at the expense of consumer goods, and, above all, the identification of Soviet patriotism with the communist system.

On one anniversary of the outbreak of the war in June, *Pravda* remarked in a typical editorial: 'The farther the war years recede, the deeper do we realize the magnitude of the immortal heroic achievements of the millions of Soviet patriots. Soviet patriotism is in the flesh of the citizens of a developed socialist society. Great affection towards the homeland, which is organically inherent in the Soviet peoples, blends with boundless devotion to the socialist system, to the communist ideals.' The paper went on: 'No one has been forgotten, nothing has been forgotten! The Soviet people always remember at what heavy price peace was won.' As the Russians' attitude to the continued imprisonment of Rudolf Hess makes clear, they will not let the world forget what they suffered. Too much political capital has been invested since 1945 to allow the memory to fade away.

Most Russians accept without question the official version of their country's heroic role in the war. Indeed, many have only a vague knowledge of the participation of other countries, as virtually nothing is said or written about the extensive American war aid, or the British convoys to Murmansk. No official memorial has been erected in that Arctic city to the allied sailors who lost their lives, and most inhabitants seem unaware of the lifeline that passed through the port. The war was a Russian war, and it was Russia that saved the world from fascism, history books state. They also assert that it was really the Soviet intervention in Manchuria in the final week of fighting that was decisive in forcing the Japanese to surrender, rather than the dropping of the atomic bombs. Few dispute the fact.

But the official version of more contemporary events is increasingly regarded with considerable scepticism. Russians have long grown used to the gap between facts and propaganda, and are able to digest this official double-think with remarkable equanimity. But to be sure of what is going on around them, they tune in, where possible, to foreign radio transmissions, especially those of The Voice of America, the BBC and Deutsche Welle. No one knows the listenership of these 'voices', as the Russians call them, but it runs into millions. Ever since jamming was reimposed at the height of the Polish crisis in 1980, thousands of people, especially sophisticated city dwellers, daily seek out a wavelength that occasionally escapes the jamming devices. This naturally infuriates the authorities. There are regular diatribes against Western radio stations, which ironically only reinforce their credibility. I remember a remarkable testimony to the popularity of VOA when a senior official giving a press conference on price increases began his statement with the announcement: 'The reason for recent price adjustments is absolutely different from that given by the Voice of America today.' Since most Western journalists do not listen to VOA in Russian, few knew what he was objecting to. I was once startled by a priest, who enjoyed good relations with the secular authorities, remarking when out of official earshot that I had written a harsh commentary on the Soviet intervention in Afghanistan. I asked how he knew, and began to explain that it was of course a point of disagreement between our two countries. 'I heard a summary on the BBC,' he replied. 'I listen every day. I agreed with your comments.'

But the popularity of foreign broadcasts has taught the authorities one important lesson: their own propaganda apparatus is in need of drastic overhaul. In 1979 a party decree admitted that much of what appeared in the papers was 'twaddle', which insulted the intelligence of the readers. It said the greatest failing was the refusal to admit failures and the attempt to gloss over criticism. The point seemed lost on Tass, the official news agency, which carried the full text of the decree on its English language service but left out the single paragraph with these telling indictments of the media.

For almost four years the Russians have been debating how their propaganda could be improved. The recommendations were always the same: make it more informative, more lively and more frank (meaning truthful). But ingrained habits die hard. The party bureaucrat or government official cannot admit failures that might reflect on his competence. The ideologue dare not depart from safe clichés laid down years ago for fear of overstepping the limit of permissible debate. And a defensive national psychology makes it hard for the Russians to admit any shortcoming lest this be taken as proof abroad of the failure of the communist system. I once asked Viktor Afanasyev, the lean, austere and dedicated editor-in-chief of *Pravda*, whether he had ever regretted publishing three controversial articles on economics in 1977 which called for thorough-going reforms and bitterly criticised the inertia of the present system. He replied that he supported opening up *Pravda* to wider debate and more public discussion of contemporary issues. But he had got into trouble over the articles – not because of what they said, but because they were reprinted in Yugoslavia – 'by our ideological enemies', as he put it. That fact alone had gravely embarrassed the Soviet leadership.

It looks as though much may change in this field under the leadership of President Andropov, however. Virtually the first major speech the new Soviet leader made on assuming office was noteworthy for its forthright language, hard-hitting criticism and absence of all tired clichés. He appears to have fewer qualms than his predecessor in naming names and stating bluntly what the issues are.

The aspect of Soviet propaganda subject to the most blistering criticism has been the compulsory political education sessions, endured alike by students and workers with indifference and apathy. Frequently television shows meetings of workers called together for an ideological harangue or to approve some new policy. Their faces are masks so devoid of emotion that it is impossible to tell their thoughts while they clap in ritual applause. At the last party congress Brezhnev said young people found compulsory political lectures so boring that they simply switched off, sitting out the allotted hours. They wanted 'real answers' to today's questions instead of 'fossilized' propaganda, as he put it. Meanwhile the country's 'class enemies' were improving their propaganda and stepping up attempts to demoralize the population.

Such is the public scepticism of all official information that rumour takes the place of news and spreads throughout cities with extraordinary speed and exaggeration. Some rumours are based on genuine information leaked by those in the know – impending price rises, for example, or the scandals and foibles of those in high places. Moscow was abuzz with rumours of the most salacious kind in the spring of 1982, linking President Brezhnev's daughter Galina with a flamboyant former Bol-shoi performer, known as Boris the Gypsy, who was apparently caught with a director of Soviet circus management in a diamond-smuggling racket. The ripples of this spicy scandal gradually spread further and further, taking in the mysterious death of a former career chief of the KGB, a magazine article that seemed to call on Brezhnev to retire and an apparent – and in hindsight probably real – struggle for power within the politburo, until it seemed that the whole power edifice of the Brezhnev regime was brought to the point of collapse because of some shady dealings in the circus.

Nothing was ever said officially, of course, and in the end the stories fizzled out. But clearly something or someone had sparked the gossip, which in turn led to more rumours about the source. Officialdom is extremely sensitive to stories about the private lives of Soviet leaders, who are veiled from public view. When news began to leak out that Grigory Romanov, the party secretary of Leningrad, had borrowed some priceless Tsarist china from a museum for the wedding party of his daughter and some of this had been smashed by the guests, he is reliably reported to have been severely reprimanded by Mikhail Suslov, the veteran politburo ideologue.

Some rumours are hardy annuals: the suggestion for example that all money is to be halved in value in an attempt to wipe out the huge amount of private savings that distort the economy, or that a gang of especially dangerous criminals disguised as police was terrorising the city, flagging down cars at night and murdering the occupants. These stories usually begin as a suggestion once canvassed by the party but rejected, or an exaggerated account of a real crime that was not reported in the press.

Perhaps the most typical Russian rumour is the weather scare story. This predicts that there will be a natural catastrophe outdoing anything previously known, and it is caused by the refusal to believe any official announcement, including even the weather forecast. I can see how such stories start. New Year's Eve in 1979 was one of the coldest on record, at minus 40 degrees in Moscow. But apart from television warnings not to take the children outside, and not to drink alcohol – greeted with derision by the entire population – no word was given of the serious economic consequences: severe disruption of transport and a break-down of most of the city's heating and hot water system. Instead the news showed pictures of heavy snowfalls in West Germany and central Europe and the chaos there. When it warmed up, I was sufficiently sceptical to half believe the assurances of a taxi-driver that in his block of flats alone sixty people had frozen to death. Meanwhile, the *babushki* forecast an unprecedented cold snap of minus 50 degrees. When I checked this extraordinary forecast with the meteorological centre, an angry official asked why I believed rumours rather than the official denial, printed in all the papers. Of course the predicted great freeze never arrived.

One result of the diminishing effect of ramming the party message down the throats of a sceptical population is that the Russians are now appealing more and more to public opinion in the hope that persuasion will take over where exhortation failed. The first difficulty is to find out what the public, for many years ignored, really thinks. This is not easy in a society where the average citizen has long been used to expressing only those opinions he thinks his superiors want to hear. But the Russians have discovered the pollster in a big way, and anonymous questionnaires are now pouring forth in their thousands, with surveys on a multitude of subjects (though not politics) directed at youth, pensioners and other designated groups. The pollsters are generally sociologists, a science that after years of suspicion has been enlisted by the party as a valuable aid in keeping the leadership informed. Soviet sociologists also have a second task – the moulding of public opinion and research into ways this can be used to back the party line.

An older and more effective gauge of public opinion, however, are letters to the press, which Russians pen in their millions. In 1981 *Pravda* received 513,984 letters, giving it the largest postbag of any paper in the world. The letters section is easily the largest in the building, employing more than seventy staff. Each letter is read, sorted, and passed on to the relevant ministry or local authority and answered (though often perfunctorily). Letters play a vital role in resolving disputes, and papers pride themselves on championing their readers' causes, cutting through bureaucracy or rooting out abuse. But letters are also vital in taking the pulse of the country, and party thinking is often modified on this basis. Only a tiny proportion is actually printed – and those selected always support party policies or are indicative of official concern over the issues raised. Sometimes letters are selected to stir up debate, or arouse public opinion on an issue, and readers' comments pour in by the sackful. An example was the debate on the widespread practice of stealing and skinning dogs for their furs. This began with a letter in *Komsomolskaya Pravda* from a distinguished theatre director, and was followed by numerous articles and reactions. Not all the letters condemned the practice, as some people said it was no worse than skinning a fox. On such a question the authorities may have a point to make, but are not interested in bulldozing public opinion.

Russians who write in disagreeing with officially sanctioned views receive a curt, printed card that simply regrets they do not agree with the position of the newspaper 'which also represents the views of our party and government'. But no measures are taken against those expressing contrary views, as this is one of the few means the party has of gauging popular reaction. Reports summarizing the topics provoking correspondence are circulated to the politburo and top political and security organs. As one official remarked privately: 'Our leaders do not pay attention to the views of 40,000 people. But if 40 million people make the same point, then they listen.'

The party also elicits public opinion more directly from the questions asked at public political lectures. These talks, organized by the *Znaniye* (Knowledge) Society are popular as they deal more frankly than the press with topical issues. In 1980, as the Polish crisis was just beginning and there was renewed fighting in Lebanon, I went along one evening. We sat in tiered rows in a big lecture hall facing the stage, about 250 people in all. My neighbour was a serious-looking middle-aged woman in a green jersey, woollen stockings and sensible shoes. On my other side was a young man who had obviously just been to Moscow's main toyshop, as he put down a bulging bag with children's plastic building blocks peeping out. There were a lot of grizzled pensioners, some long-haired students, two army officers in uniform, a policeman and the odd foreign diplomat trying, rather unsuccessfully, to blend in with the crowd. We had our notebooks ready on our desks as the panel came on stage – a bearded chairman, familiar to television viewers, and three smartly dressed journalists. The first speaker began to talk about Lebanon. He knew a lot and spoke in refreshingly straightforward language, laying out the aims of the Christians, the Palestinians and the Israelis, how much control each faction had, the effects of Camp David (calling it an 'agreement' instead of the usual pejorative Soviet term 'deal').

My stern neighbour was writing it all down furiously in a book in huge handwriting (Russians are taught at school to write in very big letters). Perhaps she would have to give a briefing later to her factory. The speaker then moved on to the Middle East in general, with quotations from Gromyko's latest speech to the United States, a frank résumé of what the Americans accused the Russians of doing in the area, and the Iran–Iraq war which had just begun. 'Aha,' murmured someone behind me, and my neighbour's husband opened his eyes. As the speaker expounded imperialism's plots, little pieces of paper with questions were passed down from row to row to the stage.

The next topic was Comecon, the Soviet trading block. This was heavy-going – a convoluted history of how the Americans had tried to strangle the socialist countries by a trade boycott after the war, and how the communist countries were integrating their economies. There were difficulties, he admitted – Czech cars were poorly made because the steel plants were old. But 'problems are being solved in a constructive way,' and Comecon was posing an increasing challenge to the Western economies. A question on Afghanistan evoked a small groan from my dutiful neighbour (who by now had filled almost an entire book with notes). 'Comrades, you all know why the Soviet army is there, to foil the intrigues of reaction, protect the borders . . . anyway if you read the papers you will get plenty of details in this.' Iran–Iraq was more interesting. 'Which one is more guilty?' 'Well, it's hard to say,' he replied and drifted off into an old and obscure Russian proverb. 'Which side do we support?' 'Comrades,' he replied, 'we have a peaceful attitude to all the world. We would like to see the soonest possible end to the conflict.' Then a more ingenious question – 'Since we provided arms to Iraq, shouldn't we now give arms to Iran to preserve our neutrality?' The answer was that it was not known (at least, officially) whether the Soviet Union was still giving Iraq arms, and the question therefore did not arise. 'Anyway, it has never been our policy to provide arms to both sides so that they could kill each other.' 'What would we do if the United States intervened?' 'Take decisive measures.' And so on.

Questions then moved back to Comecon. No one seemed to have much interest in that except where it had a direct bearing on everyday life, such as 'Why are shoes from Czechoslovakia of such bad quality?' (Laughter all round.) What people wanted to know about was Poland. Conveniently there was an expert on hand. He outlined the 'serious situation', making fun of Lech Walesa as a figure in denims who was idolized by the Western press but was really no more than a 'routine anti-communist'. Unfortunately he had forgotten that while he and perhaps the panel had all read about Walesa in their privileged copies of the Western press or in the special, fuller reports Tass provides only for the party leadership, the average Russian, if he did not listen to foreign broadcasts, had not officially been told anything at that stage about the Solidarity leadership.

The speakers admitted that in a socialist economy strikes were 'an extreme measure'. 'But why didn't our press print the strikers' demands?' someone persisted. 'That would have constituted interference in sovereign Poland's internal affairs at a time of great difficulty,' was the smooth reply. And then there was more about Poland's inefficient farming, its large debts, some plain talk about 'free and independent unions', and after a loud protest from a pensioner that he had forgotten her question about the Pope, an admission that the Roman Catholic Church played a 'positive and responsible role' during the crisis – a judgement that was sharply reversed two years later.

The questions looked as though they would go on and on, and the pensioners, who had come mainly for the travel film about New Zealand that was to follow, were getting restless. My neighbour had already filled up her book. Eventually the chairman called a halt. The session had been informative enough – and the questions, carefully noted by the KGB and foreign diplomats who take these lectures seriously, certainly revealed more than the answers.

These lectures are voluntary. But others, held in factories a year later up and down the country as the Polish crisis worsened, were not.

Thousands of workers were convened to hear diatribes against the 'provocations' of Solidarity and officially organized 'protest meetings' were televised and publicised as part of the Soviet psychological campaign against Poland. The workers have no say in these political rallies, nor in the drafting of the thousands of spontaneous letters protesting against this or that aspect of American policy. It is a political ritual, something done *pokazukha* or 'for show' in an attempt to show the world that the propaganda claims indeed represent the will of the masses. Indeed, as the economy stagnated, a party decree even re-marked rather tartly that too much time was wasted in factories on empty meetings (though this did not refer to political rallies). But despite the coercive and contrived nature of such exercises, they do sometimes strike a responsive chord, especially if, as the anti-Polish rallies did, they appeal to patriotism or Russian nationalism.

Patriotism in the Soviet Union knows no bounds. Russians are brought up from kindergarten to honour the motherland, to respect their leaders, to treat Lenin with religious reverence. They may – and do – joke about the party, the leaders and the communist system. But they do not make fun of their country, and find it hard to shake off the almost mystical awe surrounding the cult of Lenin that begins with the regular pilgrimages as schoolchildren to the local statues of Lenin (there is at least one in each town), to lay flowers on the pedestal on 22 April, his birthday. Young Russians, however unpolitical and materialist, are unashamedly chauvinistic. They complain to foreigners about short-ages, beg for jeans and records, and yet all the time clamour for approval of their country and system. Never having been outside the Soviet Union, many argue passionately about the superiority of their way of doing things. By definition 'ours' must be better, because it is ours.

And here we come to the dilemma posed by the state's policy on information and propaganda. People want to believe what they are told, want to hear that things are getting better, want to be reassured that they live well. But they cannot accept it all because experience proves it is not true, and, in the old days especially, the claims were too utterly removed from reality even to seem plausible. The defence against this vexing conflict of feelings is to develop one's own form of double-think. Many Russians are quite able to assert with enthusiasm some fact or view they do not really believe, because they know it is the 'correct' fact or view and therefore they should believe it. And in the end they often convince themselves. On a personal level this means the party line is generally accepted, and strongly influences people's views of society and the world. On a national scale it is more dangerous as Soviet officials and policy-makers frequently end up believing the interpretation that best fits the propaganda line, and get a rude shock when events in the world do not turn out as this line predicts. Afghanistan is an obvious example.

Some Russians, rejecting what they believe to be propaganda, end up disbelieving everything. They paint to themselves a far rosier picture of the West than is the case, simply because they refuse to accept the less pleasant, but true, aspects given prominence in the Soviet media. Perhaps only in the Soviet Union does the American dream still exist.

The propaganda policy under Yuri Andropov appears to be a general tightening up in enforcing the party line, but a greater readiness to admit unpleasant truths, at home and abroad. In this way the conflict between claims and reality is lessened, and the resulting cynicsm reduced. There is not likely to be much let-up in the flow of information from outside – the cut-off of automatic telephone dialling in 1982 was almost certainly prompted by KGB worries that too much uncontrollable information, of all kinds, was going in and out. To know is still to have power. But rigid suppression of anything that is awkward for the propaganda apparatus to handle is too naive a policy for Soviet society nowadays, as the authorities clearly realize. And though propaganda remains a central concern for the leadership, it has gradually become less rigid, more persuasive, more broadly grounded, more open to sophisticated argument. And under Andropov, that trend will certainly continue.

CHAPTER SEVEN

The Russian Character

Few people can sum up the Russian character – it seems to be a mass of contradictions. A Russian can at the same time be servile and haughty, warm-hearted and cruel, hospitable and xenophobic, emotional and inhibited, suspicious and fatalistic, fearful yet also reckless. The Russians themselves speak of their 'broad nature', meaning their dreamy emotionalism, and admit they are a blend of the Oriental and the European. To a Russian, for example, saving face is of great importance, and this Eastern characteristic colours not only individual actions but policies and attitudes in dealing with other countries. Indeed, many national policies can only be understood by reference to the Russian character.

Despite their official commitment to a 'revolutionary' philosophy, to the changing of old attitudes and a 'progressive' outlook that welcomes innovation, the Russians by nature are intensely, almost obsessively, conservative. Perhaps a better word is orthodox, for in politics nowadays, as in religion in Tsarist times, the Russians believe that the way laid down in earlier days is 'rightly guided' and cannot – or should not – be altered. While lip-service is paid to the need for an evolution of political thinking and for institutions to keep pace with the developments of modern society, in fact the Soviet leadership has regarded any innovation with great suspicion, and the bulk of the population has stoutly resisted change. Soviet society is increasingly traditional in its workings, and harks back almost unashamedly to pre-revolutionary times. Visitors may wonder where the old Russia they read about in Tolstoy and Gogol has gone. But it is there beneath the surface, living on in a thousand attitudes, expressions and reactions. One wonders sometimes if anything has changed.

The harshest feature of the many harsh sides of life in Russia, to an American, is the utter absence of constitutional rights. Individuals have no rights in Russia. They exist in peace and breathe the air outside a prison cell solely on the sufferance of the police, whose authority over them is practically that of deputy despots in their capacity as representatives of the Czar.

When I first reached St Petersburg, I wrote home of the agreeable impression that was made on me by seeing the Czar driving freely about the streets, with scarcely any escort. Before leaving Russia, however, I discovered that in order to make this sort of thing possible, the Czar's chief of police summarily expels from the capital no less than 15,000 persons every year, or an average of over 40 a day. Tourists and casual visitors from America and Europe see the Czar driving about in this manner, but they know nothing of the other side of the picture – of the steady streams of 'suspects' and others driven from the city, three fourths of whom are probably innocent of evil intent, and so they come away with rosy and erroneous impressions, thinking they have seen Russia.

Those who have seen merely St Petersburg and Moscow have seen little or nothing of real Russia, nor even if they have made the grand tour across the country by rail, and up and down the Volga. These tourists have glided over the surface of Russia, their path made smooth and agreeable by the imported polish of the West, but they have not seen it. Russia has within its vast area resources that should make its future as promising as the future of the United States. Hopeless as the outlook seems at present for the masses of the Russian people, all history teaches that the day of their emancipation will, sooner or later, come. The best solution of the situation that could be hoped for, would, perhaps be a progressive and liberal Czar, who would have sufficient courage and energy to give the country a constitutional government.

That was written in 1891. It is the foreword to one of the most remarkable of many accounts of pre-revolutionary Russia by Western travellers, called *Through Russia on a Mustang*. The author, Thomas Stevens, was a witty, cynical and swashbuckling man, who had already travelled around the world on a bicycle before conceiving the idea of buying a horse in Moscow and riding through the villages of Russia and the Ukraine down to Sebastopol in the Crimea. He missed nothing, scouting out traditions, beliefs, going into people's houses, getting arrested, battling with bureaucrats and always asking, asking.

The chief of police in one village seems to have been a far-sighted man. 'The only enemy we have is Germany. England doesn't understand us, and so she hates us. The countries of the future are America and Russia. Our people have more good qualities than bad. People at a distance remember our faults and forget our virtues. As a people, we have no talent for detail, and for that reason our administration is defective. We are the kindest-hearted people in the world, but a Russian is too easily contented with things as they are.'

Stevens agreed wholeheartedly. On the train to Moscow he noticed that 'at nearly every station was seen the inevitable drunken moujik, stupid and happy. One of them happened to pass through our car. He stumbled over a bundle. "Nichevo," he said in a maudlin voice, as he scrambled up, "Never mind." "Nichevo" is the most frequent exclamation one hears in Russia. It means anything of a negative degree. Nichevo – never mind! Nichevo – pray don't mention it!'

In Moscow Stevens bought a horse and engaged a university student, Sasha, to be his interpreter. The young man was 'singularly warm and impulsive, and strangely unreliable, contradictory, quixotic and inconsistent.' He started out with great enthusiasm, boasting of the glories his ride would bring to his regiment. After three days he abandoned the idea of writing a diary, saying he would translate Stevens' account when it was written instead. After a week he was complaining of fatigue. And only twelve days before Sebastopol he gave it all up and went home.

Apart from the constant difficulties of being overcharged at the inns they stopped at, Stevens and Sasha were the victims of unwelcome curiosity. He concluded, rather uncharitably, at the end of his book 'If anyone were to ask me what trait of character is most conspicuously developed in the Russians, I would answer – suspicion. On reflection I might perhaps hesitate between suspicion and superstition, and bestow a passing thought on servility; but whichever of these three graces prevails, the Russians are to my mind the most suspicious people under the sun.'

In almost every town he was called in by the police, who would not believe he was not a foreign spy, and could not understand his American passport. At one point he sat down, uninvited, in the police station, and cocked his feet on a wooden table. The officials almost had a fit, and asked Sasha to remind him he was talking to the Czar's representatives. Stevens told Sasha to reply: 'He knows you are police officers, but he is an American, and in America it is the police who humble themselves before the people, and not the people before the police.'

Stevens concluded that 'In Russia almost every conceivable thing a man might do is regulated by the written law. The Russian idea of governing the people is in direct opposition to the conceptions of the West. With us everything that the law does not expressly forbid is permitted; in Russia everything is forbidden that the law does not expressly grant, which means next to nothing at all.'

I make no apology for such a long quotation from this fascinating book, long out of print unfortunately, as it sums up in words that are hard to rival many contemporary attitudes to foreigners and to foreign journalists in particular. How often have Russian friends of Westerners in Moscow been questioned by the KGB about these connections, and how common still today is the general attitude of 'nichevo'! The point is that Russian attitudes are far, far older than the Soviet system, and have made that system what it is. That unacknowledged influence is hotly disputed by anti-communist Russian nationalists such as Alexander Solzhenitsyn. But to take an everyday example – foreign governments who complain of the restrictions the regime imposes on their diplomats have only to look back in history to see that this obsession with secrecy and security dates back to Ivan the Terrible. Even in those days merchants and envoys were obliged to live in specially allocated foreign ghettos in Moscow – as they still are.

Hundreds of thousands of square miles of Soviet territory are also permanently sealed off from foreigners today. Moscow and Leningrad, open cities (except for certain areas) are ringed by vast stretches of closed countryside and areas in Siberia as large as France and Spain along the Chinese frontier are closed.

Until the Second World War it was theoretically possible for the few Western residents in the Soviet Union and tourists to travel anywhere they wanted, though such trips were frequently frustrated by the creation of bureaucratic obstacles. But at the beginning of the Cold War in 1947, Stalin drew up a list of places officially closed, and that list, with a few changes, has remained in force ever since. The reasons for the restrictions vary. In some places, such as the huge closed zone in Kazakhstan, military considerations are uppermost. Semipalatinsk, in this area, is the centre for Soviet underground nuclear tests and for advanced weapons testing. Nearby is the Baikonur cosmodrome where Soviet space shots are launched.

Other areas surrounding military factories and key production plants are closed to stop Westerners visiting them. Gorky, for example, a large old town 250 miles east of Moscow, has an aircraft factory as well as several car factories. Since it is permanently closed, it was a suitable place to exile Dr Andrei Sakharov, the Soviet dissident leader, so that he could no longer meet Western correspondents. All along the frontiers with Norway, Finland, Turkey, Iran and Afghanistan access is prohibited within 25 kilometres of the frontier, presumably to stop anyone seeing the elaborate border defences. Naval bases at Sebastopol, Balaclava and other parts of the Crimea are off limits, and so is the desolate and inaccessible strip of coastline on the Bering Sea facing Alaska.

Other more accessible areas are closed, however, not for security reasons, but because the authorities do not want foreigners to mix with the local population, which may be strongly nationalistic. This is particularly true of the Baltic republics, where only the capital cities and certain nearby tourist sites are open.

The regulations are easy to enforce. A foreigner living in Moscow cannot just get in his car and drive off. On all roads leading out of every Soviet city there are permanent police check points. Unless a foreigner has advance clearance, he will be stopped and turned back. A resident journalist cannot buy an internal airticket without notifying the Foreign Ministry two working days in advance. Even if he got on a train or bus and was not recognized as a foreigner, he could not stay anywhere, as Soviet hotels accept bookings only if the visa has first been endorsed for the visit.

Periodically the regulations are changed. They were amended in 1966 and again in 1978, when large tracts of land adjacent to the Chinese frontier, including the Jewish autonomous republic of Birobidzhan in the Far East, were put out of bounds. But the principle of sealing off the countryside from prying eyes is firmly rooted in pre-revolutionary practice.

Russians are increasingly recognizing their pre-revolutionary heritage. As today's food shortages and the pace of urban life fray the nerves and patience of young and old alike, a growing wave of nostalgia for the good old days is washing over the country. The past, for all its poverty and much trumpeted injustices, seems to many a golden age, and remembrance of things past is a burgeoning industry. It is summed up in the joke, hard to translate because of the play on words: 'Which came first, the chicken or the egg? First (meaning also, in the past) there was everything.'

Incredibly, even the darkest days of Stalin's rule are beginning to seem attractive, especially to the older generation. There was terror and hardship, they admit, but there was still idealism and a belief that the new system was leading somewhere exciting. People long for the days when workers put in a full day's work and accomplished genuine heroic feats with projects completed ahead of schedule. People compare the law and order of those days with the crime, corruption and drunkenness of nowadays. With selective memory, they speak of shops stocked with meat and caviar, of good furs that the average person could afford, of prices that were regularly lowered. Nowadays, they grumble, everything is exported and prices keep going up.

But the real nostalgia is not for the 1930s or the 1940s: it is for the way of life in pre-revolutionary Russia. Few would define it as such, or openly regret the Revolution. But people have written to newspapers asking why Russians no longer sit around the family samovar drinking tea as they used to, why old-fashioned courtesy has disappeared and why workmanship is no longer what it was. Art exhibitions of pre-revolutionary scenes, religious and traditional Russian life, have drawn huge crowds. Novels and films about the end of the Empire have caused a sensation. Young people have started digging out old family albums, and scions of old aristocratic families no longer feel the need to conceal their origins. Antiques of all kinds have soared in value.

It is in the arts that the renewed interest in the past is most marked. The painter Ilya Glazunov owes his popularity and notoriety to his persistent playing on nostalgic themes. His famous art exhibition in Moscow's Central Exhibition Hall in 1978 enjoyed a *succès de scandale* because it included pictures on religious themes, of old villages and figures from Russian history, and made specific and pointed comparisons with the drabness of modern society. Glazunov raised enormous interest by including the figure of Tsar Nicholas II in a painting the authorities did not allow to be shown. Other painters, including a talented East German artist, Elizavetta Kluchevskaya, of Russian origin, have taken old churches and street scenes as their theme – Kluchevskaya's water-colours of the Moscow that young Dostoyevsky knew have been exhibited at the Union of Writers club, at the new publishing house of the Russian Orthodox Church and have been bought by the Ministry of Culture. These exhibitions were particularly welcome as many old quarters of Moscow have been torn down to make way for new developments, much to the sadness of many Muscovites. Indeed, the wholesale destruction of the twisting streets and lowly nineteenth century buildings has been halted only just in time. Khrushchev had already bulldozed an eight-lane highway – Prospekt Kallinina – through the old Arbat quarter, raising huge glass and concrete blocks as monuments to Soviet progress, and there were plans to modernize the quiet, historic eastern side of the city in the same way. But public pressure has forced the city planners to think instead about adapting the old buildings to contemporary needs.

Pre-revolutionary history attracts especial interest as it is so confused by official rewriting and overladen with ideological taboos. The closer the subject comes to 1917, the greater the risk of falling foul of the currently sanctioned interpretation of events, and the greater therefore the attraction. Russians are still reticent – almost embarrassed – in discussing what happened to the last Tsar. A novel about the Tsarina and Rasputin, *At the Final Frontier*, published in 1980, was the talk of the reading public and was vigorously criticised for false conclusions, anti-semitism and sensationalism. A year later, during the Moscow Film Festival, the authorities permitted the showing of a powerful film about Rasputin and the turbulent events of 1916 which portrayed the Tsar with considerable sympathy and, unusually, showed there were honour-able men in the Duma, the Russian parliament, apart from the Bolshe-viks, who had tried to save Russia from the coming catastrophe. But the film, *Agony*, lay on the censor's shelf for eight years before this showing. It has not been publicly screened in Moscow since.

Nostalgia lies behind the identification of the regime with past glories, and has spurred the new zeal for restoring old monuments. Some 90 million roubles are being spent on a ten-year programme to repair the Kremlin complex, and experts are now turning their attention to some of the smaller churches and monasteries which have been left to crumble or used as warehouses for the past fifty years. The nostalgia is Russian, not Soviet, and is closely allied to growing Russian nationalism. This in turn has fuelled nationalist sentiment in other republics, and there is fierce pride in Uzbekistan in the Muslim heritage. Vast sums are being spent on restoring the glories of Samarkand, on researching the times of Tamerlaine and Ulugh-Beg.

As conservatism asserts itself, the regime no longer feels so threatened by the past. But so much has been destroyed that the record is now hazy. Nothing is so sought after from foreigners as old books on Russia, collections of photographs that show not only the oppressed workers, but the lives of the bourgeoisie, biographies of men whose reputations did not survive the rewritings of the past fifty years. A well-known member of the Soviet intelligentsia once showed me one of his most precious possessions. It was a broken piece of wood tracery. He had taken it from the house in Ekaterinburg – now Sverdlovsk – where the last Tsar and his family were shot. For many years the house remained standing, but it was finally decided to obliterate all traces of the event. My friend went there shortly before the bulldozers moved in, and down in the cellar jumped up and broke off a piece of tracery from the window over the door where the executioners came in. 'This,' he said, handing me the piece of wood, 'was the last thing that the imperial royal family ever saw.' I too felt a shudder of awe.

If the regime is slowly rehabilitating the memory of the Tsars – with the exception of Nicholas II – this is not true of a later and bloodier ruler, who has been consigned to perpetual limbo. Only in one small town, two hours drive through the lush Georgian countryside from Tbilisi, is there any remaining statue to the man who built the Soviet Union as it is now, Joseph Vissarionovich Dzhugashvili, better known to the world as Stalin. In Gori, his birthplace, a grandiose structure stands over the simple cobbler's cottage where he was born. Close by, the marble-columned museum, redecorated for Stalin's centenary in 1979, still displays all the memorabilia and fawning tributes to the dictator. Locally produced souvenir portraits, wall plaques showing him in his marshal's uniform and photographs of an avuncular figure lighting his pipe are on sale. Georgians, who suffered more than most at the hands of their native son and his Georgian secret policeman Lavrenty Beria, now revere the name of Stalin out of nationalist pride. But elsewhere in the Soviet Union his name is still taboo. Students leaving university have only the vaguest idea of what role he played in consolidating the foundations of the Soviet state. Soviet textbooks speak of the heroic achievements of the 1930s, of the industrialisation of peasant Russia and Stalin's wartime leadership in very general terms. They acknowledge repression and mistakes, but give no details. No one knows how many men Stalin sent to their deaths, and no one believes the figure runs into millions. Yevgeny Yevtushenko, the poet, was profoundly shocked by this ignorance, which inspired his powerful poem 'The heirs of Stalin'. The ignorance is even deeper nowadays, as those who lost relatives grow old and the press imposes a complete silence on the purges and the terror. No biography of Stalin is on sale in the Soviet Union today.

Yet ignorance breeds curiosity, and there is pressure for rehabilitation of Stalin, symbolized by the popularity of privately produced photographs stuck on the windscreens of cars and lorries. Such a move would unite the intelligentsia and divide it further from the working class, as well as causing an immediate crisis in Soviet relations with Eastern Europe. The movement for a reassessment reached its height after the overthrow of Khrushchev. Criticism of Stalin was halted, and no more of his victims such as Bukharin were rehabilitated. Destalinisation retreated just as it began to lap at the records of those in power. But Stalin was never restored to a real place in history. And on the centenary of his birth the party decided on the definitive assessment, which is unlikely to alter. His birth was noted, his wartime leadership praised, and the 'considerable damage' caused by the cult of personality admitted. But the party was disassociated from Stalin's excesses: it had upheld Leninist norms, and could not be blamed for Stalin's errors, the assessment declared. And the press vigorously denied there was ever such a thing as 'Stalinism'.

Much of Soviet society retains the pattern Stalin stamped on it, however. To question Stalin's actions would be to question the legitimacy of the party's heritage, and many of Stalin's principles, such as the strong belief in centralism, still dominate ideology. On the other hand to emphasize Stalin's role risks emphasizing his methods as well. The party realizes that any return to arbitrary terror would set the country back economically. It would discourage individual initiative altogether, inhibit decision-making and lead to cultural and scientific dead-ends that did such harm to Soviet genetics, cybernetics and other sciences straitjacketed by Stalin. The party knows that in adopting drastic, simplistic solutions to the complex problems of an industrialized society – as it is under pressure to do – it would itself probably be the first to suffer, as it was in the purges. None of this debate touches the mass of the Soviet people. They murmur about the 'good old days' of law and order, but for them Stalin is already fading into history.

His monuments remain, however. The skyline of Moscow is dominated by seven bizarre Gothic skyscrapers, all built immediately after the war in an attempt to give Moscow the titanic landmarks that Stalin believed befitted a super-power. The largest of them all, Moscow State University, overlooks the city from the summit of the Lenin Hills, its huge central tower reaching 787 feet into the sky, its heavily ornate wings and its capricious spires reminding one of an enormous stone wedding cake.

Russians have grown fond of these fantastical structures, used as the symbol of the Moscow Olympics. They are impressed by superlatives. To a Russian, big is beautiful. The idea of breaking things up into smaller units for greater efficiency not only runs counter to all Soviet doctrine, but is alien to the most basic Russian feelings about themselves, their country and society. Planners and economists have long been mesmerized by what they see as economies of scale – although one of the most pointed indicators of the new thinking now going on was a

Pravda article soon after Brezhnev's death which called for an end to the tradition of building huge industrial plants for the manufacture of everything from nuts and bolts to packing cases. But up till now everything that could be put under one roof has been. There is, for example, one big complex at Sumgait, on the Caspian Sea, for producing the basic ingredients of household detergent. And when that broke down, as it did one autumn, there was no washing powder in the country for six weeks.

Soviet buildings are larger than anything conceived elsewhere. Intourist is especially fond of hotels as big as small towns where all tourists can be accommodated together. When the Rossia, opposite the Kremlin, was built to cope with the increasing number of foreign tourists, dozens of historic little streets were levelled to make way for the biggest hotel in the world. The Rossia, a grandiose square block, has entrances on each side, and if you cannot tell north from south or east from west, you can walk half a mile down carpeted corridors searching for your room. But even this hotel has been outdone by the new one at Izmailova, put up for the Olympics: five 28-storey buildings with 10,000 beds, a 1,000-seat cinema and underground transport tunnels.

The Russians insist that things have to be big in a country so vast. New generating stations are being put up with a capacity of 1,200,000 kilowatts whose walls are 300 feet high and with a boiler as tall as a 25-storey house. Even Tass remarked defensively: 'The building of such gigantic plants is not due to ambition nor is it the engineer's caprice. There is a definite economic policy to obtain maximum output with minimum expense.' Down in Kazakhstan they are now using a rotary excavator in open-cast mines that can churn out 5,000 tons of coal an hour. In one year three such machines dig as much coal as Britain's total output. And a new ammonia plant now produces more than all the chemical plants in the country in 1948.

For coal and ammonia, size may be fine; making smaller consumer products in huge centralized complexes is less efficient, as some experts now recognize. But doing things on a big scale is still the norm. Russians are impressed by roads that are up to sixteen lanes wide, by city squares where whole army divisions can assemble, by war memorials that reach up to the sky, as Mother Russia does at Volgograd, by gargantuan meals that take a whole day to eat. Even in Tsarist days they were producing bells so big they could not be rung, cannons so cumbersome they could not be fired, and books and operas so long that you need Russian-sized bottoms to sit comfortably through them.

Time for Russians also comes in large units. If you drop in on friends, you stay for hours, even days. If you go ice-fishing in winter, you remain immobile beside the hole in the ice almost until you have frostbite. If you go mushrooming, you tramp through the woods from dawn till dusk. No one thinks twice about waiting three hours in a queue, travelling four days on a train or letting their grandmothers spend five hours at a Russian Orthodox Easter service.

Size also affects behaviour. In a country so vast, in a bureaucracy so oppressively omnipotent, ordinary people have little time for the courtesies of genteel living. Indeed Russians can be, and often are, extraordinarily rude in public. People push and jostle; shop assistants are snappy and unhelpful; officials answer inquiries with monosyllabic surliness; and there is always some grim-faced *babushka* ready to wade in with a sharp lecture on this or that aspect of your behaviour – and especially your child's. Pushing, swearing, and general boorishness so typify the daily struggle of life that the average Muscovite returns home in a bad temper and with a scowl for the outside world.

Yet the grumpiest are often warm and considerate at home and to their friends. Their public aggressiveness is part of that impersonal mask they wear in crowds, a protective cover to shield them from disappointment and daily bruising encounters. Sometimes an unexpected kind word, or a small child, can transform a sharp-tongued busybody into a friendly grandmother, and the occasional even-tempered shop assistant with a smile and a joke for everyone lightens the mood all round.

Foreigners, if they are obviously foreigners, tend to be better treated. Russians instinctively try to impress outsiders, and anyone dealing with tourists is carefully schooled in courtesy. I remember going into a shop in the provinces and being unable to make myself understood. 'Why can't you stupid Latvians learn the language?' the cashier asked crossly. But when she discovered her error, she could not have been more helpful and apologetic.

Russians offer various explanations for their public rudeness. One is that many townspeople, especially in the provinces, have recently arrived from the countryside and have not lost their rough peasant ways. It is said that when generations have lived in towns, people will be as considerate as they are in Leningrad, one of the most cultured cities. Other excuses include the harshness of life over the past fifty years when there was no time for courtesy in the struggle to survive, and the spoiling of children which makes them selfish later on. The press has also blamed acquisitive materialism, the breakdown in traditional values and the tiring lives of women, who seem to be the main offenders. One Soviet journalist gave a familiar example of the kind of behaviour he found so annoying. 'I went to the ticket desk of the bus station where they were having a meeting. Three women were enjoying the details of some piquant gossip. The cashier, smartly dressed with the hair-do of a lady, was leaning back in her chair and laughing gaily. I asked the good ladies to sell me a ticket. The cashier turned round with a hostile glare – it was amazing how quickly her expression changed – and barked out, "No tickets." "But you've only just started selling them. May I have a look at the reservations list?" "And who do you think you are, Mr Big-Wig? A minister?" "Minister or no minister, kindly give me a ticket." "I said there were no tickets, so clear off." Even the intervention of the chief cashier did not help. The woman refused to sell me a ticket, though her list showed that only two had been sold. I shouldn't have interrupted the merry gathering, and now I had to pay the price.'

Queue-jumping provokes the sharpest outbursts. The same journal-ist was in a long queue when a frail seventy-year old man went up to the assistant and showed his invalid's certificate. From the back of the queue a plump, rosy-cheeked woman got up. 'They've even got in here! Isn't one shop enough for them? Everywhere they push forward their red invalid's card, ready to snatch up everything. Why should they be privileged? We all suffer the same.' And she began swearing at the old man in front of everyone in the shop.

The press has campaigned for years for better public manners, criticising officials who shout at their employees, people who play loud music during funerals, children who do not give up their seats for adults on crowded buses. All this does not mean the Russians have no manners, however. On the contrary, they have a strict interpretation of what is seemly in public. The word *nekulturni* (uncultured) is one of the strongest terms of reproach.

An aspect of public behaviour that puzzles foreigners, especially Americans, is the readiness of any Russian placed in a position of authority to behave like a petty dictator, barking out orders, scolding all and sundry. Amazingly, most people meekly obey – a reaction that has much to do with the instinctive respect for authority and the recognition of power. A very large number of people do find themselves giving orders in one way or another – as organizers of neighbourhood commit-tees, volunteer police (*druzhiniki*) helping direct traffic and control crowds, supervisors and functionaries. Many pensioners, old women

supplementing their lowly income as lift operators, cloakroom atten-
dants, ticket collectors, underpass cleaners, usherettes, snow clearers,
have no hesitation in bawling out abuse at anyone who infringes their
authority or who fails to heed the rules. A sure way of getting a lengthy
lecture is to hand in a coat without a loop to hang it up by, or to attempt to
go through the left door in a theatre when your seat is on the right. I
sometimes think these elderly crones, who seem to see their job as a
perpetual battle to enforce their authority on an anarchic crowd or as a
challenge to ensure that no one is so brazen as to ignore their suzerainty
in their patch of terrtitory, are the real rulers of the Soviet Union. They
are certainly the most effective and the most unpopular instruments in
ensuring social discipline. A generation ago these old women were put
to more sinister uses. I shall not forget an incident when I went with a
young Russian to visit an artist in a studio on the top floor of a block of
flats. As we were talking beside the lift, a door across the passage opened
a crack. A wizened face peered out and a voice demanded sharply: 'Who
is that person? What does he want?' 'We're just visiting a friend, old
mother,' my companion replied affably. 'Where is that man beside you
from? He's not one of ours,' she persisted, looking suspiciously at me.
'That's not your business,' he retorted, as we stepped into the lift. 'You
see,' he said to me smiling, 'the generation of Stalin.'

A characteristic Thomas Stevens found particularly marked in Russians a hundred years ago was superstition – a literal belief, especially
among the peasants, in devils and omens, in fortune-telling and divine
retribution. One of the boasts of the communist party is that it has
overcome these ancient beliefs: science has liberated the ordinary citizen
from the mumbo-jumbo of religious obscurantism, has blown away the
chimera of tyrannical superstition. Much of this claim is true. Today's
young engineer has only an amused disdain for the folklore his grandparents took so seriously, and little interest in observing the religious
rituals that governed the lives of his ancestors. But superstition has by no
means died out. It has been replaced by a new 'scientific' fascination
with unexplained phenomena – flying saucers, the abominable snow-
man, the Bermuda triangle, the lost world of Atlantis, biorhythms and
telepathy. For millions of Russians these things are a source of endless
interest, and speculation about them, official and unofficial, is almost
obsessive. The papers are for ever discussing new theories, expeditions
are sent off to look for Atlantis or the yeti or the mysterious vortex in the
sea. Russians devour every scrap of information they can get hold of
about similar searches overseas. *The Times* once received in London a

letter from a man in deepest Siberia complaining that he had ordered dozens of books from the West but none had arrived. All of them dealt with some aspect of the occult.

The mystery no Russian can resist is flying saucers. 'The sky was black, cloudless with many stars and the constellations were easily seen,' a reader from Omsk told *Pravda*. 'Among them I saw an especially bright star from which there came a glow. I thought at first it was a satellite, but over the lake the "globe" began to descend, and the cloud around it grew larger. In the sky above the mountains an object moved rather fast and high in an upward trajectory, leaving behind a wide, straight white tail, very similar to the trace of a plane though much wider. There was no sound or noise of any kind.' *Pravda* declared the reader was mistaken: scientists did not even recognize the term UFO. Everything could be explained by cloud formations or atmospheric conditions.

Nevertheless scientists spend a great deal of time writing about flying saucers, investigating reported sightings and trying to convince crowded lecture halls that the little green men do not exist. It seems to be a losing battle. The greater the anti-saucer propaganda, the more obstinately the belief grows.

Some years ago there was a tendency to deny outright the existence of any sort of unidentified flying object and appropriate statements by prominent scientists were used to back up this argument. In 1968, for example, the director of the astronomy council of the Soviet Academy of Sciences told *Pravda* that any object flying over Soviet territory could not fail to be identified by scientists or by the military authorities. But popular beliefs were not shaken, and have been reinforced by suitably embellished reports of sightings abroad. And so in a more recent explanation *Pravda* quoted the director of the Institute of Earth Magnetism and Ionosphere saying that many atmospheric phenomena observed by people were indeed hard to explain. He said these events had to be classified as 'objectively evaluated', but no attention should be paid to the 'inflamed fantasies of those seeking sensations'.

Some of the things Russians claim to have seen in the heavens include unusually bright stars, discs, globes, cucumbers, cigars, double and single crescents, triangles and squares. Most of these things, the paper said, could be put down to atmospheric effects at dusk. But when several geophysical research rockets were launched, leaving a brightly coloured sodium cloud floating in the sky, there was a new wave of saucer sightings.

The campaign against UFOs has been broadened to enlist the

services of sociologists and ethnographers. The journal *Soviet Ethnography* maintained a few years ago that the popular idea that the saucers were piloted by what the Russians call 'ufonauts' or 'humanoids' was nothing more than a modernized version of the old fairy stories about people encountering evil spirits – devils, witches, wood-goblins, water-sprites and so on. Another paper maintained that unidentified flying objects were really only zones of very highly ionized air. Depending on its chemical composition such a zone could assume all kinds of hues, and an encounter with one could have fatal results for the pilot of an aircraft. This explained, for example, the disappearance of a whole flight of American military aircraft above the notorious Bermuda triangle.

Popular theories are far more exotic. A woman maintained that icons painted hundreds of years ago included uncanny resemblances to descriptions of UFOs. And one young man I know now refuses to visit his uncle because he cannot stand the constant talk of flying saucers. The belief now has such a grip on the population that it has assumed ideological overtones, and the anti-saucer campaign is being directed at the highest party level. This means that all public discussion of the matter is subject to political authorization. The Soviet Academy of Sciences is said to have a number of bodies that have been investigating UFOs for years, but its members are reluctant to talk publicly, and the Academy has not published any reports on its research.

People say that Soviet cosmonauts have seen flying saucers, and this was one of the first questions put to the cosmonauts who spent the best part of six months in the orbiting Soviet space station Salyut-6 in 1980. 'Ground Control cheerfully told us once that flying saucers were floating around,' Commander Georgi Grechko replied. 'We looked at the video-scanner and in fact there was something rather similar not far from the spaceship, but it turned out to be containers with our rubbish, which followed Salyut-6 until we changed orbit.'

Pravda once asserted that no Soviet cosmonauts had ever seen a spaceship from another planet. But to ufophiles, this is no more convincing than Khrushchev's reported statement, demonstrating the falsity of religion, that Yuri Gagarin had never seen an angel. In any case the press is still speculating over the unexplained evidence of a colossal meteorite that hit Siberia some seventy-five years ago. And other supernatural phenomena are taken so seriously that large sums are spent investigating them: a prominent dissident was arrested and accused of passing over state secrets when he gave a Western journalist copies of Soviet research into telepathy and telekinesis.

There are regular expeditions to the Pamir mountains, bordering on Afghanistan, in search of the yeti, the Soviet equivalent of the Loch Ness monster, and a number of reported sightings. *Komsomolskaya Pravda* sponsored one search, involving 120 enthusiasts, and printed the breathless account given by one expedition member. She had set up camp near a sandy river bank where she had seen footprints, and was awoken one night by the sound of knocking stones and indistinct murmuring. 'I got up as I felt something was looking at me. Sixty feet away stood a very hairy person, about seven feet tall. His figure was massive, almost square. He stooped and had a very short neck. His arms hung loosely. I went about fifteen feet towards him. I remember his sparkling eyes. He looked at me piercingly but without malice. I had with me a toy bird which I squeezed to make a noise. But he turned and went away, moving over the stones smoothly, almost as though he was gliding.'

This expedition concluded that the yeti did indeed exist, and scientists announced that the creature could be a form of Neanderthal man from one of the branches of man's genealogical tree. I met one of the participants in the expedition, who had with him a huge plaster cast of a footprint that he maintained was made by the yeti. It certainly looked like the print of an enormous ape-like creature.

The persistence of superstition is perhaps allied to the tendency of Russians to extremes. The 'golden mean', the ancient Greek ideal of moderation, is not a concept that finds an echo in the Russian character. On the contrary, Russians deliberately court excess: when hospitality is offered it is overwhelming, with no thought for expense; when Russians are happy, they display an exuberance and uninhibited enjoyment of life that sometimes verges on the manic – one thinks of all those stereotyped revellers dancing on the tables; when they are sad, they weep unashamedly and seem cast in the depth of despair. And, typically, they often display both emotions in extreme at the same time.

Emotions, worn on the sleeve in Russia, are almost tangible. In a harsh world where suspicion is universal and most people develop a protective reticence to hide their real thoughts and attitudes from strangers, friendship is deep, long-lasting and highly valued. Qualities such as trust and loyalty are important to Russians, and betrayal – whether of confidence or emotions or in the form of political denunciation – is seen as particularly despicable. No one is regarded with more contempt that the *stukach*, the informer. It takes many years before one Russian trusts another fully. Foreigners have found, to their cost, that nothing is so disastrous as to introduce two Russians who do not already know each other. The icy atmosphere of wary suspicion while each tries to determine the relationship of the other to the foreigner can be guaranteed to ruin the entire evening. (One American friend had a cynical maxim: 'If you introduce one Russian to another, each thinks the other works for the KGB. And one of them is usually right.')

Surprisingly, in spite of – or perhaps because of – this general wariness, the Russians have developed an effective safety valve: the joke, and especially the political joke. Soviet humour comes as a surprise, for it seems everything the people are not – light, subtle, self-deprecating, flexible and swift. But it is one of the Russians' most endearing characteristics, and one that lightens every aspect of life in the Soviet Union. People vent their feelings in jokes, which have a characteristic bitter-sweet quality. In a country where open political comment is unwise – only a generation ago careless talk cost lives – the Russians have a way of joking about their lives and their system that says it all but without necessarily identifying the speaker with the sentiment. (The leadership, the butt of most jokes, would do well to listen to the latest anecdotes if it wants to gauge the public mood.)

The jokes cover everything, especially the party, the leadership, the ideology and the system in general. Most play on official slogans, turn common clichés back to front, use the language of propaganda to make an opposite point. Some of the short question-and-answer kind occur again and again in new forms: 'What is the difference between communism and capitalism? Capitalism is the exploitation of man by man. And communism is the exact opposite.' 'What was the first people's democratic election? When God created Adam and Eve and said to Adam: "Now choose a wife."' 'Why is the capitalist world on the edge of a precipice? So they can get a better view of us down here.' 'What would happen if all the North African countries went communist? In five years time they would start importing sand.'

Others are more topical, and swirl through the cities within days of particular events – the party congress, an important state visit, a politburo speech. There were two contradictory jokes after the 1981 congress. In one, the party delegate returns to his small town and presents his report to a workers' meeting. From the platform with other party officials he begins: 'Comrades, in the next five year plan we shall have more to eat. We shall have more cars. We shall get better medical treatment. We shall see our living standards rise . . .' Finally one of the workers at the back puts up his hand and asks plaintively: 'And what about us?' In the other joke, the official returns home with a bleak report: 'Comrades, we are approaching difficult times. There will be shortages of food. We shall have to spend money helping our socialist neighbours. Industry is facing problems . . .' He is interrupted by two men who call out: 'We shall work overtime.' He goes on with his forecast and again they interrupt: 'We shall work double shifts.' He has more news of tough times ahead, and they call out: 'We shall work round the clock.' After he has finished he asks where these keen men work. Back comes the flat reply: 'At the morgue.'

In 1983, as President Reagan stepped up his campaign to deny advanced computer technology to the Soviet Union, the Russians came up with a joke that was a clever satire on the clichéd propaganda line that everything in the Soviet Union is the biggest and the best. On learning of the embargo, the joke runs, the Kremlin decided it had to put through a crash programme to develop a native computer industry in Russia. And so they published a suitable slogan for the shock workers in the field: 'The Soviet micro-chip – the biggest micro-chip in the world!'

An old device that has been going many years is the mythical Radio Armenia, where the radio station supposedly gives politically double-edged answers to naive listeners' questions. For instance, one person asks: 'How do I escape from an impossible situation?' and the radio replies: 'We do not discuss agriculture on this programme.' Or another asks: 'What is a musical trio?' and the radio replies: 'A Soviet quartet that has been to the West.'

Officialdom is sensitive to jokes (though many of the best are privately told by senior officials themselves), for they imply a cynicism that cannot be officially admitted. Those dealing with the leadership are seen as insulting to Soviet dignity and *amour propre*. Not telling jokes in print, especially those about Lenin, who is regarded with particular reverence, was virtually my only conscious act of self-censorship as a correspondent. The offence caused would have been out of proportion to the amusement afforded readers. But I must have heard scores, mostly from the intelligentsia. The ordinary worker's humour is coarser, less political, more slapstick. But even less sophisticated people have a quick appreciation of satire, as the many cartoons in *Krokodil*, a satirical weekly, and the regular satirical articles in *Pravda* make clear.

CHAPTER EIGHT

The New Materialism

The Soviet communist party frequently justifies its monopoly of power by pointing to the material successes achieved under communism. Every party leader's speech boasts of the rising living standards, of the consumer goods available to the masses, and of the plans for the betterment of people's lives. The propaganda apparatus is forever producing mind-boggling statistics: how many television sets are manufactured, how many new flats built each year, how much wages have risen and so on. Comparison is constantly made with the situation in pre-revolutionary Russia: in 1917 so many kilowatts of electricity were generated, whereas today the figure is far higher; since the communists came to power the output of clothing, food, books and almost every creature comfort has gone up by so many hundred per cent. It never appears to strike anyone that similar comparisons can be made between England or the United States in 1917 and today.

Even when things are not going well and the papers have bad news about poor production figures, a bad harvest, waste, inefficiency or unsatisfied demand, the reports are wrapped up in a general optimistic package telling people how much better off they are now than they were. Great publicity is given to the worker who cast the millionth ton of pig-iron, the machine minder who achieved a record output of cloth, exhibitions of new furniture and the opening of new blocks of flats. The message is plain: the communist system works, and you have only to look around to see the evidence.

For many years the boast was fully accepted. There was a great leap forward in the early days of industrialization. And after the devastation of the war, people saw the rebuilding, the gradual improvements. They did not see how gradual these were – Stalin's iron curtain around his country made comparisons with other places impossible. Communism encouraged 'scientific materialism', and Russians have been urged to judge the system by the goods it delivers.

In many ways it has been a disastrous propaganda line – as Andropov now appears to realize – for it rings increasingly hollow. Standards of living are improving only slowly, and in some important areas such as food are actually slipping back. The falling economic growth and gloomy projections of manpower and resources mean that the next decade is going to be increasingly tough on Soviet consumers, who may have already seen their best days. The country cannot afford both guns and butter as it has in the past, and as the international situation darkens, the new leadership will, as always, prefer to be secure rather than fat.

But expectations have been unleashed that cannot now be controlled. A younger generation, who did not experience the trauma of war, is chafing at the slow pace of change, the absence of those consumer goods so often promised for tomorrow. And this generation has seen beyond the increasingly rusty curtain. It has glimpsed the good life overseas, and wants the same at home. Ironically, détente is largely to blame. Brezhnev, who was committed to improving living standards, fuelled dissatisfaction by emphasizing the needs of the consumer while allowing him a taste of prosperity. And that appetite has grown on feeding.

Now the party is trying to row back, attempting to dampen demand and pouring scorn on the growing acquisitiveness of most people and 'bourgeois' materialism. While still holding to the propaganda of success – though there seem to be doubts about the wisdom of this in light of the Polish experience – and proclaiming 'You've never had it so good', the party is trying to make people understand that possessions are not everything, that there are values above crude materialism, and that people's lives can be distorted by trying to keep up with the Ivanovs and ruined by wealth.

Izvestia, in a typical broadside, depicted some of the victims of the new mentality. One was a respected war veteran from Kharkov, who had served at the front, won his medals, and lived simply with his wife. But when she died he remarried, and his new wife, twenty years younger, had no time for his old feats of glory. To her, his medals and certificates had only one use – to enable her to jump the queue. She shamelessly dragged her husband from one shop to another, using his official privileges to lay hands on anything old, rare or in short supply. The aged hero, to his embarrassment, had to push through the queues, endure the curses of fellow shoppers and show his veteran's documents at the counter to obtain women's blouses, imported wall-units or anything else that took her fancy.

His sister visited him and was so shocked that she wrote to *Izvestia*. What was this mania for acquisitions? Was there no cure for rampant consumerism? The paper said there was none. But the young wife was no isolated instance: the paper had received letters from all over the country complaining of the same thing.

> You come into our flat and it's stuffed full. All the walls are covered, all the corners piled high. There is no room to breathe, but my daughter-in-law keeps bringing back more and more. Not just to keep up with other people, but to make these people burst with envy. But in fact nobody is jealous of us, and it's becoming harder and harder to live here. However much I try to convince her to buy things in moderation, she doesn't listen. And now even I, an old man, haven't got even a little corner to myself . . . dear editors, try to tell such people that they're ill.

Izvestia identified the disease as unrestrained acquisitiveness, damaging and alien to the Soviet way of life. 'The father has to be shoved into a little cupboard so that he does not get in the way. People are afraid to walk about in their flats in case they scratch the commode or break the pseudo-Saxon vase. Things for us have become things on top of us.' The paper called the phenomenon an 'inclination to material things to the detriment of a person's spiritual and moral qualities'. It concluded that once consumerism had got a grip, friends and families suffered. One was able to own many useful articles that made life easier, and still be their master, but one could also become a slave to trifles. The paper illustrated the point with a letter from Smolensk:

> Our neighbours – a pleasant, intelligent couple – recently acquired a Zhiguli car. There was nothing extraordinary in this: they worked hard and saved up their money. But literally from that moment on they changed. They almost pray over the car and already regard 'carless' people with disdain, making it clear in their behaviour that we have nothing in common to talk about. The neighbours have lost all respect for, and interest in, them.

Consumerism, *Izvestia* remarked, was catching. It cited a letter from a woman who asked the paper where she could get a 500-rouble (£330) carpet to give her daughter as a present for her fifth birthday. 'As a mother,' she wrote, 'I want to provide my girl with comforts no less than others enjoy.' Children were influenced by their parents' acquisitiveness: one parent gives her child at school gold ear-rings and the whole class is upset until every other pupil has something equally valuable for her ears. 'It is particularly upsetting to see children exhibiting such petty bourgeois values,' the paper commented.

But children have few qualms – indeed many young people are quite prepared to break the law to get what cannot be found in the shops. 'What's wrong with being a black market dealer?' Svetlana asked. 'Thanks to him you can wear Western brand-name clothes, listen to marvellous records. I am a black market dealer myself. 'I've got lots of Western things: jeans, tape-recorders, sports shoes. We buy and sell these things – though for a higher price than they cost, of course.'

Svetlana is a sixteen-year-old from Gorky. Her aim in life is to look smart, wear fashionable clothes and satisfy the demands of her black market 'clients'. She believes she plays a worthwhile role, and was bold enough to write to *Komsomolskaya Pravda*, to tell them so. 'No one has stopped me in my "work",' she said. 'Everyone is grateful to me and many depend on me. We only let those people join our circle who are able to get hold of things. Even my mother helps.'

She said she never had a bad conscience, and made enough profit for herself and her mother. But when a reporter from the newspaper went round to find out why her attitude is so typical of Soviet youth, she had second thoughts and tried to avoid him. Black market trading is a serious criminal offence. However he tracked her down. Her room was filled with pop records and super-quadrophonic equipment. How did she see her life in ten years time, he asked.

'I'll get married. I'll live in Moscow,' she replied. 'I won't work – let my husband provide for me. I'll find a well-off man – not someone with an ordinary Zhiguli, but someone with a Mercedes.' (A Zhiguli is a mass-produced car; very few Russians own a Mercedes.) She said she became involved in the black market after her mother was divorced. The mother was always complaining they did not have enough money. But when they found that a relative had a job that took him abroad often, and he was able to bring back the precious Western goods, both mother and daughter saw their chance to riches and set themselves up as distributors. Respectable aunts and uncles helped, introducing Svetlana to eager buyers. No one reproached her – they kept themselves out of her life, took the goods and left her the money.

It is not the illegal trading that so worries the authorities – almost all the country is on the fiddle to some degree – but the attitudes behind it. Lev Kukhlin, a Soviet writer, gave an example of what he called 'predatory consumerism', which he saw as a threat to real culture. He related how he once spoke to an audience of teenagers. Most were well-dressed, few knew much about art or literature and none had any interest in it. They began to listen to him only when they found out he also wrote song lyrics and knew some famous singers. One youth, in American jeans and wearing a cross, the current fashion, asked him how much money he 'raked in' from his songs. Had he got a colour television, a car, a country cottage?

Kukhlin realized he was being judged, as he said, 'in the Western fashion', and so he cut the ground from under the youth by feigning surprise that the young man had never heard of his West German Uher tape-recorder, which he said 'cost 1,500–2,000 roubles in our money'. 'I am still not sure whether I won that moral duel with this representative of the "jeans culture",' he wrote in a monthly journal. 'I told them that if Alexander Pushkin was alive today he would probably own a Volga car, since he loved riding fast, but recently a great poet, Anna Akhmatova, lived in Leningrad who did not own even a beat-up Moskvich. Did that make her any worse than me?'

Cars are indeed the ultimate criterion by which Russians judge not only wealth, but influence and position. Mass production really only got going when Khrushchev, who thought all cars smelly, wasteful and unnecessary, was succeeded by Brezhnev, who in his more athletic days had a notorious penchant for fast driving and had a stableful of most of the smartest Western models. And in spite of the export success of Lada (the export name for the Zhiguli, built in a factory supplied by Fiat), only 6 million Russians – one in every forty-four people – own their own cars. There are still twice as many motorcycles on the roads.

The idea of a car as a status symbol has become institutionalized. The Russians manufacture six different kinds, and each serves a separate function. The small Zaparozhets, made in the Ukraine, is the cheapest and is also given to those lucky invalids who qualify for a free government car. The Zhiguli, the most popular car, is the money-maker and in its various marques is sold abroad in increasing numbers. The Moskvich, also a medium-sized saloon, has fallen out of favour because it needs constant maintenance. Higher up the price ladder is the Volga, manufactured in the huge car works in Gorky, the Soviet Detroit. It is also the government car *par excellence*. Painted yellow or greenish-cream, it is used for taxis because it is tough enough to withstand Soviet roads, Soviet drivers and the Russian winter – usually a lethal combination for Western-made cars. Painted black, it rules the road as the official car of a thousand government departments. Black Volgas race about, obeying only those traffic signs they do not consider a hindrance, flashing at lesser breeds and overtaking with a daring commensurate with the status of their occupants. Their drivers can be found waiting outside ministries, slumped back in the seat, a fur hat pushed down over their faces, snoring, or hanging about ready to make a quick couple of roubles as unofficial taxis.

Next come Chaikas. They are all black and not for private sale. The older models, based on American cars of the 1950s, were all chrome and fins, and arrogantly belched exhaust from twin pipes concealed in the back bumper. The new ones are sleeker and smoother, conveying dignitaries from place to place at breakneck speed. Top of the pyramid comes the Zil. Hand-tooled, vast, bullet-proof, it is available only to members of the Politburo. Zils travel down reserved lanes in the centre of the road, and police clear the way in advance. Russians take little notice of fire engines or ambulances trying to fight through the traffic. When a Zil appears, everyone scatters.

Cars so rigidly define status that you can tell the importance of state visitors by the cars sent to meet them. A third world diplomat related how a delegation from his country received the Chaika treatment when their opposite number to Pyotr Demichev, a candidate Politburo member, arrived in Moscow. At the state banquet the best caviar was served, the tomatoes were lush and the crabs enormous. When another delegation arrived, the visitor held a higher position in his government at home, but his Soviet opposite number did not. They got the black Volga treatment: inferior caviar, smaller crabs and tomatoes that were less succulent.

The Russian love affair with the car is only just beginning, but already popular lust for this symbol of success – for which the waiting list is at least two years – has a powerful grip. Georgia, where automania has tapped all the resources of the Soviet Union's wiliest entrepreneurs, boasts some unbelievably flashy models, including, it is said, a number that made their way down there from Brezhnev's own collection. A recent British ambassador was once rash enough to take his elegant old black Rolls to the southern Republic, and his entourage had to fend off prospective buyers who produced wads of roubles inches thick from their pockets. Even in Moscow I was once approached as I got into my modest yellow Zhiguli by a swarthy man with a moustache and gold teeth who wanted to buy my car on the spot.

Judging your friends by the cars they drive, even deciding your marriage on this basis, is another unacceptable face of consumerism. A newspaper once related the sad story of Anna, a young lady whose romance began with a car and ended with bickering over the cost of candies. Yaroslav, an uncouth fellow who lacked the refinements of good conversation, used to promise her, as he polished the bonnet of his shining Volga, they would sail through life together 'with the wind in their hair'. He showered her with presents: French perfume, a new wardrobe, cases of brandy, leather-bound books. He introduced her to his friends and 'connections', and eventually the comely PhD student overcame her scruples about his lack of education. Yaroslav splashed out lavishly on wedding preparations. But Anna began to notice his shortcomings: all his time and energy went into acquiring possessions. He divided his acquaintances into those who were 'necessary' and those whose friendship was unprofitable. He was busy with speculative deals on the side. When she wanted to give one of his books to a friend, he charged her an exorbitant price – 'just like the black market,' he explained. And so two days before the happy day, she packed her bags and went home to mother.

He took it calmly: he asked for all his presents back, and sent her a bill for what he had spent on her – so much on meals, so much on films, on sweets, on cigarettes. He even sued her for breach of promise, sending his claim to the family counselling unit of the institute where she worked. The hapless Anna was hauled before the busybodies at work, who asked many embarrassing questions, tittered over the piquant details, and in the end produced a report reprimanding her for her light-hearted attitude to marriage and for falling for such material blandishment.

But it is not only such as Anna who can be bought for those precious consumer goods. Almost any article in short supply can command favours and large sums on the black market. Antiques can be bought for good Western shoes, recalcitrant officials converted to models of helpfulness with a few packs of Western cigarettes or a fashionable little gadget. The problem is not finding the money – on any day of the week dozens of people walk down Gorky Street with at least 1,000 roubles in cash in their pockets. The secret of success is access to limited stocks. For although the Russians do manufacture virtually all consumer goods from refrigerators to pocket calculators, there are never enough, and repeated calls by the leadership for more and better quality goods fall on stony ground. Too often consumer products have been last in a long list of priorities, coming after the demands of defence, heavy industry, agriculture and crash programmes such as the new trans-Siberian railway or the gas pipeline to Western Europe.

In 1981 it did seem as though the party was ready to put its cash where its propaganda lay: President Brezhnev told the party congress that consumer goods would be given priority over heavy industry and would have a higher growth rate during the forthcoming five-year plan. But it is more than just investment and priority rating that have held back production of soap powder or vacuum cleaners. The main problem is the very low quality of consumer goods, indifference in the wholesale trade, lack of any consumer research, poor distribution and retailing, sloppy handling of finished products and sluggish responses to changes in fashion and demand.

As a result the press is for ever detailing stories of gluts and shortages, waste and frustration. In one town shops stocked only 40 watt light bulbs, while in the neighbouring town they had only 100 watt bulbs. Small items such as bicycle tyre valves are so impossible to obtain that it is easier to throw away the whole bicycle and buy a new one rather than replace the defective valve. Summer dresses and beachwear cannot be found in the shops in summer months whereas skis and sledges are on sale in June but not in December. Every single refrigerator arriving in one large shop was unusable because the door was bent: workmen had unloaded them from a rail wagon by dropping them on to an old car tyre placed below.

Pravda once investigated the complaints of villages in a remote district who said that the only local shop did not stock kettles, tcapots, cutlery, nails and a range of other everyday items. A reporter who went there found the shop full of nothing but large zinc buckets, and the manager complained that this was all he was able to obtain from the factory. The factory director readily admitted that his plant produced little else, but said buckets were the only way he could fulfil his plan: other items were costly and time-consuming to manufacture and did not use up the required amount of metal allocated to the factory.

Attempts to remedy these bizarre situations have concentrated on two main failings: the poor selection of goods on offer and the lack of quality control. The party is for ever calling for better made goods. But since the departments of quality control depend financially and administratively on the factories they are supposed to check, they have little incentive for throwing out defective products, especially as the factory would lose its bonus if it fell behind the plan.

Factories can theoretically be sued by warehouses for supplying defective goods, but the fines are low and no one has any interest in stirring up trouble; after all, even substandard goods can be sold, as the choice for the customer is simply take it or leave it.

Despite obligation to stock a proper assortment, shops have had little success in improving the range of consumer goods. Regular official 'raids' on stores reveal an almost total absence of small items and spare parts: plugs, valves, nibs, nail-brushes. In one memorable article a paper sent its reporter to a hotel for a night in a big town without his overnight case and left him to see what he could buy on the spot. After wandering around all day in search of a razor, toothbrush, flannel, pyjamas and so on, he found virtually nothing and spent an uncomfortable night in the hotel.

One fairly successful experiment has been to link shops directly with their suppliers, so that they carry the full range of the factory's output. Stores are opening called for example 'Everything for Baby', and the network of such specialized shops is growing. But for most people it is still a frustrating process scouring the town for what they need, hoping to catch a consignment in those precious moments before it is sold out. I remember a funny scene in Gum. A crowd of women surrounded the make-up department, where lipstick, at that time very hard to find, was being sold. Suddenly the supply ran out. Loud arguments began until someone spotted a shop assistant bringing over a large box. They insisted she open it, though she kept protesting the goods inside were not lipstick. No one believed her, the box was ripped open – and dozens and dozens of pairs of dark glasses fell out.

Being first in the queue is often the only way of getting what you want – and not always even then. There is a joke about a shop where a long queue formed an hour before it opened. At 10.00 the store manager comes out and asks if there are any Jews standing there. Four or five people raise their hands and the manager tells them to go away. 'We're not serving Jews,' he says. They mutter a protest but leave, and he goes back in. An hour later he reappears and asks whether there are any Armenians in the queue. A few others raise their hands, and they in turn are told they will not be served. He goes inside, and later comes out to ask about Georgians, who also have to go. Then he asks about Estonians, Tatars, and so on, until towards evening only Russians are left standing there. The director then appears and announces: 'Sorry, this shop is not open today.' 'You see,' one Russian says to another, 'the Jews always get the best of everything.'

Tourists imagine that Gum (standing for State Universal Store) is virtually the only shop in Moscow. Certainly hundreds of thousands jostle through its three glass-roofed galleries each day, wearing down still further the deeply hollowed stone steps in search of everything from exercise books to frying pans. But the great birdcage, built before the Revolution, now about to undergo a major facelift, is no longer prestigious or practical. The average housewife nowadays goes to the food-shops and big stores springing up in the tower-block estates that ring the old centre of Moscow. Some are quite smart – bright tiles, wire trolleys, proper check-out counters. But the selection is erratic and disheartening: yards and yards of apple juice or mineral water, a whole shelf of mustard, the odd bag of unwashed carrots, blocks of plain cheese and tins of tuna fish. Some scarce produce remains in crates: it is hardly worth unpacking as it will be snatched up in minutes.

Self-service shops are increasingly popular, but elsewhere the three-queue system is still common: queue to find out the price of something, queue then at the cashier's to pay, and queue to present the receipt and collect the goods. Even self-service hardware shops are none too fast. After buying an appliance you have to find out if it works by taking it to another counter where it is unwrapped and inspected. And when you leave it has then to be checked again to ensure the article corresponds to the receipt: the three-queue system again.

Being the capital, Moscow is better supplied with consumer goods, and especially food, than provincial towns. Muscovites complain, with justification, that it is the outsiders who swarm in who cause the shortages. About a million extra people arrive in the capital each day, some coming from hundreds of miles away, to shop for themselves and their neighbours, while local inhabitants have to wait until the end of the working day when the shelves are bare. You can see the provincial raiders thronging the main stations in the evenings, laden with their loot. Most offices in the city manage to find one volunteer who can slip away from her desk for the day and do all the shopping for herself and her colleagues – though regulations preventing bulk buying and hoarding means she has to go from shop to shop to get all the different purchases.

The time wasted is enormous and public anger is rising. More and more people rely on their connections or turn to the black market. It is expensive and can be dangerous – during the great make-up shortage, two women improvised packs of eye-shadow out of boot polish, and did a flourishing trade from a suitcase near a metro station. Their concoction severely irritated people's eyes and, as the prosecution alleged when they were inevitably picked up, could have caused permanent damage.

One outlet that is still available, surprisingly, is the bespoke tailor – something I always regarded as quintessentially the mark of a rich capitalist. Small *ateliers* even advertize their services in local papers, promising to make coats, dresses, shirts or boots. Soon after arriving in Moscow I tried one – a small dimly-lit workshop, like something out of the nineteenth century, on the top floor of Gum. I wanted a pair of hand-made shoes, relishing the idea of such individual attention in the communist world's most famous shop. Such is the demand – mostly for women's boots – that orders are normally taken only between eight and ten o'clock in the morning. But as a foreigner I was allowed to go along for a fitting at 11.00 to avoid the queue.

I selected from a glass display case an ordinary looking pair of black leather lace-ups from the twenty-four current models on offer, and was ushered into a fitting room with green baize curtains. An assistant drew a pattern of my feet on a piece of paper, sent me to the cashier to pay 41 roubles – only a few roubles more than a pair of shoes from an ordinary shop – took my name and address and told me to return in six weeks. The collection point, when I went back, was at the other end of the building, past the workshops where women were huddled over sewing machines. An assistant produced the shoes: soft leather, nicely stitched, fresh smelling. I tried them on, but could not stand up. They were so small that the toe-cap which seemed like cast iron held my toes curled up inside. I protested I could only lace them up by leaving each alternate hole undone. The assistant was nonplussed. She disappeared to consult the master cobbler, and then told me to come back three days later. When I did so, the shoes looked just the same. 'Push your feet in,' the woman insisted. 'You'll get used to them.' There seemed little point in further protest, and so hoping the shoes would slowly mould my feet to their shape, I took them and left. But I never wore them and gave them away a few weeks later.

I had more luck with a suit. But this time I did what most Russians do – go where they have a friend and a recommendation. The designer who found the material spent weeks waiting for the stock to come in. He personally introduced me to the master-tailor and supervised the fitting. The result was a magnificent light summer suit, made within a week and of a style and workmanship that would credit any Western boutique.

Good clothes are what every Russian seeks, and it is perhaps in this area that the most striking progress has been made in the past twenty years. The Russians have been determined to bury their dowdy image – those old newsreel shots of women in headscarves and shapeless garments, men in knitted shirts and badly fitting suits. It has not been easy: good material is hard to find, and buttons and trimmings virtually unobtainable. The Central House of Fashion produces creations based on what was current in France or Italy the previous year, and invites clothing factory design directors to view its collections. But they in turn simplify the design in order to speed production, or eliminate any features – hooks, buttons, bows – which they know cannot be supplied by the Ministry of Light Industry. The result, a year later, is a dress that has little elegance or fashion.

But nevertheless much has been achieved. The Baltic republics are renowned for good design, and the collections produced by the best Estonian factories have flair and originality. Increasingly the Ministry is authorizing the import of material from Eastern Europe, Japan and the West, which has done much to brighten things up. Indeed Western clothing imports are substantial, though expensive. But people will sacrifice much for elegance, cutting back on food, willing to forgo other available luxuries for the sake of well-made winter boots, a cashmere jumper or a real fur hat.

One man who has done more than most to liven up the scene is Slava Zaitsev, the Soviet equivalent of Christian Dior or Pierre Cardin, and virtually the only Russian who has successfully attempted haute couture that can hold its own on a world stage. A vivacious, emotional, energetic man, intensely Russian in outlook and attitude, he fits with difficulty into the anonymous world of a ministry, and has finally been given the opportunity to develop his own style with a large four-storey fashion centre on one of Moscow's main streets. It holds regular fashion shows and sells off-the-peg clothes of flair and elegance that are within the range of what is available and possible to afford. He used to be the chief designer at the House of Fashion, but became disillusioned producing exquisite clothes that were too far from daily realities to have any real influence on contemporary taste or fashion. He is now too well-known to be constrained, however, and has spread his influence in various areas – he designs stage-sets for the Sovremennik Theatre, produces clothes for special occasions such as the pageant at the opening of the 1980 Olympics, travels to East Germany and Hungary to stage Russian plays, sells his designs for licensing by the state overseas, produces autumn and spring collections, publishes books on fashion, lectures to clothes manufacturers and students and appears frequently on television and in the papers. Single-handedly he is trying to mould public taste, a sense of style in a country long used to utilitarian uniformity.

His hints on what to wear and how to make up are just the kind of thing you used not to find in Soviet weekly magazines: shoes should be so, or so, colours matching or contrasting, make-up subdued. 'Don't cake your eyes with eye-shadow, remember you are all pale after the winter, and could do with skin toning,' he tells those thronging the presentation of a new collection. But he will not dictate: 'Be individual, be exclusive, decide your own personality.' He speaks fast and wittily: Russian women are so lucky, he says, because each can decide her own style, the length of the hemline, and is not subject to the tyranny of fashion. The audience – mainly young women, friends from the arts world, with a fair sprinkling of men and plumper, more matronly figures – laugh loudly at the irony.

Zaitsev holds out the vision of a world of consumer elegance Russians long for. His clothes, modelled by slender women with far from typical figures, conjure up the evening party, the opera, the discothèque, the long lost luxury of the 'age of Anna Karenina' and the contemporary, casual scene of the independent young man. There are formal suits, high-shouldered, square-cut in contrasts of navy blue and red or black and white, unadorned knitted dresses, matching skirts and jerseys in olive greens or lilac and purple, flowing summer dresses with loose belts, bright yellow coats and romantic white chiffon evening gowns. The male models sport brightly coloured loose shirts, jackets with narrow lapels and sloping pockets, something to wear to a picnic, something to dance in. It is an indulgent fantasy, egged on by Western pop music, coloured spotlights, Zaitsev's commentaries as he whirls and turns on stage, microphone in hand, or recites some of his own emotional declamatory, extravagant poetry.

The official attitude to him is ambivalent. His career began with a scandal: after graduating from the Moscow Textile Institute and doing his obligatory stint in a small factory specializing in workers' uniforms and protective clothing, he began designing clothes with folk themes that harked back to the gay peasant costumes of old Russia. Officials found it all a bit impractical, but his portfolio caught the eye of *Paris–Match*, and the magazine published photographs of him, his flat, his creations and billed him 'Dictator of Moscow fashion'. He was just twenty-five. Soviet officials were not amused: publicity of this kind in the West for a young Russian with neither rank nor official sanction can be disastrous. It smacks of personal prestige in a land of collective anonymity, it arouses jealous and petty feelings among bureaucrats who believe seniority rather than talent should determine acclaim. Zaitsev however survived, his own self-confidence increased. Since then he has received considerable publicity abroad, and is a personal friend of leading Western fashion designers. But he still lives modestly in a two-room flat and has difficulty getting hold of foreign fashion journals. Whereas a comparable figure in the West would have dozens of associates and helpers to provide the necessary materials, and arrange programmes and contracts, Zaitsev himself has to get hold of the materials, crayons and drawing paper he needs, and periodically defend himself against anonymous charges that he does not work in the spirit of a collective – in other words, is too individual, too demanding, too well-known. 'I love my country, I want to bring honour to it, to show the outside world that we too are capable of the best. But how can I make them understand that?' he asks in exasperation. It is a question artists and members of the intelligentsia often ask themselves.

Clothes in the Soviet Union are expensive, but Russians will happily pay for quality. There are few outlets on which consumers can spend money, and luxury articles are therefore as much in demand as everyday items. Good books, jewellery, gold, furs, carpets and antiques are snatched up, visible symbols of the new consumerism. The authorities have responded by raising prices by up to 100 per cent in attempts to dampen demand and mop up surplus cash that otherwise fuels the black market. But paradoxically this has only increased demand. Inflation officially does not exist, but many things have gone up steadily in recent years, and Russians are now looking for investments where their money will hold, or increase, its value. State savings banks are already overflowing with cash. There are of course no outlets for private citizens to invest money in industry in a communist society. And luxury goods therefore look increasingly attractive as prices rise.

Nothing is more sought after at the moment than gold. The Soviet Union, one of the world's largest gold producers, is obsessively secretive about the precious metal. The location of the mines in Eastern Siberia, long worked with convict labour, their output and development are all state secrets. No word about Soviet gold sales ever appears in the press. No statistics are given that could lead to deductions about reserves or the role gold plays in financing Soviet trade. Gold as such is not for sale in the Soviet Union. But people can buy jewellery, have their teeth filled with gold and of course buy gold wedding rings – available at a reduced price for first-time marriages. In a society where prices often bear little relation to real costs or the world market, gold goes up (though not down) with alacrity whenever the price in the West does.

No smart woman nowadays is complete without a flash of the yellow metal somewhere about her. The shop assistant lingers as she hands over goods, displaying huge gold rings. The young man on the train usually leaves his shirt unbuttoned to reveal gold chains and a gold cross. Theatre-goers proudly display heavy gold ear-rings, and on the beach the young sophisticates wear gold bracelets and rings to set off their bikinis. Even schoolgirls appear in class decked in brooches to make their classmates jealous.

The craze has been gathering momentum for the past five years, and the state jewellery factories have turned it to advantage. It is hard nowadays to find any precious stone set in silver or platinum – all is gold, and the more the better. Long queues form outside the jewellery shops before they open, especially after the price has gone up. Pensioners stand in line for their daughters, prompting one newspaper to comment acidly: 'They stand patiently as only their generation knows how to. They used to stand in line for hours for bread, and they learnt patience. Now that experience is serving them well: they are queuing for gold. Yes, we live much better now than we used to; but just think how many worthwhile things could be done in that time and with that money if all this wealth were used intelligently.'

That money is also spent on antiques. Until recently revolutionary ideology and the sheer struggle for survival combined to render virtually worthless the artifacts and religious symbols of pre-revolutionary Russia, and after the war people were ready to sell for a few roubles those family icons that had not already been cast adrift in rivers or left to rot outside. All that has now changed. The state has begun to regret the drain of the precious treasures that for years were sold to foreigners or smuggled out of the country – a loss not only of the Russian cultural heritage but of valuable hard currency commodities. And as the prices in the West have risen dramatically, icons, samovars, old books, porcelain and crockery made by the famous Kuznetsov firm are all now prohibited from export. Meanwhile the growing nostalgia for past splendour and craftsmanship has sent the prices paid in the state-run second-hand shops rocketing. It has become chic to own a vast, carved mahogany chest even though it hardly fits into today's small flats. The intelligentsia and Russian nationalists are not afraid now to express open admiration for the religious works of art that meant so much to their ancestors, and are willing to pay thousands of roubles to those peasants who have had the foresight to hang on to their icons.

While welcoming public appreciation of Russia's heritage – and savouring the prices Western museums are willing now to pay for Russian antiques – the state has nevertheless become worried by the mentality that regards antiques as an investment. It savours of personal profiteering, opens too many black market possibilities, has led to a sharp rise in the burglary of churches and smuggling by foreigners, especially third world diplomats. Cartoons frequently sneer at the nouveaux riches – a phenomenon new in communist society – stuffing their flats with samovars, icons, grandfather clocks, carpets and whatever they can lay hands on.

Nothing so annoys Russia's intellectuals as the speculation in rare books, for it exacerbates a shortage of good reading material that is at painful odds with the official boasts of the vast output of books in the Soviet Union. It is certainly true that the Russians publish more books than almost any other country. But the state does not publish what people want to read, but what it wants people to read: volume after volume of ideological propaganda, tracts for and about the party, books on atheism and – while he was alive – the collected speeches of Brezhnev and other fellow Politburo orators. (The books mysteriously vanish from the shelves once the man has died.) Go into any Soviet bookstore and there is little else, apart from scientific literature. For a nation of readers as avid as the Russians – almost everyone on the metro has his head in a book – this is intensely frustrating. There is an admirable and unsatisfied demand for good books – the Russian classics, poetry, encyclopaedias, art and foreign literature. Even the Greek and Roman classics are making a comeback: a recent book of ancient Greek myths was in hot demand, and Herodotus is also a best-seller.

New editions of Tolstoy's works sell out immediately, and speculators grow fat on the profits of selling classics on the black market. Even during the anniversaries of Tolstoy's birth, or Dostoyevsky's, their works could not be found. Pushkin, Gogol, Yesenin are equally hard to find, and fine poets such as Maria Svetayeva and Anna Akhmatova, who have only recently been officially recognized, are published in such small editions that it is hard to get them without good connections. Writers complain that the print order for good modern poets is never large enough – although obscure and sometimes poor poets from the non-Russian republics are readily translated and published to demonstrate the commitment to the cultural equality of all the Soviet nationalities.

The official excuse is always the same: there is not enough paper. Indeed the most heavily forested country in the world has to limit its newspapers to four or six pages because of the paper shortage. There is not enough cardboard to pack vegetables, or paper to wrap goods in shops. And the most painful shortage of all is the lack of toilet paper, a commodity that has achieved an almost mystic value to those who tire of the discomfort and irony of using *Pravda*. There was a paper shop near my office and I could always tell when the toilet paper was in stock – all around people could be seen walking away garlanded with dozens of rolls on a string around their necks, as though they had just arrived in a sanitary version of Hawaii.

Defensive officials argue that 2,500,000 acres of forest are felled each year to provide paper, and that shortages are due to hoarding the waste. The 3,200 publishing houses – all of course state-run – are said to put out an average of 5 million books and booklets each day. Most of them gather dust on shelves of bookshops and in street kiosks, and to get rid of them shop assistants bundle them up in packs of four with a book in much demand. You can only get a copy of Yuri Trifonov or another contemporary writer if you agree to take books on scientific atheism or the speeches from the last party congress. It is a situation that, as often, suits everyone except the consumer: the bookshop fulfils its plan, the propaganda apparatus is happy that such worthy tracts sell so well, and the publishers know they can safely give the public more of this healthy fare next year.

Public libraries reflect this situation. Shelf after shelf is devoted to Lenin and the party, and a lot of space is taken up by PhD theses on agriculture or some safe subject – printed in large editions to increase the prestige of the research and then dumped in libraries all over the country. But there is little popular fiction and even classics of Russian literature are in short supply. Patriotic tracts, especially books on the Second World War, are considered especially edifying, and entire bookshops are devoted to this subject. But few thrillers or light entertainment stories are published, and then only in periodicals and monthly magazines. The gap is filled by entrepreneurs who produce underground *samizdat* (home-duplicated) literature. By no means all of it is pornography or political dissent: duplicating machines have been used to produce Russian translations of Western best-sellers such as *The Godfather* and spicy romances.

Those who can boast the collected works of Pushkin or Western books published overseas and not for sale in the Soviet Union impress neighbours not so much with their erudition as with their proven ability to lay hands on such precious commodities. More impressive still are pre-revolutionary books in fine bindings. Cases are often reported of thefts from libraries and special collections of old books in institutes and universities.

Russians have never known a world free from shortages, nor a time when they did not need to buy things immediately for fear they would not reappear in stock for many months. The typical city dweller has always carried a string bag, the celebrated *avoska* (from the old word *avos*, meaning perchance) to carry home kilos of oranges that appear in boxes on street corners, or into which you can stuff a fresh fish kept under the counter for you by a friendly shop assistant. The more sophisticated now have shoulder bags or a capacious briefcase, but the principle – and the contents – are the same.

Nothing is predictable: pillows, umbrellas, tins of Greek orange juice, kitchen units appear without warning. You need good ground intelligence, a pocketful of cash and a ready excuse – especially nowadays – to take time off from work to snatch up something you may not need now but will not find when the moment is pressing. And it is no use buying one tube of toothpaste, or a single East German mohair scarf – better to get six, as the extra ones can be stored in reserve or used as well-timed gifts or traded with neighbours in exchange for other 'deficit' commodities.

This situation, the vicious circle of hoarding that leads to shortages and shortages that lead to hoarding, has exaggerated the old Russian characteristic of living from day to day, of spending everything in a reckless orgy of indulgence without thought for tomorrow. Today's material delights are tangible, but tomorrow's are only promises. As a result, Russians are often in each other's debt. Wages and salaries are paid out in cash twice a month, and by the end of the fortnight people are broke and borrow shamelessly.

However it is not only the party that regrets today's emphasis on the material aspects of life. Several of the more thoughtful people I met said they believed one of the strengths of the Russians was their ability to do without the pampering Westerners have grown used to. They of course were frustrated by shortages and queues, but at the same time believed – with justification – that the absence of all the creature comforts taken for granted in the West made Russians more aware of the spiritual and emotional sides of life. People in the Soviet Union, they said, were faced more starkly with what was essential, with what was really valuable. It is, alas, these very qualities that the new materialism and the growing acquisitive ambitions of the younger generation now threaten to smother.

CHAPTER NINE

Soviet Youth

The communist party has two images of youth: the girl from Kirghizia, born to a shepherd family, sent to a primitive school where a thirst for knowledge is awakened by a compassionate teacher – a long-standing party member; struggling against the Islamic beliefs of her village, she announces her intention of studying medicine at university, and despite poverty and attempts to force her into marriage, she returns home and triumphantly delivers a sick villager of a baby. The other image is of the fourteen-year-old boy from a steelworker's family in Smolensk. 'Don't worry Mamochka,' he told his weeping mother when the Nazis took away the father, 'I'll not let down the motherland.' Now, years after he was shot as a partisan, a statue of him stands in the village where he risked his life to give warning of a German attack.

Both images are ingrained in the minds of the elderly party leaders, brought up during the social revolution in Central Asia and living their noblest moments during the Second World War. They are the stuff of a thousand films on television, of edifying tales in textbooks to teach Uzbeks Russian, of leaden reminiscences in weekly magazines. The middle-aged film producers and flabby propagandists half convince themselves that Soviet youth still aspires to this heroic mould. But at home their twenty-year-old sons in Levis and printed T-shirts argue about the use of the family Zhiguli, play Abba on their Japanese cassette recorders, get drunk at parties and ask for more Kent cigarettes from the party shop. Their daughters, in furs and Chanel perfume, are mixed up with divorced actors and flaunt their jewels and privilege.

Unlike the West, there is no generation gap in the Soviet Union, assert the little booklets published for distribution overseas. But at home *Komsomolskaya Pravda*, the organ of the Communist League of Youth, pours scorn on the thrusting university students who marry the daughters of the party establishment for their connections, denounces the pop music dominating the mentality of a generation, asks what should be done to strengthen the moral foundations of the young and instil a sense of 'social responsibility' in the jeans generation.

The Russians are worried by the alienation of youth today. Day after day the press berates its materialism and lack of values, its petty protests and disrespect for the older generation. Where is the patriotism and commitment that should have been inculcated from the first day at kindergarten? Where is the selflessness that should typify the communist? People see young men today as 'soft', mollycoddled at home and lazy at work, interested in after-shave and the after-life and apathetic to the class struggle.

Whereas the middle-aged careerists look back to the disciplined days when they proudly pinned up their class photographs, their sports trophies and Komsomol awards, today's 28-year-old gives pride of place in his room to a centrefold from an old edition of *Playboy*. He covers his door with Western cigarette cartons, and counts among his status symbols a plastic model of an Italian racing car, several battered records of The Rolling Stones and Cleo Lane acquired from a friend who runs a lively exchange racket in Leningrad with Finnish tourists, imported platform shoes and of course a pair of jeans, for which he paid 90 roubles.

Dzhinsy (jeans) hold a peculiar fascination for Soviet youth. It is not simply that they are hard to get and quintessentially American, the symbol of the hippy and the protester and the rock star. They are in themselves a protest against the clumsy disapproval of officialdom, a way of telling the conservative older generation that enforced conformity can go only so far. Every Western tourist has stories of being approached and offered fistfuls of roubles for his jeans. It does not matter if they are old, patched or shabby, or what size they are, so long as they carry the right label. A tall thin Englishman told me he had once barely sat down in a restaurant before he was cajoled by an insistent waiter, in broken English undertones, to sell his jeans on the spot. He returned from his room with them discreetly wrapped in a plastic bag, wondering how they would fit the short and stocky waiter. He had not long to wait: the man soon reappeared with them, bulging grotesquely over the waist but gleaming with satisfaction and ready with the cash.

Prices can range up to 200 roubles for the right label, depending on distance from the tourist towns, the principal source of supply. A young Russian woman we knew once appeared in a denim suit and showed it off with girlish delight, boasting that it cost her only 300 roubles – almost twice her monthly salary. Those who have jeans wear them all the time – to work, parties, the theatre, at home. I have heard Russians argue at length whether Levis were superior to Wrangler, and a paper once related how a young man, to please his fiancée with a stylish wedding, had an entire suit made up of denim he had purloined. But when she saw him in it on the wedding day she called the whole thing off, insisting she could not marry a man with so little taste as to appear in jeans without any label. A writer on the phenomenon said pupils in Moscow secondary schools were divided into three categories: those in the 'de luxe' class had Lee, Levi and Wrangler jeans. Second came those who could sport jeans made in Malta or Finland. And bottom of the class by a long shot were the unlucky ones who could only get hold of jeans from Bulgaria, India, Poland or – worst of all – the Soviet Union. Cases have even been reported of fifteen-year-old girls in Georgia slashing other girls with razors to get their jeans.

But jeans are only a symptom of a wider phenomenon the authorities appear powerless to counter: the cult of Western fashion, taste, music and even language. It is chic because it is taboo, but also because it suggests a life-style that no Russian, however privileged, can follow. Blouses, T-shirts, handbags, corduroy trousers, Adidas shoes, disposable lighters, anything with a brand-name and all the paraphernalia of Western consumer society find a ready echo. A smart plastic bag is a real find: apart from those issued to tourists at the *Beriozka* hard currency stores, Soviet shops do not have them. When a tattered Selfridges bag we used for carrying buckets and spades once blew off the sandy bank into the Moscow river, a young man nearby waded in to retrieve it, delighted with his unexpected trophy.

In summer you see any number of young people wearing T-shirts with printed Western slogans, preferably in English – young men proclaiming themselves to be a member of the Los Angeles Police Department, a G.I. in the U.S. Army, a student at this or that American university, a smoker of Marlboro cigarettes, a drinker of Guinness and a fan of assorted pop singers. Walking ahead of me through the twisting streets of old Tbilisi, I once saw the elegant figure of a Georgian girl with the British royal crest covering her back, a souvenir of the Queen's Silver Jubilee.

I often wondered whether the twenty-year-olds whose clothes announced 'I shot J.R.' had any idea who J.R. was, or realized that the gentle bearded man emblazoned on their chests was meant to be Christ. Few passers-by took any notice: the T-shirts could only have come through the black market or illegal dealings with tourists, but the police did not seem to care. The authorities do, however. There are periodic onslaughts on the T-shirt fad, ridicule of those who so value their jeans that they sleep in them, and calls for Russians to produce their own equivalent status symbols (the only ones with any apparent success are the white sports kit bags with USSR and CCCP in bright blue and red letters on the side).

The reproofs used to be gentle. 'Don't wear jeans to the Bolshoi; it's not smart,' a fashion designer wrote. After battling unsuccessfully against jeans, pop music and long hair, the authorities appeared ready to swim with the tide. Negotiations were opened with American firms for production under licence of genuine American jeans. Western pop music was played on the radio. But as the international situation darkened in the wake of Afghanistan, Poland and Reagan's America, the party clearly decided that the westernization of Soviet youth had gone far enough. The tone changed: Western T-shirts were now said to be 'openly hostile to socialism'. Young vigilantes were encouraged to pounce on their owners and engage them in ideological debate. 'The eradication of Western symbols is a serious matter. This is part of the education of young people to ideological maturity, political understanding and aesthetic culture,' a party newspaper asserted in 1982.

But not only clothes came under attack: it was time to do something about Russia's 'gilded youth'. For years the sons and daughters of the party bosses have enjoyed the spoils of privilege: imported clothes, the chance to travel, an education at the sought-after special English or French speaking schools for those talented in languages and then a place at Moscow State University or the equally prestigious foreign language institutes. They have an automatic entrée into the bohemian world of Moscow's pseudo-artistic circles, can afford semi-dissident friends, secure in the knowledge that Papa's position will protect them from exposure by snoopers or bullying by the KGB. They have time and money to go to the smart parties, be seen at the latest theatre sensation, frequent the 'Blue Bird', the nearest Soviet equivalent to a Western night-club and discothèque, where only those with connections or large bribes are able to get in. They affect a nonchalance about their position and wealth, tell jokes about the party and system, drop names and sleep around. They know when and how to demonstrate loyalty to the system, what rituals to go through and whose palms must be greased. When safe to do so, they flaunt their expensive perfume, good English, knowledge of Western life, and pour scorn on the provincial bumpkins who are struggling to make the scene.

Everyone is jealous of these spoiled children, with their snobbery and affectations. Sometimes they go too far: a discreet warning to Papa about his daughter's 'undesirable' friends is followed if necessary by a smoothly phrased 'conversation' with a KGB officer and perhaps later by an unpleasant confrontation when all the courtesies are dropped. Black market trading is permitted to go only so far: many a party man has been ruined by a *skandal* over his son's currency dealings or his daughter's friendliness with foreigners.

The gilded youth has a jargon of its own, a kind of Russified English culled from Western films, advertising slogans, the jet-set language. 'OK,' they say, 'bi bi.' It infuriates their patriotic, monolingual elders. Students nowadays, an indignant doctor of philology complained to a newspaper, sounded as though they had just dropped in from Texas or California – wearing a *pulover* and *dzhinsy*, they were interested only in *rok-music*, the latest *disky* in the *khit-parad*. Their parents are known as *Mazer* and *Fazer*, they boast about their new *shoozi*, *voch*, *beg* (shoes, watch, bag), *stripovi dzhamper* (striped jumper) and its *leibel*, their *flat*, their *bokser*, *poodl* or *buldog*, where they are going at the *vikend*, the *girl* they want to *ringanut* (ring up).

Russian is already loaded down with foreign borrowings, especially in the fields of technology – *komputer*, *kompressor*, *nokhau* (know-how), *program* and sport – *futbal*, *penalti*, *referi*, *champion*, *trainerovka* (training), *sportsmenka* (female athlete), *partnyor* (partner), *nokautirovat* (knock out). Even ideology has had to borrow terms – *partiya*, *kollektiv*, *miting* (a meeting). But the new flood of English – or rather, American – words is seen as part of the general insidious corruption of today's youth. These linguistic '*khuligani*' (hooligans) were said not only to be contrary to the character of the Russian language, but 'evidence of an ignorance of and disrespect for the national spirit of Russia'. 'You won't find irrigation workers in Pskov, milkmaids near Moscow or sailors in Leningrad using such terms,' the irate doctor of philology added.

He is of course right: the gilded youth survives only in the rarefied atmosphere of the capital, and with considerably less élan in Leningrad and one or two of the other big cities. A different breed lives in the villages, the wastes of Siberia or the mining towns of the Dombas: heavy, solid men with large hands and rough ways, pasty women who marry early and smell of garlic and sweat. A foreigner to them is someone from another town. In quilted working jackets or knitted skirts and dowdy jerseys, they know nothing of imported whisky and Boney M, eye-shadow and video tapes. (A video recorder is the ultimate status symbol of the parvenu, the item most commonly stolen from foreigners' flats.) Getting drunk is the main interest at the weekends.

But the urban sophisticates have worried the party sufficiently to provoke an outburst from Boris Pastukhov, the 49-year-old secretary of the Komsomol until his replacement in December 1982. At his last Komsomol congress he lashed out at T-shirts and jargon, pop music and pessimism as something 'alien to the Soviet way of life'. A few days after his speech a young friend was summoned to the Central Committee in connection with his application to take part in a five week tour in the West. It was clearly a serious affair: there would be a thorough examination of his references, political loyalty, behaviour and intentions. 'I haven't any idea of what's going on in the world,' he told me. 'Tell me what I ought to know.'

I told him about Brezhnev's latest proposals on arms talks in Europe, I outlined in terms he should use the essence of the Falklands war, then in progress – 'Rejecting attempts to remove colonial rule from a small group of islands, British imperialism . . .' He came round two days later. The interview had indeed been tough: three senior party officials questioned him for over an an hour. Tell us about Comrade Pastukhov's speech, they said. He confessed he knew little about it. 'We advise you to read it carefully,' they said. 'And one more thing: why are you dressed so strangely?' He had long hair, and was wearing jeans and a bright T-shirt with two pictures on it – Mickey Mouse and Minny Mouse. There were some icy reminders about communist standards of dress. Amazingly, he got his visa.

The lure of the West gives birth to dreams in many young Russians of going there. They know it is virtually impossible. Only if you are an exemplary member of the Komsomol, a reliable activist quick to report anti-Soviet behaviour and seemingly immune to the material blandishments of the West, can you hope for a chance of a cruise with a youth group on a Soviet ship, closely chaperoned when on land, to selected sites in Copenhagen, Amsterdam or London. But this does not stop young Russians working out all kinds of schemes to get abroad, embellishing their fantasies with scraps of information they glean from books, films and tourists about life 'over there'.

I once met a young man who had risked everything in an attempt to get to England. He had somehow been invited to a cocktail party in the flat of another correspondent: a small, nervous figure, clearly out of place amid the banter and guffawing of Western journalists, who see each other every day. He latched on to me when I talked to him, explaining in excellent, earnest English that he was the secretary of an independent Soviet–British society. I hardly believed him: there are no 'independent' societies of any kind in the Soviet Union – certainly none that have any dealings with foreigners. I gave him my phone number, and he then called repeatedly, insisting the society wanted to entertain my wife and me for supper. Eventually we set a date, and met at the entrance to the compound where we lived. He was with a dark-haired friend in a leather jacket – another society member, he explained.

We set off in our car, winding round unfamiliar parts of Moscow, seven storey panel blocks with rough concrete balconies and battered entranceways, cracked kerbstones, heaps of rubble on open patches of ground that were green with dandelions and tufted grass. At one point he asked us to stop, dashed out into a nearby peasant market and came back with five tired roses in cellophane, which he thrust into my wife's hand. His flat was large by Soviet standards – heavy musty furniture, a grand piano covered with a Victorian-looking embroidered cloth, and a bookcase with dusty editions of the Russian classics. His parents were clearly people of wealth and culture. They were out.

The Soviet–British society of course existed only in his mind, and the friend and he were the only members. But his room was a shrine to England – a tourist map on the wall, calendar pictures of British cathedrals, a few Penguin books, postcards of the Queen and Piccadilly Circus and a collection of empty German beer cans. In an awkward, unreal atmosphere he produced drinks – vodka and whisky from a dusty bottle obviously kept for special occasions. His story was a sad one: he had had a job helping as a tourist guide but had become too friendly with some of the tourists, even inviting some to his parents' country dacha. There had been warnings, which he had ignored, and he was sacked. He could not find another job and wanted to emigrate. He believed the KGB were after him, and hoped that getting to know foreign correspondents would protect him. He also spoke a lot about his 'sponsor' – a British businessman who appeared to have befriended him on a couple of visits to Moscow and seemed to be part of this self-styled Soviet–British society. As we were talking and eating a chicken he had prepared, a call from London came. It was the sponsor. I was immediately introduced on the phone and asked to speak to him – a silly, embarrassing conversation with neither quite knowing what the set-up was. The call had clearly been pre-arranged. The young man had hoped that those listening to all overseas calls would note that he was befriended and supported by Western correspondents.

His dark-haired friend was much less nervous. He turned out to be Jewish, had already applied to emigrate and had no job while he was waiting. He spoke mostly to my wife, and gradually steered the conversation round to the price of diamonds in the West, and how much silk scarves cost and how easily they could be imported. We smelled a rat, and resolutely changed the conversation. Only outside, under the plane trees in the small courtyard where I had parked the car so that the foreign number plate could not be spotted by nosey neighbours, did he put it bluntly: could I bring in bundles of material and scarves through the diplomatic bag, as he could then sell them for vast sums of money on the black market? I laughed and explained, as tactfully and firmly as possible, that this was absolutely out of the question. But inwardly I was angry that we had landed ourselves in such a dubious situation. It was my last attendance at the Soviet–British society meeting, though I heard that other correspondents also enjoyed chicken and whisky there.

Another young man we knew, Kolya, also wants to emigrate, but has a more plausible reason: he has married an American girl. It happened almost by chance. He met her while she was studying Russian at the prestigious Pushkin Language Institute. But none of his friends believed it. 'You can't imagine how jealous they are,' he told me. 'They keep asking me how I managed it, what I had to do to get her to agree. And what's so funny is that they're all the gilded youth who looked down on me till now.' Kolya indeed has long hovered on the edge of that society. He is from a modest background, virtually abandoned by his parents and brought up by a grandmother. But he is quick-witted, strikingly good-looking and has a genial, rather naive amiability that has helped him move into Moscow's arty set. I first met him at a party where he was playing American folk songs on his guitar. He sang well, as do many young Russians, and was clearly in command of his audience as well as his English. The Joan Baez – Bob Dylan style still has a strong influence in Russia, and Kolya, though without musical training, has been invited to play at various private shows and soirées. He knows Scottish ballads and things to make his audience laugh: 'There was an old woman who swallowed a fly . . .' as well as lyrical songs in Georgian he used to sing with his Georgian girlfriend until her family suddenly married her off to a Tbilisi millionaire.

In the summer he used to go down to the Black Sea coast with a group of other students, and almost consciously like American youth they would sit around camp fires, drinking and singing to guitar music. Kolya has a good mimic's ear, and can imitate Vladimir Vysotsky, the witty, rebellious balladier who died at the early age of forty-two during the Olympic games and who has become a cult figure in a nation that has almost deified this voice of the post-war generation. The Vysotsky style – rasping, daring, slightly coarse, mocking the nouveaux riches, the pampered party bosses, singing about the little fellow struggling to get by and the miseries of prison camp life – has become almost a cliché; now safely dead, his works are being officially recognized, issued on record and praised in the press, while the Taganka Theatre, where he acted, was – when I left Moscow – still struggling with the censors to be allowed to stage his life. Kolya can produce the photographs to prove he knew Vysotsky and can give a good imitation – part of the repertoire he is building up to sing in the West if he gets an exit visa.

At twenty-four Kolya has come a long way on good nature and the friendship of others. He spent several years at a medical institute, but his heart was never in it. The only excitement was the time he joined the anti-doping team for the Moscow Olympics and daily attempted to cajole hulky English-speaking athletes into filling up bottles with their urine. Like many others, he wants to be a photographer – a job that seems to combine glamour, prestige and a certain amount of freedom to do what you want. The limiting factor is always the equipment. Soviet cameras do not have the range and versatility of Japanese models, colour films and development equipment are expensive and hard to come by. Kolya has had a few commissions: some magazine covers, some fashion photographs. But he has given up his medical studies because the next stage would include the compulsory military course, the alternative to three years' national service that until recently used to be available to students in higher education. After taking such a course or serving in the army men are not allowed to emigrate for at least seven years.

It is a precarious life without qualifications in any field, but so far he has survived. Sometimes he is cast into the gloom of depression that grips all Russians when they see only blackness ahead. He was reduced at one point to night work unloading crates of fish from trucks to earn a few casual roubles to help pay the exorbitant cost of occasional phone calls to track down his wife in America. However he is resigned to the fact he might never get there, 'especially if relations between our two countries get any worse'.

Kolya does not think much about politics – though was once commended at his institute for writing a paper, the kind all students have in their political education classes, about the Chinese threat. But he cannot ignore the general political atmosphere. When there is a tightening-up, as there seems to be at present, everything becomes more difficult. Pop music especially is feeling itself under attack – not only Western pop, but some of the best Soviet groups who have been vigorously attacked in the press.

Russian youth today is as much the pop generation as ever it was or is in the West. Pop music, which began as the surreptitious imitation of the Beatles and other Western groups, has taken firm root and, in spite of the stuffy disapproval of the party oldsters, has drummed itself into every section of Soviet society. It is one of the few things that a sophisticated Moscow student has in common with a working youth in the provinces. When John Lennon was murdered it was a shock to millions. The papers carried long articles about his life and influence, admirers begged foreigners for magazines that carried commemorative obituaries, and a large crowd of young people gathered for several hours in a vigil outside Moscow University before being dispersed by police. Some young wits refer jokingly to the central metro station 'Biblioteka Lenina' at the Lenin Library as 'Discothequa Lennona.'

But tourists, deafened by Abba and other familiar over-amplified voices in hotel restaurants or surprised by last year's hits coming out on a summer's evening from every block of flats, miss the more important phenomenon: the extraordinary dynamic development of Soviet pop music. It is vigorous, inventive, not over-commercialized and without doubt has an unprecedented influence on the young in a country that discourages any build-up of show-biz personalities. Some groups can rival any in the West for style and impact. Many of the best come from the Baltic republics, where Soviet pop music really began. Until the recent crack-down, the local radio in Estonia used to play all the latest Soviet and Western hits, whereas in Moscow you had to tune in to Radio Moscow's English service.

Pop music tends to be livelier in the provinces, away from the political spotlight. Georgia and Armenia hold yearly festivals of music, the equivalent of open-air rock concerts in the West: exuberant affairs, where thousands of Russian '*khippis*' – hippies, who really do exist – with rucksacks and sleeping bags from all over the country gather for four days of non-stop pop. Every year they spawn new stars, discover new talent at the competitions. An Armenian, Stas Namin, bearded like Marx and a grandson of the old Bolshevik Anastas Mikoyan, a former Soviet president, is a rising composer and group leader. The Ukraine, with its strong folk music tradition, has produced several pop singers, including Sophia Rotaru who frequently makes the Soviet *khit-parad*. And a new group has just been started in Kiev by Alyosha Bordkevich, for many years the lead player with '*Pesnary*' (The Singers), more lyrical and folk in style than rock, who headed the charts for ten years but are now giving way to harder and more daring stuff. Bordkevich is the antithesis of the tawdry and ephemeral figures in the West who seem nowadays more the creations of the record industry than the embodiment of talent. A highly educated architect and a great admirer of Einstein, he is accompanied on tours with his new group by his diminutive wife, Olga Korbut, the former Olympics gymnastics star.

Perhaps the word 'charts' is misleading, for there is no organized pop scene as in the West. The key role is played by the composer. In the absence of a competitive recording industry, managers, promoters and all the hangers-on in the West, the composer has a lone struggle to find his singers, manage and promote them and cajole Melodiya, the state recording company, into risking a recording. There are constant attempts to channel pop music into staider, more conservative moulds, to emasculate it of any suggestion of beat, protest, nonconformity or Western influence. Many of the best groups fall foul of the authorities and are forbidden to record or perform in public concerts. But their music is still known, thanks to the rapid spread of cassette tapes, whose copying and private distribution, like *samizdat* publishing, is well developed.

One of the most talented composers at present is David Tukhmanov, small, intense and Jewish. After a string of successes, his haunting 'Farewell Moscow' was chosen as the theme of the 1980 Olympics and was an instant hit. For this he was awarded the Friendship of People's Medal – rather like the Beatles getting the MBE. Most of Tukhmanov's songs are written for the top male singer, Valery Leontev, a stylish performer with sultry looks, a Western casualness and a mane of curly hair. His hit 'There in September' was constantly played on the radio. Even better known is Alla Pugachova, the leading female singer. Her records sell by the millions, and she has made many. She is vivacious, temperamental and extremely rich. Indeed, for those performers officially approved by the state, the earnings are substantial – though of course outlets on which to spend them are as limited as for everyone. And even then the groups have difficulty getting hold of amplifiers, guitars and equipment.

Soviet pop groups have never been sure how much they can get away with. There is always an element of risk – censorship, a sudden change of programme, cancellation of facilities – and this adds a frisson to their best performances. They have to bargain with officious watchdogs, sometimes over almost every line, and cannot make their repertoire too Western or too avant-garde. But away from the limelight, in youth clubs or colleges, they can be very daring. Perhaps no group better illustrates this or has come under fiercer official attack than Time Machine. They are by far the most popular and influential Soviet group. They wear startling clothes, use all the aggressive suggestiveness on stage of Western pop and raise roars of applause with lyrics that are savage, witty, verging on outright rebellion: 'I do not believe in promises, and I won't do so in the future. There's no point any longer in believing in promises.'

They have not been allowed to perform in Moscow but concerts on the outskirts of the city in factory halls are always packed to capacity. There are no advertisements, little advance publicity. Word of mouth spreads news of such things quickly. In 1981 a Moscow youth paper, which runs a full page on the pop scene each month, made a perceptive comment about them: 'It is no secret that native rock music plays the role for youth which for older people is filled by literature, cinema, journalism. It is in rock music that many young people seek answers to questions troubling them. And Time Machine, with the almost missionary character of its lyrics, to a certain extent influences the lives of young men and women.' This, the paper added, put a heavy responsibility on the group. Clearly, the party realizes that if you have a Soviet equivalent of the Beatles moulding a generation, it is important they say the right things.

Pop singers know this well. They have bought a limited freedom to move into fields and styles that only a few years ago would have been unacceptable with healthy patriotic songs of the 'I love the Motherland' and 'We're off to build the new Siberian railway' variety. Some are not bad, though the audiences want stronger stuff. But nevertheless in the wake of Poland the party has displayed increasing nervousness about the messages being put across, and in the summer of 1982 launched a full-scale attack, picking, significantly, on Time Machine. The policy of limited tolerance which was evolving appears to have been decisively reversed by conservatives, who appear more worried by native Soviet pop music – which has a much stronger hold over Russians – than by the steady inflow of black market records of Western groups.

It is the uncontrollable nature of pop music that is anathema, the ability to excite emotion and unloose feelings that have few other outlets. When Elton John came on a tour of Russia in 1979 – an event of some significance – he was amazed at the tameness of the audience. A few rushed up to the stage in the first concerts in Leningrad, and there was a certain amount of stamping, whistling and spontaneous outburst. But all that was quickly suppressed by stewards, and by the time Elton John came to Moscow, word had gone out that there were to be no chances for the audience to let out their feelings or leave their seats. (The Moscow concerts were also rather tame because the audience consisted largely of middle-aged senior officials. Tickets were so hard to obtain that the gilded youth had to rely on their parents' connections. And the parents, assuming that the performances were therefore something special, decided to use the tickets themselves. I saw dozens of solid square-jowled bureaucrats and senior officers in military uniform sitting in disapproving silence as the wilder numbers throbbed out from the stage.)

Soviet pop groups are formed in clubs, factories and colleges – there are about 5,000 in Moscow alone, but few are recognized by the Union of Composers. And though amplifiers, synthesizers and good instruments are hard to obtain, the Russians lack nothing in ingenuity. One of the best groups I ever heard was formed by students at the Institute of Electronics in Novosibirsk, who built all their equipment themselves. The lead singer, a long-haired androgynous figure, could give a devastating imitation of every well-known pop singer, and had the charismatic, leather-jacketed director of this go-ahead institute beaming with amusement at his take-off of Alla Pugachova.

The sad thing is that as soon as a group becomes official it has to conform to regulations – put in a specified number of concerts, tour the duller outbacks, tone down its repertoire and cut out spontaneity and innovation. The best groups therefore often refuse to perform professionally, and sacrifice everything for the music which they play now and then in odd halls or experimental theatres. I went to one such performance. It was a remarkable evening. The show was literally underground, in an improvised theatre in the basement of a block of flats. The only way in was down dark, rather narrow concrete steps. There was tiered seating for about 100, but that quickly filled up, and people kept coming in: students, earnest young women in woollen skirts and boots, long-haired men in jeans, leather jackets or anoraks, slim good-looking people in tight-fitting blouses and chunky jerseys. They sat round the tiny stage, crowded round the walls, perched on ledges or the lower steps of the exit. There was a buzz of conversation, a thickening warm fug. I wondered anxiously, as I have in many Soviet theatres and confined spaces, about the fire risk.

The four young men were at last ready to begin. They were astonishingly versatile, ranging from loud, raucous satire 'The Samovar of Ivan Ivanovich' to gentle, haunting melodies based on Pushkin or Burns poems. They clowned, mimicked, threw out energy that seemed to burst the confines of the rough, concrete, black-painted walls. Several of their songs were religious, sung with a spirituality that was profoundly moving. Others were jokes at the expense of authority, *babushki* and the nouveaux riches. The spotlight picked out images of total commitment: Volodiya, the lead guitarist, forced feelings and emotions into the microphone, the veins on his slender neck bulged blue; Seriozha, a diminutive elfin face, leaped about the stage, squeezing ever higher and faster notes from his instrument; Andrusha in a tight white satin suit with fair, shoulder-length hair and a dreamy smile seemed like an apostle of flower-power quietude; and Sasha, fuzzy-haired and stocky who has a worldly-wise air and a clown's sense of timing, and held the performance together with the percussion, flute, and home-made rope and drum that harked back to the old days of skiffle.

Like most Russian pop singers, all four are articulate, well-educated and cultured people. Volodiya, tall, thin, with gentle eyes and a face like an apostle in a Russian icon, is a serious composer, a full-time student of music. His feelings are intense and immediate. He can recite Pushkin and other Russian poets at length, forget time and place in discussion of Russian history and culture. He cares little for material possessions except books, his guitar and his antique piano with delicate candle-holders. He is intensely religious, a profound believer in the ceremony and mysticism of the Russian Orthodox Church. For him, his wife and friends it was absolutely natural that we should pause, crowded round the kitchen table in his flat, while he blessed the food and said grace. Volodiya embraces age-old Russian qualities with the outlook of his generation – an idealist (though not in a political sense), emotional and spontaneous in friendship, but distrustful of authority, wary of 'them'. He knows the limits of what is permitted, and there is black humour in his rather cynical view of the frustration of daily life, but no bitterness.

Andrusha also is too gentle to be angry, though life is not easy for him. He does not have a permanent residence in Moscow, and although only twenty-two has already separated from his wife – 'things didn't work out,' he explained apologetically. He has no real job and little money. What he earns is spent on food and on the needs of the group. But he has a fierce pride and absolute commitment to the group. So has Sasha, the group's 'manager'. He was married to an American student in Moscow, and because of this got permission for something almost unheard of for any Russian – an individual visit to America. Having never been abroad before, he went straight to California: a change so extreme that he found it hardly real. But though Sasha learned some Los Angeles slang, enjoyed the beaches and was quick to pick up the television advertising jingles, he was far from won over by the Californian way of life. He knew his place was with the group in Moscow – though his only job is as a lowly nightwatchman. Perhaps he is one of the few Russians who does not believe in the American dream. Seriozha, the best musician of them all who has studied professionally, has a quiet confidence in himself and an instinctive feel for the preoccupations and responses of his generation.

The group – apart from Andrusha – has been together six years, has been praised in the Soviet press, played on Moscow radio and television, made recordings and given concerts. But it lacked official status and recognition, and although it won acclaim in the open-air summer festivals in the fields outside Moscow, the constant struggle was wearying. Eventually, in the summer of 1982, they decided to split up, some joining other groups, others engaging in part-time music study. They hope to get together again and repeat their success. They are some of the nicest people I met in Russia.

CHAPTER TEN

Life in the Country

More than any other European country, Russia has been and still is a rural nation. Almost half the population still lives in the countryside. Despite social transformations brought by the Revolution, peasants as a class continue to exist in the Soviet Union. Stalin bled them white to fund the industrialization of Russia, their land was taken away from them by collectivization, and their homes were burnt and destroyed by the Nazi invaders. But the Russian village survived much as it always was. The community, which in Tsarist times was organized into a virtually self-governing unit known as the *Mir*, adapted to work on state and collective farms. The peasants continued to live in beautifully decorated wooden houses, drawing water from wells, keeping ducks and pigs and tending their private plots of land.

Since the war, however, progress has steadily undermined the old order. Young people have left for the factories in far-away towns, schools and rural institutes have opened horizons, the granting of internal passports has finally given the villagers the right to come and go, and roads and buses have given them the means to do so. The flight from the land has become a stampede. In many villages only the old people are left. And attempts to upgrade the skills of the agricultural workforce by training young people to use farm machinery and in scientific skills has hastened the exodus, as those with any qualifications have immediately found jobs in the cities.

But the villages remain. In winter they are inaccessible, cut off from the world; in spring they are a sea of mud; and in the summer they present an idyllic picture of pastoral peace. But all over the country these ancient ancestral homes, settlements that have existed for generations, are now under threat. The state has decided that thousands of them no longer have any economic future, and wants to close them down, moving the population to large consolidated towns. The peasants themselves refuse to move. And the bureaucracy is confronted with one of the most profound challenges to the Russian way of life for generations. What should be the future of the Russian village?

Only occasionally was I able to visit a proper village. Foreigners tend to go just to the big cities in the Soviet Union, and not only is it difficult to strike out on your own into the rural depths, but it arouses considerable suspicion if you try to do so. Villagers themselves are unused to strangers, especially those from abroad, and do not like you snooping around. On the other hand, they are open, warm-hearted and straightforward people, who say what they think and offer spontaneous, rough hospitality: neither of which is encouraged by the authorities who monitor foreigners' contacts and movements.

The real villages, those in deepest Siberia, have often no contact at all with the outside world. A Western photographer who visited some said he was treated like a medieval prince: the entire village gathered together for a speech of welcome and for the sumptuous banquet laid on in his honour, and feasting and drinking went on for hours. No foreigner had ever been there before and their curiosity and gratitude were boundless.

Nearer to Moscow less fuss is made. My wife and I wandered round a village not ten miles from the city one autumn afternoon and were astonished that it was so rural. Most of the houses were wooden, with tin roofs and intricately carved and painted window frames. They were rather ramshackle, one-storey buildings with outhouses at the back and small plots in front, each marked off with green painted wooden fences. Some appeared virtually abandoned, unkempt and rickety – one mournfully displaying a rusting plaque 'Best kept house in the village.' In others smoke came from the chimneys, chickens clucked about and logs were piled up neatly beside the wall. Rows of vegetables were growing in the garden and women in headscarves were busying about. The houses had electricity but no water: a standpipe in the muddy lane served the small community instead.

We were only a few miles from a capital city of eight million people, yet the overwhelming impression was one of primitive isolation. The decaying church, half bricked up, was used as a store for electric cable. The only brick building seemed to be the party centre, where a small red flag hung over the door. Everywhere there was mud – thick, rich, glutinous mud that seems to exist only in Russia. A broken boat was lying upside down on the bank by the river. A wooden hut nearby called itself *Medpunkt* (medical centre), but was clearly no longer used – the door was swinging open, the window broken and inside there were only broken bottles. It seemed a dreary sort of place – though I imagine in summer there was more life, more colour.

Probably this village, like many others, had seen better days. Indeed for most of the Russian countryside the last twenty-five years –
especially Khrushchev's period – have been a particularly disruptive
time. His restrictions on private agriculture sharply cut back the
incomes of many peasants, and his grandiose schemes for urbanizing the
countryside hastened the disintegration of villages. So many were left as
empty shells that the authorities drew up a master plan for the comprehensive reorganization of the countryside. Resources were to be chan-
nelled into certain well-to-do villages marked for expansion as regional
centres while others were to be allowed to die. No new investment would
be made in villages considered 'futureless', and the inhabitants would be
encouraged to move out of their wooden houses to blocks of prefabricated flats in the new rural centres.

This plan has drawn intense opposition from many quarters –
especially the villagers themselves. The unattractive blocks of flats are
shoddily built, and, without private plots attached to them, threaten to
cut down private agriculture just when the state has decided to reverse
Khrushchev's policy and give maximum encouragement to this vital
sector.

The flight from the land is slowing down, and in some areas has been
reversed, especially in Siberia. Large incentives and priority supplies of
consumer goods have induced many young people to emigrate – if only
temporarily – to the development towns and the settlements springing
up along the new Siberian railways. But this has not helped the older
villages. Houses and cottages lie boarded up and abandoned. Many
could be inhabited by city dwellers wanting to retire to the countryside if
it were not for legal and ideological obstacles. For all land in the Soviet
Union is nationalized, and some cottages are owned by the collective
farm on which they are situated. The press has campaigned for a
relaxation of the law that would allow people to buy and restore these
dwellings, but objections to such forms of private enterprise have
so far prevented this.

The defence of the village has been taken up by the Soviet intelligentsia in recent years, for an important school of writers has grown up
which idealizes the Russian village as the fount of Russian culture, and
deplores the destruction of traditional values. The arguments are
refreshingly free of ideology, and a genuine debate is now going on in
public. Opponents of the current policy point out that more than 80 per
cent of all rural housing, apart from that owned by collective farms,
consists of individual, privately-owned homes (nobody is allowed to own

land in the Soviet Union, however, only the buildings on it). Resettlement plans aim to change this figure drastically so that state-owned rural housing would account for at least 70 per cent. But this would be fearsomely expensive. It costs around 5,000 roubles (£3,300) to resettle each villager, according to official figures, and to carry out such a programme would therefore cost from 6,000 to 7,000 million roubles each year over the next two decades alone, plus proportional increases in spending on municipal services. It is a completely unrealistic aim, and the policy has therefore come under question.

Economists argue that instead of building a few consolidated towns, it would be better and cheaper to link all the existing hamlets by road to regional service centres. And although multi-storey prefabricated blocks of flats are cheaper to put up than individual houses, the overall costs to both state and individual are higher. Peasants earn a quarter of their income from their private plots, which would be lost in resettlements. And of course the state would lose the valuable produce from the private plots.

Nevertheless, wholesale resettlement is still official policy. In Perm province, in central Russia, there were 5,642 rural communities in 1980, of which 5,170 were classified as 'futureless', and earmarked for extinction by the year 2000. In the last five year plan about 1,740 villages – occupied by 12,000 families – were supposed to have been eliminated. But less than 3,000 families had been moved out in the first three years. Many preferred to stay put. One woman who raised nine children in a remote village far from schools and doctors told *Literaturnaya Gazeta* why.

'It would be a shame to lose the sense of freedom. Here we have everything right around us – fields, woods, crystal-clear springs, places for gathering berries and mushrooms. What is there for us older people to do in Stryapunyata (the central consolidated village)? Loaf around in the shops by the hour? No thanks, that life isn't for me. I'm used to getting all my own food from my own farm.' At a time when food supplies in the towns are increasingly precarious, the argument is telling.

It is not just the older people who want to stay. The young are just as dismayed by the prospect of moving into cramped flats with no gardens. In the whole province of Perm not one newly-built resettlement block included any out-building for private agriculture. The urbanization of rural life held such appeal for some officials, however, that one respected chairman of a collective farm in the Urals wanted to put up a

100-unit block of flats and gather under one huge roof all the families from fifteen hamlets! He got no support, but other farm centres in the province have built five-storey buildings where retired peasants have no opportunity for private gardening, and the consequent economic losses are considerable. State purchases of privately-raised meat in the province are now only a third of what they were five years ago. One resident of a futureless village complained that the new brick buildings in the new towns were monotonously similar to the worst urban development. And whenever it rained, the street was a sea of mud. She lived comfortably in an old wooden house with carved window-frames and cornices. If she had to move, would it not be better to move the entire solidly built pine house, and add on a modern kitchen and bathroom?

In Belorussia, with a large rural population, almost 90 per cent of all villages are to be written off by the year 2000. The republic's new rural centres will, according to the plans, include enterprises relating to farm production: canneries, feed plants, veterinary clinics, farm machinery divisions, fertilizer centres, airports for crop-dusting and so on. Each centre will have a department store, a cultural centre, hospital and medical centre, hotel and sports complex. It sounds ideal – but this is so far only a project, and even officials admit that it is a long time before a network of these model settlements can be established.

Meanwhile peasants have begun to appeal to the party against decisions hastening the death of their communities. When the only shop in the village of Kochugurki, population 148 souls, was closed, one resident wrote to *Pravda*. He complained they now had to go four miles to get bread, salt and sugar, and fourteen miles to get anything else. 'As a communist, I don't think people should be treated this way,' he wrote. He said he had written to the local party committee, who promised eventually to send round a mobile shop, but nothing happened. However, the letter to *Pravda* had an effect: a party delegation went to Kochugurki, and within a few hours, according to the newspaper, a shop was opened there. Life was restored to the modest village club and a film, the first for years, was shown. Steps were taken to discipline those who had been too quick to write off the community.

Another letter complained that a thriving village in rich pastureland was melting away because no one would build a three-mile road to link it to the outside world. The medical aid station was closed, and the children had to walk to school through mud that was impassable even by a tractor in some months. The inhabitants of another village where all the young people had left said there was no well, and the old people had to haul water five miles every day. The local council said the village was futureless and would do nothing.

Pravda declared that the amalgamation of hamlets was an 'important shining goal' to which thousands of peasants were drawing near. It was therefore 'all the more distressing' that on the path to this goal some officials were closing amenities ahead of schedule.

However, not all villages are short of money. Many are now richer than they have ever been before, as the state pours money into agriculture and rural wages have risen faster than the national average. Many people, especially the writers who idealize the traditional way of life in the Russian village, argue that this prosperity, a result of the massive state effort to upgrade standards in the countryside, is often artificial and accompanied by a growing material acquisitiveness and spiritual emptiness. Villagers are becoming lazy, living on government handouts. Drunkenness is growing, creative initiative has been destroyed and a sense of malaise has overtaken the small communities.

In one of his last novels, *Home*, the celebrated writer Fyodor Abramov painted a bleak picture of a village called Pekashino slowly going downhill. He was probably referring to his own home village of Verkola, in northern Russia, which in a startlingly frank letter to *Pravda* he depicted as nothing more than a rural slum.

It could have been a paradise. The meadows produce rich and plentiful grass, the scenery rivals that of Finland or Sweden, and comfortable new houses have been built for the villagers. But the cattle are starving, the grass is unmown, the fields untilled, stray dogs roam the village, the dairy is filthy and the workers indolent. Verkola is living on state subsidies. In the ten years up till 1980 a hundred new houses were built and equipped with refrigerators, television sets and modern fittings. The average monthly wage is now 209 roubles (about £150 – more than usual for the countryside), and dairymaids, shepherds and tractor drivers often get 300 roubles. Tractors, combine harvesters and lorries are plentiful. Government allocations to the state farm total some 2 million roubles.

Yet none of this is justified by increased productivity. The amount of land under cultivation has fallen by thirty hectares. Fewer sheep are raised then ever before. The yearly milk yield per cow has gone up by only just over a quarter in fifteen years. Though the little village is drowning in luxuriant grass, it is a rare year that there is enough fodder for the cattle in the winter. In a typical year the cows get only four pounds of hay a day, and in the spring fodder has to be imported from the

Ukraine because nobody bothers to help cut the grass. At haymaking time in 1980 only 41 out of the 117 men in the village went to work in the fields, and even they worked half-heartedly.

Abramov asked whether the villagers had forgotten the habits of generations. 'On the contrary, they are working on their private plots from early morning until late at night,' he said. Such plots were all very well, but Verkola had a large state farm and lived by this. In July, a few months before his letter, eight calves died of starvation because there were not enough people to look after them. The herdsmen and the dairymaids worked round the clock with never a day off, but when one was sick there were no replacements.

He suggested giving away some of the cows to a farm nearby, but concluded it would be impossible without handing over pasture land, and that would signal the end of Verkola. It was not a question of mechanization or a shortage of labour. The fault lay in people's attitudes. Nowadays, he said, the villagers could not care less about their villages. Fields that used to supply 2,000 haywains full of hay were left uncultivated. Tractor drivers routinely drove their tractors through fields of wheat. Wages were paid on the basis of labourers' own assessments of how much work they did – 'and some have absolutely no conscience'.

Abramov complained that even in Tsarist days the *muzhiks* never went on holiday during the harvest period. But today's *muzhiks* were often away in the summer period. Former pride in neatly ploughed fields and mown meadows had disappeared, as had love for the land. Villagers nowadays lacked self-respect – the cause, he said, of the present wave of absenteeism, lateness and drunkenness. Verkola could be a beautiful village. But no one took any care of it. Abandoned dogs bit the children but nothing was done. Healthy young people stayed in bed until 11.00 a.m. A club built for the village a few years ago was filthy. The local dairy stank so much that people had to hold their noses when passing it. The 207 pensioners in the village (a high proportion, and indicative of the demographic problems of many villages) were too busy on their private plots to help with the haymaking on the state farm.

Abramov's letter was a devastating criticism of the state of rural Russia, and it took some courage on the part of *Pravda* to print it. For the obvious conclusion is that the system of state agriculture as organized by Stalin has failed, and the massive investments poured into the countryside over the past twenty years have neither brought greater efficiency nor stemmed the haemorrhaging of rural Russia. The discrepancy between town and country is widening, and village life continues to be hard. Surveys have shown that women have an average weekly work load of eighty-eight hours, and the last census showed that young women are leaving for the towns even faster than the young men.

It is not so much a shortage of money as the suffocating boredom of rural life that prompts the flight. It also prompts a frightening insensitivity and cruelty, which co-exist side by side with warmth and sentimentality in so many Russians of peasant stock. One incident, detailed by *Literaturnaya Gazeta*, gives an indication of the brutish callousness found in villages where young people have neither hope nor ambition.

It was New Year in the village of Bakhmuta, and the teenagers had nothing to do. They hung about on the street, looking for girls, hoping for trouble to liven up the day. Someone suggested going to Stupki, a village nearby. It was dangerous, because, as often in Russia, the villages were rivals, and the local beauties were jealously guarded. But it promised a change from the monotony. The Stupki teenagers were waiting for them with crowbars, however. The moment the gang from Bakhmuta arrived, they were outnumbered and beaten. One had his skull cracked, two lost teeth, the rest were cut and bruised. Returning home, they swore revenge. No one thought of calling the police – neither their parents, nor neighbours, nor the doctor who patched up their wounds.

The youths chose as a leader a cool-headed seventeen-year-old who had not taken part in the fight, armed themselves with iron bars and bottles of petrol, waited ten days and then set off one winter evening for Stupki. Music and lights came from the club house where about sixty people, mostly schoolchildren, were at a dance. When one boy came outside, the leader of the Bakhmuta group struck him in the face. The others surrounded the building, fused the lights, smashed a window and hurled their petrol bombs inside.

As the building caught fire, the dancers tried to escape. Their attackers blocked the exits and beat them back into the inferno with iron bars. There were screams as the dry New Year's tree went up in flames and the young people's hair and clothes caught fire. The attackers withdrew, and threw their weapons in the river, setting the bridge on fire so that they could not be followed.

Twenty of the young people in the club were severely burnt. And none of the attacking gang, who were caught and imprisoned, showed any remorse. They mumbled phrases about regretting their actions to the Soviet journalist who interviewed them, but their eyes sparkled when they described the attack and the fire. They still considered the seventeen-year-old leader a hero.

The Kremlin's difficulty is how to make village life attractive, up-to-date and economic without altering its character, destroying ancient communities and in the process further damaging Soviet agriculture. Ironically many of the measures designed to educate and hold young people have the opposite effect: schools encourage a thirst for better things, and inculcate the system of values the teachers bring with them from their training colleges in towns. Attempts to give young men in villages a proper technical grounding to enable them to use agricultural machinery give them instead an education which allows them to go off to the towns and find jobs there. Bringing television to the countryside means that today's young generation of farm workers, salaried and rewarded like ordinary industrial workers, prefer to sit at home watching television in the evenings rather than cultivate their own private plots as their parents used to.

Attracting qualified professional people to work in the countryside is a ceaseless struggle. Many are university or college graduates sent to remote villages for the obligatory two year first posting which every Soviet student faces at the end of his studies. For many, it is like banishment. They find it hard to adapt to the isolation, and as soon as the two years are up they return to the towns. The problem is particularly acute with teachers and doctors. But in their efforts to improve efficiency on the state farms, the authorities are also sending out scientists – agronomists, engineers, managers – who have little feel for the land and whose presence is resented by other farm workers. The high turnover rate does not make for long-term stability of consistent planning.

The mechanization of Soviet agriculture has been a prime target ever since the communists came to power. But it still has a long way to go. The reason is not a lack of machinery: Soviet industry turns out millions of tractors and combine harvesters, and profitably exports many of them. But those deployed on farms are so poorly maintained that they break down within months, and are either botched together or left to rust. The tractor has become a virtual symbol of Soviet power in the countryside. It features in every poster, its operators beam out from the front pages of *Pravda*, and the sturdy beast is deemed a suitable object for socialist realist art and literature. But the percentage that are out of operation through a lack of spare parts, a shortage of drivers and unsuitable terrain is astonishing. Matters are not helped by the shenanigans of those responsible for repairing them: *Pravda* had a richly typical story of the difficulties facing farmers in the Leningrad region. They were told that a new tractor engine repair plant had been built to handle 14,000 engines a year. Designed by a special institute, it was considered a modern industrial miracle. It was handed over by the state contractors to the relevant ministry in December 1978 and was formally declared open two months later.

For a full year it was in operation. But the production statistics were unsatisfactory, and showed large losses. Collective farms in the north-west reported great difficulties in getting their tractors repaired.

In fact the factory simply did not exist. On paper it looked solid enough, but anyone following directions to the site came upon a grizzled old guard, a gate, a few foundation trenches filled with broken bricks and a number of half-built blocks. The guard enjoyed a very peaceful life: no one had worked on the site for years. The project had begun satisfactorily in 1974, but had run into the inevitable delays. Two years later the state bank had cut off further credit, and most of the builders were pulled off the project. A new start was planned for 1977. But the regional construction authority was so far behind schedule that it had no hope of ever building a factory by the target date, and the chairman decided to wash his hands of the affair. He would hand it over to the commissioning authorities as though it were complete. And so a year later, with birds nesting in the open window spaces, the building contractors officially recorded that 'all construction work has been completed according to design. The factory is now ready for use.'

The problem of getting inspectors to sign the hand-over papers was overcome by a series of reshuffles on the State Inspection Commission so that no one was left who knew the real state of affairs. Someone signed for the chief engineer, declaring he had been appointed to check the work instead. The doctor designated to work in the non-existent factory signed, though subsequently denied the signature was his. The fire inspectors had no qualms in signing: with no factory, there was no fire risk. Similarly the environmental protection agency signed without hesitation: there were no pipes discharging waste, so there was no possible damage to the environment.

Officials in Moscow, seeing all the papers were in order, concluded that all was well. And for a full year a fictitious plan was assigned to the phantom factory, while its all too substantial losses were written off. But inevitably the reckoning came when independent state auditors – the body known as National Control – began asking questions, convened a meeting and summoned all those concerned with the affair. Many were dismissed and others severely reprimanded. But for the farmers of the north-west there was a huge backlog of broken-down tractors to repair – made worse by the closing down of several smaller old repair facilities when the modern industrial miracle had been officially declared open.

But even when working, tractors have not yet taken the place of human labour on the land. Peasants have worked in the fields for thousands of years, and still do – bent double over rows of vegetables, or picking the fluffy cotton in the hot dry southern republics. Russians have always been close to the land, with close bonds of attachment to the fields and animals where they earn their living. The collectivization of agriculture weakened this bond, but it was the assault on private plots under Khrushchev that appears to have struck the hardest blow. And although official policy has been reversed, with the encouragement now of 'subsidiary farming', peasants and officials have lost interest. The peasants suspect, not without cause, that were their little patches allowed to flourish to the point where they competed with the state sector, there would be a new clamp-down and their land and livestock would again be confiscated. They do not want to work for nothing. Officials, brought up to view private agriculture as ideologically un-acceptable, an unfortunate remnant from the old days, are in no mood to supply peasants with fodder, young piglets and farm tools as they are now being encouraged to do, especially if this makes it more difficult for the farm directors to fulfil the targets set for the vast state farms.

Everyone agrees the old bonds of attachment to the land should be renewed. But how? The obvious answer, restoring private ownership of land, is ideologically impossible. Another solution, quietly canvassed by experts and economists, would turn the state farms into co-operatives, giving farmers almost unlimited freedom to decide what to grow, how much and what price to charge, making wages dependent on earnings and allowing farms to keep and reinvest the profits. For a year the party toyed with the idea of a radical reform along these lines, and the special food plenum of the party in May 1982 was expected to cast aside all existing restrictions on private plots and adopt some of the radical innovations that have made Hungarian agriculture so productive, to the envy of Soviet party officials. But in the end orthodoxy triumphed. It seems that at the last moment the aging Soviet leadership got cold feet, and announced instead a 'food programme' that simply revamped traditional formulas – more investment, pay rises for farm labourers, better transport, storage and packing of food, more fertilizers, farm machinery and technical training, the creation of more 'agro-industrial complexes' and the setting up of new layers of bureaucracy to allow farmers to appeal against the plans set for them and the prices offered. There was nothing that would strengthen the peasant's direct interest in working on the land.

This programme was one of the last important domestic issues under Brezhnev's leadership, and the new men in the positions of power now have been strikingly cool to the programme. Andropov has a thorough knowledge of Hungary, and knows that success there was not achieved this way; Mikhail Gorbachev, the young agricultural expert in the politburo, has distanced himself from the food programme, and is presumed to have pushed for something more radical. However, the leadership has clearly grasped the importance of doing something swiftly to improve the food supplies. And indeed the first winter of Andropov's leadership saw a marked change, with citrus fruit and vegetables in relatively plentiful supply, shorter queues and even the occasional appearance of frozen chicken imported from Eastern Europe and the West.

Old attitudes die hard in Russia. And this is especially true of the way Russians treat the land. Their country has always seemed inexhaustible. It is so vast that its resources have seemed limitless. There was never much need to husband wood or water, to use the land intensively, to protect nature. Like the Americans, the Russians have plundered their land for its riches without heed for the environment. And the results have been almost as disastrous: rivers poisoned, clean lakes polluted, land blighted by industrial waste, huge areas rendered unproductive.

But just as attempts are now being made to set agriculture on a firmer footing, so, belatedly, the problems of the environment are also being acknowledged. Senior economists have spoken of the damage being done, and programmes have been drawn up to control pollution by industry and oil pollution. But indifferent officials and bad planning ruin the best of intentions, and industry, always under pressure to fulfil targets beyond its means, has no time or money to clear up the mess.

A classic case is Lake Baikal – the largest and deepest freshwater lake in the world, whose legendary purity has long been a source of pride to every Russian. This 'pearl of Siberia' in a great cleft of the earth contains a fifth of all the fresh water in the world, and is fed by 336 rivers. The dense forests and the moss of the *taiga* filter the melting snow, catching impurities, and about 90 per cent of all precipitation seeps down into the rock and is again filtered before entering the lake through underground channels.

Lake Baikal however is now the centre of a rapidly expanding industrial zone, where the exploitation of minerals and timber has brought a burgeoning population. The new Trans-Siberian railway is being built close to the northern shore, and damage to the lake has been caused by the burning of forests, pollution of streams and destruction of grass cover. The damage is especially serious because of the delicate ecological balance in the extreme Siberian climate. If a tree only six inches in diameter is destroyed, it takes between 150 and 170 years to grow another of the same size. The area's rivers have only a tenth of the self-purifying capacity of the Volga or the Don.

In the early 1970s the government passed laws to protect the lake's basin. Restrictions were then laid on the big pulp and cardboard works, the main source of pollution to the lake. Industrial effluents had to be demineralized or converted to non-toxic substances, and all the factories are due to change over to closed water supply systems. But things are not getting better. Poorly treated sewage is still being discharged into the lake, increased shipping has brought oil pollution, and the floating of log rafts of two million cubic metres of timber down the lake each year leaves hundreds of tons of organic compounds in the water.

A national campaign has begun to clean up Lake Baikal, and probably has the verbal support of every citizen. But enforcing the regulations on reluctant bureaucrats, especially in far-away Siberia, is not easy. And this is true of nature protection in general. The Soviet Union with its expanses of tundra and virgin forests, its mountains, deserts and steppeland, has some of the richest fauna and flora in the world. But industrial development has taken its toll, and now many species that used to roam wild are found only in the nature reserves that have been set up in different parts of the country.

A 'Red Book' of protected species has been compiled, and the authorities pride themselves on their official commitment to saving some of the world's rarest and most beautiful creatures from extinction. But in recent years this commendable effort has been brought almost to nought by an increasing number of poachers. And poaching in the Soviet Union is not simply a case of bagging a rabbit or fishing in private waters as in the West; it is the organized slaughter of the country's wildlife on a scale that is threatening to wipe out whole species of protected animals.

Every year thousands of elks, deer, foxes, bears, bison and other animals in nature reserves are massacred by bands of poachers armed with machine-guns who roam freely in lorries and on motorcycles through the forests. The hides of exotic animals are sold on the black market for huge sums, while the meat is cut up and eaten or even barbecued and sold openly as a delicacy in towns and tourist resorts. Every year dozens of state game wardens are shot dead by poachers, formidably equipped with hand-made guns, explosives and other weapons, who return fire the moment they are challenged. Large-scale gun battles are fought in the forests and steppeland. Some 70,000 poachers in the Russian Republic alone were apprehended in 1981, and 20,000 weapons confiscated – but that is only a fraction of the total.

In some areas the forests are now almost silent. Regular raids by bands of poachers have eliminated all the larger animals, while birds, squirrels and hares have been killed by people shooting at anything that moves, just for the fun of it. Rare species bred in captivity and released in game parks for scientific study have been shot within weeks. Animals listed in the Red Book have ended up on skewers over hot coals.

A vigorous campaign has begun to strengthen the small army of game wardens, enlist public opinion in the fight against poaching and stiffen the penalties. But hunting has always been a popular sport in Russia, and many a top Soviet official, including Brezhnev, has entertained his visitors with a day's chase in the forests. Illegal hunts are often organized by senior party officials, and in a memorable scandal in 1981 the head of the coalminers' union was sacked and then prosecuted for taking part in a hunt in which bears and elk were machine-gunned from a helicopter.

Poaching is often conducted by the very people supposed to be guarding wildlife. One group, whose escapades were publicized in the press, descended on a state reserve in the Caucasus by helicopter, shot seven valuable bison, as well as goats and boars, skinned them and smoked the hides on the spot, and then took the dressed meat by helicopter to nearby towns where it fetched 12 roubles a kilo. Taking part in the hunt were a senior researcher at the reserve and the chairman of a regional society of hunters and fishermen.

Poaching from a helicopter, usually purloined from Aeroflot through a hefty bribe to the pilot, is particularly harmful to deer, elk and other large animals as it destroys the basis of the herd's existence. The large herds are broken up and are then unable to defend themselves against predators. Whereas earlier herds had numbered up to 1,500, they often now comprise no more than five or six animals. Poachers also use motorboats, snowmobiles, jeeps, hovercraft and even light aircraft – mostly those belonging to state farms or country patrol services, and 'borrowed' for a large fee. This is particularly the case in the lightly patrolled forests of the Far North and around Lake Baikal.

The press has called for more game wardens, but the shortage of meat and furs throughout the country makes poaching increasingly lucrative. In one Siberian fur farm, for example, it was found that the state received six tons of meat from wild hoofed animals each year, while poachers took eighty-five tons.

Hunting is not prohibited altogether, however. Indeed in the depths of Siberia it is the most common form of livelihood, and licensed hunters lead the tough and lonely lives they have for generations, battling against the bitter cold and trekking through the forests for days on end. Licensed hunters and trappers operate more or less as private entrepreneurs, receiving permission to carry a gun in return for an obligation to deliver a specified number of valuable furs to the state each year. Those hunting for sport go after wild boars and hares.

Ironically the wolf, for generations the scourge of the Russian village and the huntsman's prime target, has recently enjoyed the protection of the state. As a result it has become a real threat to life, human and animal, outside the big towns. All over the country the wolf population has increased in recent years. In the Russian Republic there were an estimated 2,500 wolves in 1960; now there are about 12,000. Wolves are particularly numerous in the steppes and in Kazahkstan, and the total population is now about 100,000.

According to Vasily Peskov, the best known and influential Soviet naturalist, the animals cause considerable damage. In Perm, in the Urals, they killed at least 2,000 elk and over 600 sheep and goats a year in the late seventies, and other animal losses amounted to nearly one million roubles. Attacks on people have also increased, especially on those trying to protect their animals. Children are particularly at risk.

'My legs are weak, otherwise I would have shown him,' an old peasant from Kirov told Peskov. 'I was watching television and heard someone knocking, then a dog's yelp. I went out and a wolf had its teeth in my dog's leg. I pulled one way, the wolf pulled the other. The dog got away, but it lost a leg.' Other dogs have been less fortunate. In one winter in the Kirov region, north-east of Moscow, thirty were killed and countless huskies attacked. Wolves even ventured into the city, and a large pack was discovered only a few miles away. There were twenty-one cases of attacks on humans.

Wolves do not attack in the hungry winter months but in summer when they have cubs to feed. In one bizarre incident the papers once reported how a wolf rushed into a peasant's house in Byelorussia and started eating up pillows, carpets and boots. The woman managed to barricade herself safely in the kitchen. I myself have seen fresh wolf prints in a snowy forest near Minsk. It is not hard to understand the Russian's fear of his traditional enemy.

After the Second World War wolves were numerous, but they were hunted, trapped, poisoned and even shot from light aircraft until they seemed to present no danger. The hunters put down their guns, but the remaining wolves survived and adapted. Now there are calls for a revival of the traditional wolf-hunt. This almost died out when the state bounty of 3 roubles paid on each wolf-skin was too low to encourage hunters. It was more profitable to go after elk and wild boar. But in 1979 the bounty was increased to 200 roubles for a she-wolf and 150 for a male. And the old-fashioned wolf-hunt – with rewards of a pig or sheep from grateful peasants – may soon see a revival.

Perhaps because communism has aimed its message primarily at the urban proletariat, or perhaps because Russian thought and culture has long existed almost exclusively in the few big towns that are seen as islands of civilisation in an ocean of rural backwardness, the Soviet authorities are extremely sensitive about the countryside. They want to point to progress, to the revolutionary transformations in the fields, but fear the outsider will see only peasant conservatism, traditional values and a landscape that appears little different from that described in Gogol's *Dead Souls*. Ideology may praise the peasant as the bedrock of the Russian people, but to today's city-dweller 'peasant' is now a term of abuse.

It is a pity. As a people, the Russians – indeed all the ethnic groups in the Soviet Union, apart perhaps from the Jews – are still deeply attached to the land, find refreshment and strength in their rural roots. But they do not willingly take outsiders there. Yet some of my most enjoyable memories are of the vast, unchanging country beyond the towns. In Russia itself the landscape cannot be called beautiful: it is flat, monotonous and rather ill tended. Yet it has a powerful and slightly mournful appeal. How often did I go with friends and visitors to the little village of Alexandrovka, about thirty minutes from the centre of Moscow, just to sit under the pines on a hill overlooking the Moskva river, listening to the crows and looking at the fields of maize below. And one of my most interesting days in Uzbekistan was when I went – properly chaperoned by Intourist – into the bare dusty mountains where meat was still grilled on open fires outside and life had unhurried, primitive values.

Village life is still a real form of existence to most Russians, even if they now live in towns. Unlike Western society, which seems to have lost touch with the land, Soviet life is earthy in all senses. It is something we too easily overlook in the West.

CHAPTER ELEVEN

Nationalism: Regional and Ethnic

One unfortunate effect of the West referring always to 'Russia' rather than to the Soviet Union is that people forget that Armenians, Georgians, Latvians and Uzbeks and countless others with their own languages, cultures, traditions, religions and outlooks are by no means the same as the Russians. Officially the Soviet Union consists of fifteen separate republics. But the largest, the Russian Soviet Federated Socialist Republic, which covers the heartland of European Russia and stretches right across Siberia to the Pacific, includes dozens of autonomous republics, where different peoples and races – Tatars, Yakuts, Chechens – have developed very different ways of life. The outward trappings of Tallinn and Bukhara may be the same – the blue and white trolley buses whose arms constantly fall off the wires, the police uniforms, the statues of Lenin and the obligatory puppet theatres – but these two towns are as different as Edinburgh and Tunis and as far apart. The Soviet Union is a continent almost as large and certainly as varied as Africa.

The map indicates the size, but tourists are still surprised to find that you can fly east from Moscow for ten hours on a four-engined jet, arrive eight time zones ahead and still be in the same country. While Uzbeks swelter in 45 degrees centigrade in the deserts of Central Asia, the permafrost of Yakutsk has not even begun to melt and the gold-miners of Magadan cover their faces against the biting cold which can freeze your nose within minutes.

The West imagines the Soviet Union as a uniform country with rigid control from Moscow. It is a false picture. Naturally, all the main political and economic decisions are taken in Moscow. The communist party is a single, monolithic organization, and local government has only limited powers. But the Soviet Union is the world's largest and most diverse multi-national state, and without a very firm structure and tight control at the centre, it would probably split apart into dozens of separate competing units. Regional and ethnic nationalism is strong and is growing, and despite the much-trumpeted official picture of a big, happy, harmonious family, there are tensions and quarrels beneath the surface, which are suppressed only with difficulty.

Nevertheless, Moscow does not and cannot supervise what goes on in every corner of this self-contained world. Distances are too great. Things go on in the villages of Tadzhikistan or the mountains of Georgia that are quite unknown to the bureaucrats in Moscow, even though ethnic Russians invariably hold senior positions in local party organizations. The nomads who still roam about in Turkmeniya and the hunters of Siberia rarely come into contact with the authorities and acknowledge no government. Moreover, a large number of them cannot speak a word of Russian. An Estonian and a Tadzhik have more in common with their neighbours across the political border in Finland and Afghanistan than with each other or with the Russians around them.

Since the Revolution the Soviet government has been preoccupied with the problem of nationalities, of holding the old Tsarist empire together without the Russians appearing to be colonial rulers. It was Stalin who devised the present nationalities policy, and for many years the Kremlin poured money into the non-Russian parts of the country in order to demonstrate the benefits of permanent union with Russia and to buy off any latent nationalism. The point has now been reached where people of these non-Russian republics, especially those in the south, live better than the Slavs in the heartland of old Russia. This has produced a strong backlash: ethnic Russians resent money being spent on development in Georgia and Uzbekistan while the villages only forty miles from Moscow stagnate and decay.

From travels in nine different republics, my impressions were strongly reinforced that the diversity and variety is such that no amount of centralisation can mould a single type of 'Soviet man', even if that were the aim – which increasingly is recognized as unrealistic.

Tallinn, the capital of Estonia, is perhaps my favourite city in the Soviet Union. As the train from Moscow draws in past the Gothic spires and ancient walls of the medieval city, you feel you are coming to a different world – gentler, cleaner, quieter, more friendly than the harsh, hurried, political atmosphere of the Soviet capital. Tallinn – literally 'Danish town' – is one of the most perfectly preserved Hanseatic cities of northern Europe. For two years before the Olympic Games wooden scaffolding shrouded almost every ancient structure while plasterers, painters and craftsmen laboured to get the Estonian capital into shape for the Olympic yachting regatta, held there in 1980. And when they had finished the 25 million rouble facelift to repair years of drabness and neglect, there emerged a strikingly beautiful ensemble of red tiled roofs, twisting, cobbled streets and painted façades.

Tallinn, or Revel as it used to be called, is the small capital of the smallest Soviet republic. The city has less than half a million inhabitants, and Estonia, roughly the size of Belgium, has only 1,400,000 people. With an extremely low birthrate, there are fears that the Estonians, now only 64 per cent of the republic's population, may soon be unable to resist gradual Russification as immigrants from other parts of the country come to fill the highly paid vacancies in the most efficient and developed economy of the USSR.

But the Estonians have long struggled successfully to preserve their rich national culture, though they have always been at the mercy of their powerful neighbours – Russia, Germany, Sweden, Poland. Like the other Baltic republics, Estonia, flat, sparse and stony, has been a battlefield throughout history. In 700 years they have known only twenty years of fleeting, sparkling, deeply mourned independence, from 1920 to 1940. Soviet troops occupied the independent republic in 1940, and after an election in which only communist candidates were allowed to stand, the new government 'asked for admittance' into the Soviet Union. The request was granted on July 21.

Estonia lost a third of its population during the German occupation and the Stalinist purges that came with the return of the Russians. Today the little land is resigned to the fact that it is now irrevocably linked to the Soviet Union (a link not officially recognized by the United States or by the many Estonian exiles overseas). And materially it is doing fairly well: average salaries have more than doubled in the past fifteen years, and are now about 20 per cent higher than the national average. Collective farms, more prosperous than the towns, produce more food per head than any others in the country, and export 90 per cent of their milk and meat to other republics. Industrial output has grown forty-eight times since 1940, as official statistics frequently point out, and Estonia is now a leading producer of high-quality clothes, textiles and precision instruments. People are well dressed, well educated (they spend eleven years at school compared with ten elsewhere in the Soviet Union) and fairly well-to-do. One in eleven people owns a car, the highest ratio for the Soviet Union.

The Estonians are part of the Finno–Ugrian peoples who swept across from Mongolia. They have broad, fair faces, a language that is rhythmic and impossibly inflected and a close kinship with the Finns. Tallinn is just across the Gulf of Finland from Helsinki. After the incorporation of Estonia into the Soviet Union all links with Finland were cut. But now things are easing up. A regular ferry brings hundreds of Finnish tourists over every weekend. Most come on vodka binges and spend two days in perpetual intoxication at the elegant Viru Hotel. They sell their jeans, shirts and anything else they bring to finance their drinking, which goes on until they are rounded up by the police on Sunday evening and dumped back on the boat home.

A Finn once explained that this unfortunate image of the drunken Finn in Estonia stems partly from deep-seated social attitudes. Throughout history the Estonians were the wealthier, more cultured, more developed people while the Finns scratched a living across the Gulf. Since 1940 the situation has been reversed. But some Finns still need to show off their new riches, to flaunt their freedom in bad behaviour.

Links with Finland are not simply alcoholic. All Tallinn used to watch Finnish television, which could easily be received with the help of a small adaptor fixed to the set. It came as a shock when an Intourist guide told me how much she enjoyed *The Onedin Line* and other BBC programmes exported to Finland. Indeed the head of Estonian television told me he had no objection to competition from across the water: it gave the viewers a choice of two extra channels. The Finns of course do not broadcast anything offensive to their powerful neighbour. But things have tightened up now. The propaganda offensive launched before Brezhnev's death and sharpened under Yuri Andropov has tried to stop the nightly intrusion of Western images into people's homes.

To Russians going to Tallinn it seems as though the Western way of life has arrived. 'It's our little piece of the West,' a Russian once remarked. The shops are better stocked, there are good cafés and restaurants, people are more smartly dressed. Above all, things seem to work in Estonia. There is a greater sense of initiative and responsibility. Private housing was permitted for some years after the war, and some leafy suburbs grew up on the outskirts of the old city. There is still an actute housing shortage throughout the republic, but private housing is being vigorously encouraged. Co-operatives make up a quarter of all accommodation in Tallinn, although the building of private villas, now selling for vast sums, has been banned. On farms, materials are available for labourers to build their own cottages. A farm director admitted this was cheaper for the state, more popular and encouraged a more responsible attitude to maintenance.

Russian tourists can be seen everywhere. They come to buy up everything they can see in the shops, which causes some local resentment. Mr V. I. Klauson, the Estonian prime minister, admitted at a press conference for foreign journalists that people from elsewhere in the country tended to buy clothes, shoes, meat and milk, but added disarmingly: 'Some people prefer practical things to souvenirs. Perhaps they don't appreciate some of the same things they have at home.'

The Estonians are fiercely nationalistic, but the KGB makes sure there is no organized opposition to the Russian presence. Instead Estonians show a strongly felt attachment to their language and culture, and refuse to speak Russian. Of all the republics, Estonia was the only one where statistics showed in the 1979 census that knowledge of Russian was more limited than it was ten years before. It was the only place where I found it a positive advantage to stumble and halt in Russian (though it is surprising how much of the language people will speak if they know you are a foreigner). I once told a Russian how much I liked Estonia. 'Ah,' he smiled, 'now I can see you are anti-Soviet.'

One great manifestation of Estonian culture is the national song festival every five years. Like an enormous eisteddfod, it draws singers from all corners of the republic to Tallinn, where 20,000 people stand and sing national songs to an audience of up to 200,000. It is an emotional occasion, a re-dedication of the people to their country. The Estonian theatre is also vigorous and innovative, and the ballet has a high reputation. Musically the little republic is a colossus. It came first in a competition of national republic orchestras when it was under the baton of Neeme Jarvi. I was once invited to a concert in which he gave what was probably the first performance in English of 'Land of Hope and Glory'. It was a moving occasion – I was probably the only Englishman in the audience listening to this most English piece of music beautifully sung by a local choir. Jarvi has since emigrated, and has won acclaim conducting in Sweden, Britain and America.

Estonia is not a fertile land. The rocky ground, harsh winters, sparse population, feudal heritage and rural deportations at the start of collectivization would seem to discourage agriculture. Much of the land is also being blighted by the enormous oil shale extraction works, which have aroused the wrath of the environmentalists. But Estonians, mainly Lutherans, have a Protestant work ethic that is, by Soviet standards, unusual. Farm production did not reach the 1939 level until 1960. Now it is double the Soviet average. A model farm sixty miles from Tallinn makes a profit of around four million roubles a year. It can afford a cinema, library, gymnasium and swimming pool. It sponsors motor-cycling and volleyball, builds retirement homes for its workers and allots a quarter of its 12,000 rouble turnover to bonuses and a further 10 per cent to the cultural fund.

The Olympic Games brought a surge of funds and attention to Estonia. A new yachting centre was built around the bay from Tallinn, complete with a hotel and sports complex. It has since been used for Soviet yachting competitions, though yachting is not a sport most Soviet citizens can afford. The smart sailing boats moored in the Olympic harbour almost all belong to sports clubs.

Estonia has deep fears for its future identity because of the very low birthrate. The immigration of Russians has slowed down as the author-ities are sensitive to resentment caused by the change in the population balance. Attempts to counter anti-Russian sentiments have also in-cluded a campaign to get Russians living in Estonia to learn Estonian at school. More significant are recent secret directives to step up the teaching of Russian. But nationalism is not far beneath the surface. At Tartu university, founded in 1632, there have been several student demonstrations. In recent years there have been several petitions by intellectuals over the language question and a virtual riot broke out among students and young people after a football match in 1981. The older generation looks back with nostalgia to the pre-war days, though the only records on public display of the 'bourgeois period', as the twenty years of independence are officially known, are of the under-ground activities of the small communist party. Any depiction of that time as something other than a deviation from the 'historic' Baltic destiny of union with Russia is considered anti-Soviet and therefore criminal.

All three Baltic states have always been at the mercy of their neighbours, and Latvia, to the south of Estonia, has had an equally chequered history. This is succinctly summed up in the different names given this century to the main street in Riga, the capital. Until the Revolution it was called Alexander Street; during the short-lived independent republic it was called Freedom Street; in 1941 it became Adolf Hitler Street; and after the war it was renamed Lenin Street.

The Germans were the first invaders. The Knights of the Sword, as the Teutonic knights were known, conquered the Baltic shores under the guise of converting the pagans in the thirteenth century. Bishop

Albert began a mighty cathedral in Riga in 1211 – which took 500 years to comlete – and the city became a member of the Hanseatic League. Then Riga fell under Polish domination, followed by the capture by the Swedes in the seventeenth century. It was wrested from them by Peter the Great and incorporated in the Russian Empire until 1919. And now the Russians are back.

Each wave has left its mark on the city's architecture, and what survives of the old centre is a hotch-potch of styles. The Germans set the tone and for years dominated culture and commerce. In 1899 they constituted almost half the population compared with 23 per cent Latvians. During those boom years, Riga was a smart and over-whelmingly German city within the Russian Empire. Solid, imposing blocks were erected to house the stock exchange, the first travel agency – Thomas Cook and Sons – the labour exchange and the opera (where Wagner spent a year as principal conductor). These monuments to bourgeois prosperity now serve more Soviet functions, and look rather forlorn and shabby. Unlike Tallinn, Riga is still waiting for its facelift. A master plan exists to turn the cobbled alleys and little courtyards into a tourist paradise of boutiques and cafés, but so far little has been done.

It has been enough of a job to repair the ravages of the Nazi occupation, which left half a million Latvians dead and virtually wiped out Riga's once thriving Jewish community. After the war the factories were rebuilt and the planners established new industry. This is now seen as a mistake by nationalist Latvians for, as in Estonia, labour was brought in from all corners of the Soviet Union to fill the new jobs. Russians, Ukrainians, Belorussians flooded into Riga because of the higher standard of living, and brought Russification in their wake. When the non-Latvian population reached 800,000 out of a total of only 2,500,000 in all Latvia, further immigration was stopped.

Riga, like Moscow and Leningrad, is now a restricted city requiring a residence permit. No new industry has been allowed in the capital, and the planners are trying to shift factories to other parts of the republic. The great influx has left Riga looking more like an ordinary Soviet city than most other places in the Baltic republics. More Russian is spoken more fluently than in any other non-Russian part of the country. And every year thousands of tourists from all over the Soviet Union head for the golden beaches of the Latvian coast.

A high proportion of foreign tourists consists of émigrés returning to see their families – 47 out of 200 groups before the Olympics – but numbers have been limited by a lack of hotel space. In 1970 Intourist began a grandiose 700-bed hotel to solve the problem. But the stark skyscraper, plumped in the middle of the medieval city, was soon becalmed in bureaucratic bickering and its constantly receding target date for completion became a local joke. Brochures were printed telling tourists of the wonderful view from the restaurant on the twenty-seventh floor, but until 1980 no tourist could set foot in the unfinished building to have a look for himself.

Latvians have no love for the big, blue box-structure that maddeningly outdoes by three feet the elegant thirteenth-century steeple, 380 feet of late Gothic architecture, of St Peter's church. Still, as one guide remarked, at least the building timetable was in the tradition of Bishop Albert's ancient cathedral. That cathedral was used by the Lutheran Church until the Soviet state took it over as a monument in the 1950s. It contains one of the world's most renowned organs, a magnificent 6,768-pipe structure built by German craftsmen in 1884 and still one of the largest in the world. The Nazis had it dismantled to take to Germany, but retreated before they could do so. It was rebuilt and then restored in 1961, and in 1982 underwent another major overhaul. The cathedral aisles can hold more than 1,000 people for the famous organ concerts which draw capacity crowds.

The Lutherans still have eighteen working churches in Riga. Services are in Latvian and the Church is strongly identified with Latvian culture. The Lutherans have a seminary in Riga training forty clergy, five of whom were women in 1980. Bishop Matulis ordained the first two women clergy in the late seventies without, he maintained, any controversy with the Church. They are both now working in country districts where, because of the shortage of clergy, each holds a service in three different parishes.

Latvia is the point where East, West and South meet in religion. The Russian Orthodox Church, 80 per cent of whose attenders are Russians, and the Roman Catholic Church, which ministers to the Polish minority, are approximately equal in strength, with fourteen Orthodox and sixteen Catholic churches in Riga open for services. All those I visited one Sunday morning were full.

The Roman Catholics also have a seminary in Riga with thirty students – not enough, according to Monsignor Wilhelm Nukš, the vicar-general of the main Catholic church, but a compromise figure accepted by both the Church and the atheist Soviet state. The Russian Orthodox Church also has a convent beside the main cathedral. The fifty nuns range in age from twenty-four to ninety, and Latvia is still grateful to them for saving the lives of 100 children during the war by buying them out of the Nazi concentration camps.

The war wrought greatest destruction on the Jewish population. All the synagogues were destroyed, and only one was rebuilt afterwards. That now serves a Jewish community of under 28,000 (in 1970 there were 37,000 but emigration has reduced that figure). Before Passover the cellar of the synagogue bustles with activity turning out matzo, unleavened bread. I saw twenty-five people engaged in the ritual baking under the watchful eye of Rabbi Samuel Gureyvich. Flour for the matzo is bought from the state, and parcels of the flat, crispy bread are sent to Tallinn, where there is also a small Jewish community but no bakery. From the beginning of January until Passover the synagogue bakes about thirty tons of matzo, which sells for about a rouble a pound.

Many Jews in Riga still speak Yiddish, a language that has practically died out in other parts of the Soviet Union, where Jews now mostly speak Russian. The community gets financial help and prayer books from Canada and the United States, but religious observance among the young is declining. There are only about five bar-mitzvahs a year.

Like Tallinn, Riga is a window on the West, as it has traditionally been. The republic has taken the lead in many social questions, and experiments are possible here which would not be countenanced elsewhere. At the end of the Brezhnev era it was in Latvia that a few cautious attempts were made to liberalize the economic system, with the encouragement of private enterprise in such areas as restaurants and garages. Clothes are brighter than in Russia, living standards higher, art and theatre more innovative. One of the great Soviet ballet dancers, Maris Liepa, comes from Riga, and the city's ballet school still trains those who go on to reach the top.

Latvians are proud of their esoteric language and individual traditions. They boast that the overnight train to Moscow – the 'Latvija' – is the best in the country. Certainly, it is a surprise to have fried eggs brought to one's compartment in the early morning. But even the train is becoming more Soviet. When a woman colleague tested the famed beauty salon on board, she found it locked. 'It's self-service now,' the carriage attendant explained. 'If you want to bring your own make-up and equipment you can use the room, but we don't have anyone to work here.'

More than a thousand miles to the south-east of Riga another city is also becoming more Soviet. Tashkent, the capital of Uzbekistan, is now the third largest city in the country, an increasingly important industrial and cultural centre. Yet only a few miles outside Tashkent you could be anywhere in the Middle East. Backgammon dice click against a background of Oriental music, fountains play in the town squares, the air is soft with the fragrance of roses mixed with dust and some less attractive smells, close-cropped children pleading for chewing-gum scamper after tourists and in vine-shaded courtyards old men sip green tea and recline on large, square beds.

Only the inevitable red and white slogans, statues of Lenin and grey and red uniforms of the police tell you immediately you are in Soviet territory. Uzbekistan, with its 14 million people, is where the Soviet system meets the Oriental way of life. This is the old frontier land of the Russian Empire, where only eighty years ago Russian colonial governors were just consolidating their hold on the Tsar's newly conquered territories in Central Asia. Uzbekistan was part of the larger Muslim region known as Turkestan. Emirs in three old cities – Khiva, Bukhara and Kokand – ruled in feudal splendour and backwardness. Runaway slaves were nailed by their ears to the city gates. The last public executioner in Khiva, who operated with a simple sabre, died after a long retirement – in 1967.

Tashkent does not have the historic associations or the gruesome history of the other large towns of the republic. Here all is new, planned, Soviet. The city was made the capital only in 1930 when the authorities found the monuments of Samarkand too constricting to allow future growth. And since the devastating earthquake of 1966, which razed the city centre, Tashkent is being cleared of the traditional mud daub buildings and transformed into a modern economic and administrative centre, with a new airport, tourist hotels and block upon block of high-rise flats.

The building boom shows no sign of stopping. Tashkent now has nearly 2 million people, and planners estimate another million by the end of the century. This is from natural increase not immigration from the countryside. Uzbekistan has one of the highest birthrates in the Soviet Union. The average family has seven children. But the city authorities, far from trying to curb this growth rate, are delighted. Tashkent, like other big cities, is short of labour.

There are pious hopes that some of the new generation will move north to Siberia where labour is more urgently needed. But nobody expects Uzbeks to leave their sunny climate for the frozen wastelands without powerful incentives. Indeed, it is hard enough to get them to move from the villages to the towns, and rural under-employment is quite a problem. The Uzbek party leaders are pressing Moscow hard to increase the fertility of the area, enabling them to support a larger population, by giving priority to the age-old scheme of diverting the Siberian rivers that flow north into the Arctic sea southwards into the parched lands of Central Asia. The project is still official policy, though the colossal sums involved and the doubts of scientists and environmentalists make it increasingly unlikely that it will be realized.

Cotton remains king in Uzbekistan. In Tashkent and all over the republic the targets for the valuable crop are emblazoned on the sides of buildings, strung across the roads or hung over the entrances to collective farms. Record harvests in the early eighties, that look even better by comparison with the country's dismal grain crops, have boosted the prestige of Uzbek agriculture and the fortunes of the republic's party chief, Sharaf Rashidov. It is said Uzbekistan could make a fortune growing fruit and vegetables if it were allowed to. But central planners have decreed that cotton is more valuable – it is an important export to the West – and field upon field blossoms in the warm autumn. Despite healthy statistics boasting the use of mechanical harvesters, old women can still be seen laboriously gathering the precious fluff. In all the collective farms, picturesquely named 'Marx', 'Engels', 'Lenin', 'Communist', and so on, vast white stacks the shape of houses wait for transport to the cotton gins.

Though industry has grown, the more recent boom is in tourism. Uzbekistan has a wealth of Islamic monuments which are worth their weight in foreign currency. Though the summer is fearsomely hot, this does not deter British and American tour groups, who make Tashkent the jumping-off point for a Central Asian tour. The Japanese, one guide observed, more sensibly prefer the spring. The Germans come all year round.

The best time is really the autumn. In mid-October the temperature is still in the upper 20s centigrade and the markets are full of ripe melons. The problem is that all Russians know this, and it is almost impossible to find an aircraft seat from Moscow on any flight south. The autumn is also prime conference time. When Moscow is cold and rainy, international symposia need no persuasion to adjourn to Tashkent. There are at least half a dozen a month in Central Asia – health scientists at Alma Ata, environmentalists in Turkmeniya, musicologists in Samarkand, molecular biologists or Afro-Asian writers in Tashkent. I remember seeing the Nobel prize-winners Dorothy Hodgkin and Linus

Pauling posing with a group of fellow scientists amid the blue-tiled monuments on their day off from scientific papers.

Uzbekistan was carved out of the old Asian empire as a homeland for those that speak Uzbek, a language akin to Turkish. But the peoples of this region are so mixed up that almost as many can be found who speak Tadzik, more related to Farsi, and other Asiatic languages. In Bukhara, a town of 165,000, there are eighty different nationalities. Russians swarmed south in a wave of emigration earlier, and Russian is much in evidence in Tashkent. It is also the language to learn if you want to get ahead. But many of the Russians, some third generation inhabitants of Tashkent, are now leaving. Some are going north to Siberia, others to areas where there are more jobs. Many find that as a new technically-minded generation of Uzbeks grows up, there is less and less need for the skilled Russian in the economy. Of course, Moscow-appointed Russians still hold the key jobs in the party or the security apparatus. But, unlike America, there is no brain-drain south to the sunbelt: the movement is the other way.

Uzbekistan does not demonstrate the fierce nationalism of Armenia or Estonia, perhaps because the contrast between the feudal past and the present Soviet way of life is so much more striking, and social progress more measurable. Nationalism at present takes on the more acceptable form of intense pride in past Islamic glories, and restoration of ancient monuments is now in full swing. Nowhere is this more evident than in Samarkand, a city, like Petra, that is for ever fixed in people's minds by a single quotation. But the Golden Road to Samarkand is filled now not with pilgrims but with tourists, who come to the city of Tamerlaine to see the mausoleums and monuments of the man who inspired awe even in far-away Elizabethan England.

A glittering city awaits them. Nearly six pounds of gold were used to restore the inner dome of Tamerlaine's tomb, and colossal sums have been allocated to another dome in the city centre. In Bukhara, a million roubles a year is being set aside to preserve the mosques and madrasahs (Islamic theological training colleges), and another 5 million is due to be spent reconstructing the old market place. In the most ambitious project of all, some 14 million roubles will be spent until 1985 to rebuild, almost from scratch, the huge Bibi Khanum mosque, now under Unesco protection, which has been devastated by successive earthquakes.

Since 1972 Samarkand has had a special school concentrating on ancient architecture, Arabic, Persian, tiling, woodwork and other restoration techniques. Some 400 pupils follow a diploma course and the city now has eighty-six master builders and ninety restorers who are at work on the fifty-four monuments now being rebuilt. In Bukhara 180 specialists are employed in restoration workshops. Some techniques have been rediscovered only recently – the secret composition of the oxides used for the ubiquitous blue glazed tiles being the most valuable. Some of the money comes from Moscow, but much more from the government of Uzbekistan.

But Samarkand is not just a monument to a vanished empire. It is a thriving modern city, whose youth is as intent on modern pursuits as anywhere else. You can see them on Saturday nights in the main tourist hotel, dancing to the throbbing beat of a local band, wearing tight jeans, high-heeled boots and sporting gaudy T-shirts. In Moscow they dance to the Boney M song 'Ra, Ra, Rasputin', which has the added attraction of dwelling on a subject still politically sensitive. In Uzbekistan in 1981 they had discovered the exact equivalent, and the band belted out fortissimo the risqué number: 'Gen, Gen, Genghis Khan'.

I found the incongruity extraordinary. For generations old men in turbans and long striped robes had told their grandchildren of the ravages of the Mongol invader and the destruction wrought by the hordes of the mighty khan. For 200 years the heirs of Genghis Khan held the Russians, today's rulers of Central Asia, in abject thrall. Tass, echoing old Russian prejudices, has denounced China for attempting to build up Genghis Khan as a national hero of the Oriental peoples.

Yet there they were, the heirs of Tamerlaine, drinking Soviet brandy, wearing the latest fashions obtained from planeloads of Western tourists, throwing themselves about while the band, with drooping moustaches and garish shirts, reproduced the hit tunes of the German group Genghis Khan. I wondered what the local party bosses made of it all.

They were probably perfectly happy. The crazes of modern youth might seem unseemly to their conservative minds, and certainly smack of the West, but at least they were more acceptable than the current concerns of young people 200 miles to the south in neighbouring Iran and Afghanistan. The attractions of European youth culture are less threatening than Muslim fundamentalism. But Islam, scorned by the atheistic publications that fill the shelves of any bookshop, is increasingly making its presence felt. The younger generation, ambitious, educated and materialistic, may seem to be going the way Atatürk hoped his people would go in Turkey, pulling away from the old customs towards the urban societies of the industrialized north. But young people are becoming curious about their past. And month after month turbaned dignitaries from the Middle East are escorted round the few working mosques and shrines, persuaded by their hosts that Soviet Muslims enjoy full rights and equality, while reminding the local inhabitants that Islam has become a force the Russians have now to reckon with – at least abroad.

Take a plane 1,000 miles north and you are in another world – Siberia. The very name inspires awe and dread. Both to the Russians and to foreigners it conjures up a vast frozen wasteland, a place of exile and punishment, a remote region of endless winter. But to today's planners and economists it has also come to mean the Russian El Dorado: a land of boundless natural wealth, a vast unexploited reserve of gold, coal, oil, iron ore and almost every natural resource needed for the future development of the Soviet Union.

What lies beneath the permafrost could make the Soviet Union the richest country in the world. It is the challenge of how to exploit this potential that still inspires awe. For thousands of years Siberia has been isolated, challenging man with its harshness and vastness, and there is still a brash, tough, frontier spirit among those who live in a region that covers more than 6 million square miles. The Siberians are proud of their endurance: 'A hundred kilometres is no distance. Minus 40 degrees is no frost,' they say.

It was, of course, the railways that opened up this mysterious land to the modern world and led to the founding of today's unofficial capital of the whole region. In 1893 the Russian engineers building the Trans-Siberian railway came to the mighty river Ob, the fourth largest river in the world. They built a bridge across it and on its east bank a station and a town, which was named Novonikolayevsk in honour of the new Tsar, Nicholas II. Ninety years later this town has become a city of almost a million and a half, spilt over on to the other bank of the Ob, and has a post-revolutionary name – Novosibirsk.

Though farther from Moscow than London is, Novosibirsk is still considerably less than halfway across the Trans-Siberian railway from the Soviet capital to Vladivostok. The busy, modern city belies the popular image of Siberia as a land of forest and *taiga*, mosquitos and fir-trees, salt mines and labour camps. The original wooden houses are all gone, and the remaining few threatened with the bulldozer. Novosibirsk today is a city of trams and trolley-buses, broad tree-lined boulevards, parks, squares and modern blocks of flats. By Soviet standards it would do credit to European Russia west of the Urals, and you have a curious feeling that after all the travelling you have really gone no distance at all from Moscow. Its inhabitants often compare it to Chicago – 'but we grew faster,' they say.

To an outsider the most striking thing is the climate. In summer the temperature can soar to 40 degrees centigrade. But in winter it drops to minus 35 and sometimes touches minus 50 – an incredible range of 90 degrees. In summer the Siberians flock to the banks of the Ob to fish or sunbathe. Locals claim they enjoy more sunshine than the traditional holiday resorts on the Black Sea, but in winter the Ob is covered with six feet or more of ice and you venture out at your peril. No city so far south in the world – Novosibirsk is on the same latitude as Carlisle – is so cold.

The inhabitants like it cold, and after three days there I could see why. The sky is deep blue, the sun shines and the climate is bracing. It is far nicer than Moscow where a warm spell in winter means continual slush and outbreaks of flu. And the cold also gives each citizen a home-made deep-freeze: outside every window you can see bags of food hanging in the frost until needed. Nevertheless, it is cold for the uniformed children who take turns guarding the eternal flame, changing every fifteen minutes and marching away, machine-guns on their arms, with the peculiarly chilling and depressing slow goose-step. Novosibirsk was too far from the wartime front to suffer attack, but 3,000 people went off to fight and did not come back.

The only real fighting there went on during the Civil War, when the city was occupied by the White army of Admiral Kolchak and then retaken by the Reds during that confusing campaign fought almost entirely up and down the Trans-Siberian railway. There is, of course, an appropriate memorial to the Red martyrs butchered by the Whites, and the guides expect a suitably partisan reaction to their tales of White terror.

Siberia is crucial to the Soviet Union's economic future, and Novosibirsk, as the capital, plays a central role. Though younger by some 200 years than other towns like Irkutsk and Tobolsk, Novosibirsk has outstripped them all. It lies in rich farming land and is also an important industrial and transport centre. A train passes through the station once every four minutes. Ships carry goods more than 1,000 miles down the Ob to the towns and regions of the north.

But the real key to Siberian development lies twenty miles to the south amid picturesque birch groves – Akademgorodok, a purpose-built town to house hundreds of the country's most illustrious brains. Here scientists and economists, under the aegis of the important Siberian branch of the Soviet Academy of Sciences, mastermind the future of the Siberian virgin lands, test the colossal development projects, and supervise the building of a second Siberian railway – already half built – or the reversal of the Siberian rivers to flow south to the deserts of Central Asia.

The community was founded in 1958, in the heady days of the post-Stalin thaw, and by all accounts was an exciting place. Young scientists, lured from the western part of the country by good salaries and a relaxed life-style, could start everything afresh, order any Western journals and books, join clubs that bubbled over with ideas and argument. Some of the steam has gone out of the place as the brightest and the best were enticed back to Moscow to other top jobs, and those remaining simply stayed on and grew older. The noted liberalism was curbed, some of the clubs were closed down and the experimental feel to the place gave way to institutionalism.

But Akademgorodok still has a pleasant campus atmosphere. Even the standard block of flats looks tidier, better kept. The local restaurant is rather like a faculty club, the schools educate some of the brightest children in the region, most of the researchers have been abroad, and there is a curious sense that this small township, buried in the snow thousands of miles from the old centres of West European culture, is more closely in touch with what is going on in New York, Paris or London than most other places in Russia.

Certainly culture has a good showcase in Novosibirsk. An immense opera house, built during the war in lavish classical style, can seat 2,000 people and has one of the better ballet companies in the Soviet Union. The art treasures were evacuated there from Moscow during the war. There is not much to see in the way of old churches however – only a couple of wooden Russian Orthodox churches built before the Revolution, a synagogue and a Baptist prayer house. The guide seemed proud of the fact: 'Novosibirsk is a city of youth, a city of atheists,' she proclaimed.

Technically, Siberia stops short of the regions bordering the Pacific coast, which are known as the Soviet Far East, though most foreigners think of it extending from the Urals all the way to the sea. Foreigners are increasingly common in Siberia as tourism there gets going, but so far only five cities are open for package tourists as much of Siberia is either inaccessible or closed to foreigners.

Though Siberia is very Russian (Novosibirsk's population is 95 per cent Russian, and virtually none of the population of Central Asia has emigrated north), it is so vast, so still, so strange – rather like a desert – that it is impressive even to Russians used to vast distances. And the winter really is the best time. As the old Russian proverb says: 'In Siberia the winter lasts twelve months, the rest is summer.'

Siberia is as big as a continent and still forms only part of the Russian republic. By contrast Armenia, tucked away in the mountains on the Turkish border, appears only as a small dot on the Soviet map. But this smallest republic is like a precious pinch of salt that gives flavour to the whole country. Armenians have a tragic history. Following the Turkish massacres they were forcibly dispersed from their homeland and are now scattered all over the world. Soviet Armenia is the truncated portion of the historic area of settlement, and does not include Mount Ararat, the legendary mountain that is a national symbol. The mountain is clearly visible from Yerevan, the Armenian capital only a few miles from the Turkish frontier. It hovers tantalisingly in the air, the base obscured by mist, the snow-capped peak shimmering, for ever unobtainable. The mountain appears on the Armenian flag, and Turkey once formally objected to what it saw as a Soviet claim on Turkish territory. Back came the reply: 'You have a crescent on your flag. Does this mean you are laying claim to the moon?'

In spite of – or perhaps because of – the repeated persecution the Armenians have suffered, they are a quick, lively, witty people. Almost every Soviet joke features an Armenian, and Radio Yerevan has become such a well-known formula for political jokes that the Armenians have a difficult time convincing people they do in fact have a serious broadcasting service.

One of the oldest Christian communities in the world, the Armenians have historically always looked to the Russians, their co-religionists, to protect them against their Muslim neighbours to the south and east. But they are essentially a Mediterranean people – black-haired, olive-skinned, hospitable, wine-drinking, southern in temperament and outlook – and have little in common with the Slavs, though many of the most talented have made their names and careers in the society of their northern neighbours: perhaps the Mikoyans are the most famous and influential family in post-revolutionary times. Though flung all over the world, they have a strong attachment to their barren, mountainous homeland, hot in summer and bitterly cold in winter. And this attachment is symbolized and fostered by the Armenian Church. It has its seat at Echmiadzine, not far from Yerevan, and gifts from Armenian communities in the United States and Western Europe testify to the importance of the Church's role in holding together the Armenian nation across political frontiers.

These frontiers are perhaps easier for Armenians to cross than any others in the Soviet Union, for Armenians have always been something of a special case. Even Stalin recognized the strength of their links with the outside world. He tried to persuade all the diaspora to immigrate back to their homeland, and after the war thousands returned from Lebanon and the Middle East and the West. They were encouraged to bring their wealth with them, and allowed to build private houses. But the movement was all one-way. Now many of these post-war immigrants are streaming out again. Indeed, while Jewish emigration has fallen dramatically in recent years, the trickle of Armenians going West – especially to Los Angeles – has become a steady stream.

Even those who stay at home know more of the outside world than most Soviet citizens. Every year thousands of Armenians from overseas come to visit relatives in Armenia. Until the fighting of recent years, there was a weekly flight from Yerevan to Beirut. And many Lebanese Armenians fled to the Soviet Union for some months during the 1975 civil war to escape the violence and chaos. As a result, Armenia, a republic with fewer inhabitants of other nationalities than any other in the Soviet Union, is intensely aware of its position in the world, of its history and culture. It is no coincidence that one of the finest collections of ancient manuscripts, a unique record of a people and their past, is housed in the purpose-built manuscript museum in Yerevan, and each year new scrolls and documents are received from Armenians in the diaspora. Armenians who make their name in the West often make the pilgrimage to their homeland at some stage. Occasionally they insist their ashes be interred there.

One man in Armenia has done more than many others to foster the Armenians' sense of identity: Genrikh Igitian, the director of two galleries unique in the Soviet Union – the Children's Art Centre and the Museum of Contemporary Art. His mission, supported at the highest party level, is almost preposterous in its daring and ambition. He wants to make aesthetic education so fundamental to the life of each child in Armenia that in one generation the level of culture will surpass anything achieved before by this ancient people. Already the tiny republic is producing art of a vitality and originality that stands out in the country.

The art explosion began in March 1970, when a collection of the best paintings from local schools went on display in a former wine shop in the centre of Yerevan. The young artists were excited by the attention they received and strove to do better. Others took up brushes for the first time and sent in their works. Teachers came to see what other schools were doing and went back with new ideas. Igitian, the gallery director, travelled to distant mountain villages to persuade ten-year-olds to paint the life around them, and he began to collect paintings by children in other countries.

The centre now has one of the largest collections in the world. Themes from Armenian life and history fill the upper rooms: kings, churches, mountains and villages, battles and legends, bright market scenes, fierce-looking dogs and stern-faced teachers, painted by eight-year-olds with a vigour that enthralls. There are also collages made of matchsticks, puppets, tapestries and woven designs, masks and models. Downstairs, pictures from more than ninety countries show the world of children: families, friends and fables from Bulgaria to Peru, Greenland to Jordan. Schools in some countries such as West Germany have set up links with the museum. Pictures from France came from a travelling exhibition. Harold Wilson personally arranged the dispatch of 100 paintings by British children.

Genrikh Igitian has watched the improvement over ten years. 'You cannot find paints in the shops nowadays, such is the demand,' he says. Once a year the republic organizes open-air pavement painting, when every child draws with chalk on the roads. Luckily the Children's Art Centre has captured the imagination of the party secretary in Armenia. As a tenth anniversary present Igitian was given the rest of the block to turn into a theatre where children would themselves write, direct and act. A children's workshop is being built where the gifted will receive tuition in painting, ceramics, film production and other arts. Already the Centre and the Contemporary Art museum employ a large full-time staff.

Tragedy, national and personal, lies close to Igitian, and has sharpened his determination, flecked his black beard with grey and given his eyes a sad look. He does not forget Armenia's catastrophe at the hands of the Turks in 1915. He sees a reinvigorated culture as the only answer to the genocide. More poignantly, the museum displays the magnificent paintings his son Reuben did between the ages of eight and fourteen. In 1975, Reuben together with Igitian's wife and daughter were killed in an air crash. From that day on he gave his life to the Children's Art Centre.

'I need only ten more years,' he told me in 1981. In that time he wants to build a centre for aesthetic education that will be a model for the country. The government has promised him all the money he needs. He has ambitions for classical concerts, poetry readings, individual shows by eight-year-olds, pantomime, design and decoration. He sees the mission in almost cosmic terms: 'A person who loves Mozart will never kill another. This is how we can improve the world. Every child is talented, and it is we adults who are guilty for not bringing this out.'

It will be several years still before the child exhibitors of the 1970s establish reputations as mature artists. For the moment the Museum of Contemporary Art serves as the focus for those now active. Igitian says he will hang any picture, regardless of content, provided it is art. He decides what is art, and shoulders responsibility. Some Western visitors have called him a dictator, a term he resents. But he admits that one person must make decisions, as he does. He justifies the exclusion of anti-Soviet themes not only on grounds of common sense but also because this, he says, is propaganda, not art. Refreshingly, there is little obvious pro-Soviet propaganda on the gallery walls.

His vision of a rejuvenated Armenian culture is idealistic: harmony between government and intelligentsia, positive, healthy themes, freedom of expression. Already he has achieved a freedom and independence for art that is impossible in Moscow or Leningrad, where painters are bogged down in quarrels with censors and bureaucrats. But Armenia, as Armenians remind you, is a special case.

CHAPTER TWELVE

Religion under State Control

God is never far from a Russian's lips. 'The Lord be praised!' 'God forbid!' 'My God!' are expressions as common in Russian as in English. Even Brezhnev, on signing the Salt 2 arms treaty in Vienna, told President Carter that God would not forgive them if they let down the hopes of the world. Indeed God is not far from very many Russians' thoughts, for the Russians are a naturally religious people. The 'opiate of the masses' has almost as powerful a hold over the Russian soul – though by no means as visible a role in daily life – as it did when the early communists denounced religion and the political influence of the Russian Orthodox Church. In the past decade especially, religion of all kinds – Christianity, Islam and Judaism – has been making its presence increasingly felt in the Soviet Union. And the authorities have reacted with a mixture of concern, caution and calculation to a revival that has important political and ideological consequences, at home and also abroad.

Nothing perhaps is more essential to the Russian outlook, to Russian values and feeling than Russian Orthodoxy. And the Russian Orthodox Church, still one of the world's largest and most influential divisions of Christianity, is the repository of Russian history and culture, the institution that has moulded so much of today's atheistic state in its likeness. In 1988 the Church will celebrate its millenium and mark the thousandth anniversary of the decision by Prince Vladimir of Kiev to embrace the religion of Byzantium and establish Orthodox Christianity as the religion of the Russian-speaking people.

More than sixty years have passed since the Bolshevik revolution inaugurated a period of unparalleled persecution and militant atheism. Yet the Church is now witnessing a remarkable revival. Young people are turning in thousands to the religion of their forefathers, as the Church, decimated by purges under Stalin and Khrushchev, is slowly coming back from the abyss.

No one knows how many believing Christians there are in the Soviet

Union today. The Russian Orthodox Church does not count its members, or keep written records of the children it baptises. The clergy
refuse to give figures, saying belief is a matter between the individual
and God – a sensibly cautious attitude in a country where some 10
million people are still engaged in the state-supported struggle to
enforce scientific atheism. Occasional official estimates, however, and
statistics in atheistic publications suggest some 15 to 20 per cent of the
adult population are believers, giving a total of around 32 million people.
Apart from a few Roman Catholics and Lutherans in the Baltic
republics, and some 500,000 Baptists, mainly in the Ukraine, most
Christian believers look to the Russian Orthodox Church.

Today this Church is sadly diminished from its former glory. In
Tsarist days there were 57,000 priests, helped by 94,000 monks and
nuns in 54,174 churches and 1,025 monasteries and convents. Today
there are only a few thousand priests serving about 7,500 churches.
There are three remaining seminaries (two with higher theological
colleges attached to them), fifteen convents and only three monasteries.
In every village of Russia there used to be a church, but almost invariably
it is now a ruin, left to decay or turned into a storage dump for steel
girders and other such mundane products of this material world. In a
few cases, where the cupolas are particularly beautiful or the fanciful
architecture especially striking, the state has declared the church a
national monument, and it has been kept in decent repair. But otherwise
the churches lie rotting, unattended, the rafters collapsing, the interiors
stripped, rooks nesting in the forlorn structures.

This decline is the result of direct repression by the state, principally
during the first twenty years after the Revolution when the new regime
tried to extinguish religion altogether. It was also hastened by Khrushchev, a man now revered in the West (though not at home) for the
liberalisation he brought to other spheres of Soviet life. The communists fought against the Church so vigorously because of its close
identification with the Tsarist regime and the important role it played in
the old empire – a role, the Bolsheviks maintained with some justification, that invariably sided with the ruling classes and did little to improve
the lot of the peasants and the poor.

Under Stalin thousands of priests were executed, churches were
closed and by 1939 only four bishops and 100 churches could function
in the whole country. But the war brought a sudden change. Stalin used
the Church to help rally support for the struggle against the Nazi
invaders. Some 25,000 churches were reopened and the number of

priests reached 33,000. New regulations were drawn up defining the legal position of believers, which were extremely circumscribed but gave the Church a tenuous basis on which to exist.

Today the legal position of religion is laid down in the 1977 Soviet constitution. Article 52 guarantees each citizen freedom of conscience, and the 'right to profess any religion or to profess none, to celebrate religious rites, or to conduct atheistic propaganda'. The same article also states that the Church is separate from state and school. Soviet officials and Church leaders themselves maintain that this article gives the Church an independence to conduct its own affairs that it did not enjoy before. In theory this is true. But the practice of religion in the Soviet Union nowadays is hedged around with all kinds of administrative barriers, and while the Church is forbidden to proselytize or carry its message to the world, the state gives positive encouragement in a hundred different ways to militant atheists.

An article of the penal code prescribes imprisonment of up to five years and the confiscation of property for any believing Russian who encroaches on the rights of citizens under the guise of performing religious rites. Nevertheless, in recent years the Church has found a way of accommodating itself to the legal framework. The state officially stands aside – though in fact keeps a close watch on all religious activity. The Council for Religious Affairs, which has the authority of a ministry, is responsible for administering the laws on religion. It is the same secular organization to which the Russian Orthodox Church, together with Baptists, Jews, Muslims and Buddhists, must refer in any question concerning the opening or closing of churches, the repair of church buildings, disputes with local authorities and the holding of church conferences.

For the authorities, the Council is a vitally important body. It has to hold the balance between the need to prevent organized religion offering any opposition to the militant atheism of the state, and the need to ensure the Church serves the aims of the state, especially its foreign policy. On the surface, the Council maintains good relations with religious leaders and projects an image of harmony to the world. Behind the scenes the Council leaves the Church in no doubt that if it ever attempts to overstep its severely limited role, even the freedoms it now enjoys will be removed.

Many harsh restrictions, passed during the vitriolic Khrushchev campaign against the Church in the early sixties, still remain secret. But since his downfall things have stabilized. Few churches have been arbitrarily closed – although bulldozers have demolished buildings erected by believers in the provinces. The public taunting of worshippers at Christmas and Easter services has stopped. Some of the niggling regulations designed to make life difficult for the Church have been replaced. And the Council has on rare occasions intervened on behalf of the Church when over-zealous local authorities have caused international embarrassment by preventing legally registered Christian communities carrying out their functions.

According to the law, a church may function if twenty responsible parishioners can be registered as a parish council that can maintain a church building and pay the salary of a priest. On registration, a community will be allowed to use a church building, though the land still belongs to the state. In towns these conditions pose no problem: services are always crowded, and during saints' days and at Easter the throng is so dense that the police are needed to prevent accidents in the crush (their presence, of course, also ensures that many young people are afraid to try to go to the services). The big working cathedrals of Kiev, Vladimir, Odessa and other old cities are sumptuously decorated and well maintained, but there are few of them: Leningrad with a population of 4 million has only four working churches. Moscow with 8 million is better off with fifty churches.

But in the countryside many rural parishes are suffering from the flight from the land. Small congregations cannot support the upkeep of the remaining churches often in need of extensive repair, and the law does not allow richer parishes to come to the aid of the weaker ones. If the structure becomes dangerous or the congregation of believers cannot guarantee a priest a minimum salary, the church has to be closed.

Most of Russia's famous churches have already been turned into state museums – or museums of atheism – including St Isaac's cathedral in Leningrad and the ancient complex of churches in Moscow's Kremlin. The state has the right to step in and declare a church a national architectural monument, in which case it will provide for its upkeep. But, except in isolated instances, such state protected buildings no longer serve as places of worship.

To be in a working Russian church immediately gives you a sense of eternal Russia, and makes it clear why the beauty and ritual, the sense of history and continuity hold such appeal for young people seeking spiritual truths beyond the drabness and cynicism of modern life. I vividly remember the midnight service at Suzdal on Christmas Eve: the moon glittering on the fresh snow, the decorated wooden houses looking warm and bright in the freezing night, worshippers streaming out of the white-washed church as the bells rang out the Christmas message. The date was January 6, as the Russian Church never changed the calendar after the Revolution as the rest of the country did. Christmas Day therefore falls on December 25 Old Style.

Suzdal, 160 miles east of Moscow, is one of the most beautiful of all old Russian settlements. Now a sleepy market town of only 15,000 people, it was briefly and gloriously the capital of ancient Russia before the rise of Muscovy, and its thirteenth-century splendour is still seen in some of the fifty churches that cluster round the old market place, the disused monastery and the ancient Kremlin fortress. As a parish Suzdal now falls under the sway of its long-time rival Vladimir, a large industrial town some twenty miles away. But until 1929 Suzdal had its own bishop and before the Revolution its onion-domed churches were thronged.

For the Russian Orthodox Church Christmas does not hold the same significance as Easter. But there were still plenty of worshippers in the five-domed square church. The congregation of about 200 were packed in suffocating closeness, mainly old women, in black shawls and head-scarves muffling wrinkled, harsh faces that showed a lifetime of struggle and suffering. They chanted the responses in quavering voices, shuffling about in their heavy felt boots and crossing themselves frequently before the many icons with their rows of burning candles.

Father Valentine, a large warm-hearted man with a fine, deep voice, was clearly a popular priest. He personally supervised the reconstruction of the two working churches – one used mainly in summer, the other in winter – the transfer of the icons and other valuables from the smaller dilapidated church on the market square that has now been closed, the installation of central heating and the carving of church furniture by master craftsmen. His own house, a finely crafted wooden dwelling in the traditional style, reflected the comfort and refinement in which many priests now live, with his own valuable collection of icons and ancient church literature, rich carpets and simple, traditional furniture. By profession he was a cook before he received his calling, and his hospitality is overwhelming: in no other house have I tasted such magnificent Russian cooking, which he stayed up until late in the night preparing.

On Christmas morning I attended the service in the twelfth-century cathedral in Vladimir, another ancient city in the 'Golden Ring' of historical settlements around Moscow. Here the congregation was far larger, pressed together in the oldest continuously working Russian church which contains the priceless paintings of Andrei Rublyov, the icon master whose works celebrate the Russians' victory over the Tatars. There were no hooligans to jeer the worshippers on Christmas day. But the old people inside, all far shorter than any other Russian crowd I have been in, are ever suspicious of young believers whom they appear almost to resent. There were sharp glances, muttered complaints at the sight of foreigners they felt would ignore the hallowed rituals. Amid all the jostling and shoving, it was rather like being on a Russian bus.

It was never a Christmas tradition in Russia to exchange gifts. Instead godchildren sang carols to their godparents, groups of girls on Christmas Eve and boys in the early morning. Priests and godparents were given a traditional dish of rice and wheat, nuts and a jug of home-brewed mead. Father Valentine still serves the same to his Christmas guests. For priests and observant believers Christmas marks the end of a forty-day fast, when the Orthodox are forbidden to eat fats, meat or eggs. In Suzdal there are also monuments to more strictly enforced fasts. An old monastery, disbanded in 1918, was used for many years until 1905 as a prison for dissident clergy. Some were shut in the tiny cells, now part of a museum, for over forty years, and the Father Superior had the double task of head warden as well as leader of the monastery. The last notable prisoner in this fortress where Peter the Great imprisoned his first wife was the German field-marshal von Paulus, who was held there after his defeat at Stalingrad.

Though intensely conservative in dogma and mystic ritual, and maintaining a traditional aloofness from the daily lives of its congregation, the Russian Orthodox Church has accommodated itself in subtle ways to the twentieth century. The training of priests, for example is now more thorough and in tune with the realities of Soviet life. The three seminaries are in Leningrad, Odessa – the summer residence of the Patriarch – and Zagorsk, the spiritual centre of the Church and now a prime tourist attraction some thirty miles from Moscow. The seminaries train about the same numbers that seven seminaries used to educate before four were closed in the Khrushchev era.

Competition to get in is fierce, despite the odium poured on religion in every school and by the Komsomol. All applicants have to have finished their secondary education and to prove their spiritual commitment. The syllabus is heavy, the hours long and recreation restricted. The courses, a curious blend of religious studies and normal Soviet higher education, are controlled by a church education board, and in the

Odessa seminary the director of studies, a lively tousle-haired priest, insisted the Church had never prepared its servants so thoroughly before. Seminarists learn Old Church Slavonic as well as the history of the USSR. They read the Bible and the copies of *Pravda* and *Izvestia* that lie around on tables in the library. They watch films and television as well as officiating at services. I noticed when I went there in 1979 that on one wall of the refectory were portraits of bishops and patriarchs, on the other those of Lenin, Brezhnev and Kosygin. Doubtless those last two have now been updated.

Every year the best are sent to Zagorsk, where they can pursue higher theological studies. On graduation seminarists must chose whether to become monks – in which case they take vows of chastity and may advance up the Church hierarchy, eventually eligible to become bishops – or they can become parish priests, in which case they are obliged to get married. Married priests in the Orthodox Church cannot rise to positions of ecclesiastic power.

Every year about twelve of the Odessa seminarists are sent out to serve in the parishes. But not all those who become monks are able to enter the few remaining monasteries in the Soviet Union. One of these is beside the Odessa seminary. Founded in 1824, it is in a quiet, idyllic setting beside the sea. When I visited it in 1979 it had forty-one monks ranging in age from twenty-four to ninety-five. It is self-supporting, growing its own food and imposing a traditional, closed regime. The convents in the Soviet Union also impose strict simplicity on the nuns, who lead quiet, traditional lives, having little to do with the society around them. Hospitality dictated that the Mother Superior provided a suitably generous breakfast for the group of foreign correspondents taken to a convent in the Ukraine by the Council for Religious Affairs, but I detected resentment at the intrusion from the stern-faced black-cowled women whose prayers were disturbed by Japanese cameramen. Nuns in some convents do however sometimes work in local hospitals or take part-time jobs as nurses. As with most clergy, they do not wear traditional habits outside their communities.

The Russian Orthodox Church depends for its finances entirely on donations and fees for marriages, burials, baptisms and special mention of the departed in prayers. The accounts are not published, but the Church is by no means poor. The minimum salary for a deacon in a country parish is 150 roubles – only slightly below the average Soviet agricultural wage. He receives free furnished housing, and as a matter of course can expect gifts, mainly of food, from parishioners. The rector of a seminary receives 350 roubles, and a bishop's salary is over 500, virtually the same as top salaries of leading Soviet officials.

For two decades until 1981 most of this salary disappeared in punitively high taxes, set at more than five times those paid by ordinary citizens. But the tax rates have now been brought into line with those paid by other Russians considered self-employed, such as artists and private artisans. The rate is still high, but priests are able to live well. The total income of the Church is hard to estimate. Some parishes in southern Russia and the Ukraine are rich, receiving over 200,000 roubles a year. The cathedral in Odessa, which supports six priests and four deacons, earns over 300,000 roubles (£212,000). Parishes in northern Russia and Siberia, more scattered and with fewer believers, are poorer. A typical parish at Ostyol, an ancient Ukrainian village about fifty miles from Kiev, earns 50,000 roubles a year, and the parish priest estimated there were about 5,000 believers in his flock. If each believer in the country donated on average 10 roubles a year, the Church's annual income would amount to around 300 million roubles – a colossal sum which does not seem out of keeping with the Church's apparent affluence.

Taxes, salaries and the upkeep of churches account for much of the money. One particularly harsh regulation however insists that any unspent money an individual church has in its savings bank account at the end of each year automatically goes to the state – thus making long-term savings and major repair works difficult. Nevertheless, the Church, forbidden by law to support any secular activities, contributes heavily to the Soviet peace fund, an organization giving unswerving support to government proposals on disarmament and détente. The Church also gives generously to occasional state emergency funds such as that set up after the disastrous Tashkent earthquake in 1966.

The Church has just built a sumptuous new publishing house at a cost of 2 million roubles, which has a conference hall boasting forty chandeliers – a veritable sign of affluence and standing for any ordinary Russian. Three editions of the Bible have been published in the past twenty-five years, and a monthly journal of the Moscow Patriarchate details the Church's public activities. The circulation is restricted to the clergy and other 'authorized' recipients. Near Moscow there is also a Church factory for manufacturing church plate, candles, wedding gowns, censers and other articles as well as commemorative medals and artifacts presented to overseas visitors. Not surprisingly – though somehow incongruously – this factory is run on the same lines as all others in the Soviet Union, with monthly 'plan' targets, production quotas and exhortations for greater output and quality.

No one pretends that relations between Church and state are easy, or that the practice of religion is as free as it is in most other countries. The party specifically forbids membership to anyone who is a believer. Young people who attend church regularly will find their career prospects suffer. As one Soviet official said: 'This is an atheist country, and the Church is still considered the ideological opposition.' But he said the state had a duty to allow people's religious needs to be satisfied – and that was why it allowed the continued training of priests and the limited activities of the Church. He said the state also had an interest in seeing that priests nowadays were properly educated: 'They understand the policy of our government and the situation of the Church. They are respected. It is better than having an ignorant villager serving as a priest. He might be a fanatic and cause difficulties for everyone.'

'Difficulties' have indeed occurred on many occasions when local priests have challenged the state limitations on religion, accusing senior figures in the Church of collaboration with the government in preventing the Church fulfilling its proper mission. Two well-known priests have been arrested on charges of anti-Soviet propaganda, though one, Father Dmitry Dudko, made a much publicized recantation and was allowed to resume his duties – under the watchful eye of the KGB. Another who refused to recant, Father Gleb Yakunin, was sentenced to ten years of exile and hard labour, and has staged a number of hunger strikes in his prison camp.

The Russian Orthodox Church, whose policy of not rocking the boat has prevented it from intervening on their behalf, has been gravely embarrassed by dissident clergy, both at home and abroad. Indeed the Church goes out of its way to demonstrate its loyalty to the regime. One parish priest in the Ukraine told me he saw no conflict between Marxism and Christianity. 'Marxism is a new interpretation of the Christian code. It is based on the Beatitudes. Christians believe that man should strive on earth for the kingdom of God, and Marxists strive for true communism.' It is not a view reciprocated by the party.

Patriarch Pimen, elected in 1971, frequently supports Soviet foreign policy initiatives and enjoins the faithful in his Christmas and Easter messages to back the Kremlin's 'policies of peace'. Russian Orthodox leaders, like those of other religious groups, have lent weight to Soviet campaigns against the neutron bomb or Nato's rearmament plans, and in 1982 the Patriarch called a conference of world religious leaders in

Moscow to 'save the sacred gift of life from nuclear catastrophe'. The conference was clearly intended to back the Kremlin line on disarmament, and Metropolitan Filaret of Minsk, the Church's 'foreign minister' and an ambitious man who obviously enjoys official favour, had hoped to produce at the end a communiqúe that heaped praise on Soviet disarmament initiatives and would be a welcome document in the propaganda battle for the hearts and minds of Western Christians. In fact a powerful American delegation of religious leaders, realizing that the conference was in danger of becoming a propaganda exercise (and much embarrassed by some fulsome remarks by the Rev Billy Graham on religious freedom in Russia) decided to do battle on the communiqué. They argued until late into the night, insisting on restoring balance by including a public welcome for President Reagan's readiness for arms negotiations, and in the end won their way. Interestingly, the Church leaders appeared exultant at this hard-line approach – obviously it had enabled them to return to the Council for Religious Affairs, which had had a large hand in drafting the communiqué, and report that the conference would break up in embarrassing acrimony if the concessions were not made. 'You have restored our own honour by your tough stance,' was the message clearly hinted by the Russians to the Americans – though of course never spelled out loud.

Nevertheless, abroad, the Church invariably takes a line wholly consistent with official Soviet policy. Increasingly there appears to be an unwritten bargain between Church and state to the effect that the Church will encourage allegiance to the state and its policies – a not unfamiliar role which it played wholeheartedly before the Revolution – and put forward the Soviet view in such bodies as the World Council of Churches, where it is extremely influential, in return for the opportunity to run its affairs relatively unhindered within the limits set.

Publicly the bargain works, though there are carefully concealed suspicions on both sides of the other's intentions. The Church cannot and does not approve of the unremitting campaign against religion, especially in schools, and resents the ban on religious education. The state, mindful of the Church's powers of survival, believes it is subtly trying to increase its influence and attract the allegiance of the young.

The fears of the atheists are well grounded. The Russian Orthodox Church has benefitted from the resurgence of interest in old Russian culture, in the movement to preserve historic monuments, in the general nostalgia for past glories. It is officially recognized as the fount of Russian culture, and its buildings as the quintessence of Russian art and architecture. The prominent role the Church played in history is acknowledged by cultural authorities and intellectuals who are turning to the Church as much to discover the country's roots as out of religious feeling.

This cultural attraction coincides with a resurgence of Russian, as opposed to Soviet, nationalism. Many ethnic Russians are concerned that their leading political and economic role in the country is being eclipsed by the increasing assertiveness and higher birthrates of other nationalities in the Soviet Union. They look to the Church for reassertion of the Russian element, for honour to the cultural and historic achievements of the Russians. As one senior official joked significantly: 'I'm an atheist, but I'm an Orthodox atheist.'

At the same time party officials, the press and ordinary people are worried by the consumerism, cynicism and lack of spiritual values among the young. The party of course still proclaims that communism offers the younger generation all they need. But there is a sneaking feeling even within the party that this is not so. And officials look with envious eyes at the Church's ability to attract support with its proclamation of traditional, unchanging spiritual values.

Certainly more young people are now seen in church than before, especially in areas where religion still has a strong hold, such as the Ukraine. The majority of worshippers are still old women – but atheists note resignedly that even those who are not believers become religious and start going to church after they pass the age of fifty. It was said that Nina Khrushchev, every Westerner's image of the Russian grandmother, began to attend church after her husband's death – a fitting revenge on the man who did so much to try to destroy religion.

The Church however makes no special efforts to attract the young or any concessions to modernism. Theologically the Russian Orthodox Church must rate as one of the most conservative in the world, and there is no hint of intellectual liberalism in the ruling hierarchy. Even bishops who worry that ancient ecclesiastical rules such as the long periods of fasting before Christmas, Easter and Ascension Day are impractical in the modern industrial world see no likelihood of any change. Only in its relations with other churches has the Orthodox Church shifted its position significantly in the past fifteen years. The anathema on the Old Believers, who broke away in a great schism in the seventeenth century, pronounced in 1667, was lifted in 1971. The Church has sought closer links with the Anglicans, and the present Archbishop of Canterbury has had extensive contacts with the Moscow Patriarchate. The uneasy relations with Soviet Baptists – strained because of the Baptists' successful proselytizing of Orthodox believers – and the historic rivalry with the Roman Catholics, especially in the Ukraine, have given way to more cordial, ecumenical relations.

Some of the attraction of the Orthodox Church for the young is merely modish: it has become rather fashionable among intellectuals to take an interest in religious art, music and ritual, to wear a cross and to go to church, especially at Easter, Christmas and on holy days. Like Western clothes and music, religious symbols have an element of the taboo, a hint of rebellion about them, which only increases their attraction. The party reacts now and then with predictable heavy-handed indignation. Regular diatribes in the papers denounce the wearing of crucifixes, especially by the young people who are clearly not believers but adorn themselves with large crosses as though a crucifix was an ordinary article of jewellery.

Pravda published the complaint of a woman who saw a young man of twenty-five walking down the street carrying a bag with a picture of Christ on one side and on the other a likeness of the Virgin Mary. The paintings were bright and provocative – 'just like an advertisement,' she complained. Another paper related how the Moscow police once stopped a young man with a suitcase and found he had ninety-nine T-shirts inside, each with a picture of Jesus painted on it. He was not a Christian convert, merely a sharp black market operator who knew where his market lay. He and his accomplices were sent to prison for four years for trading in Christ.

The officially encouraged institutes of atheism have been much vexed by this recent craze for crucifixes, for they see the phenomenon for what it indeed is – a symptom of the slackening of anti-religious propaganda. And, they note ruefully, while some people declare that crosses symbolize to them the invincibility of the Russian people, others, as one indignant professor of atheism wrote, 'have begun to find a certain beauty in faith itself'.

In response, atheist propagandists are urged to step up their work. Few people could maintain there is not enough anti-religious material. Every school pupil is indoctrinated in the foolishness of religion, and the Komsomol, to which most teenagers belong, enjoins 'scientific atheism' on all its members. Most bookshops have a wall of shelves denouncing religious observances, railing against Islamic customs or Christian belief. And the Knowledge (*Znaniye*) Society, which organizes political lectures for the public, has enthusiastic volunteers who will race to the scene of an outbreak of faith and attempt to spread the pure light of healthy disbelief.

The trouble is the propaganda and tactics of the state-supported campaign against religion are so crude as to be thoroughly unconvincing. One favourite ploy is to invent parallel secular customs to replace the cherished ancient religious feasts and festivals which still have much meaning for most Russians. Atheists suggest for example that infants be officially enrolled as Soviet citizens at a special 'Name Day' ceremony, where the young child receives a certificate and two friends of the family pledge themselves as his or her moral guardians. This, it is hoped, will eventually replace baptism, which the atheistic publication *Science and Religion* (*Nauka i Religia*) described as 'primitive, superstitious and unhealthy' but noted was still widely practised – in some areas a third of all babies were baptised.

In two republics with strong Roman Catholic traditions, Lithuania and the Ukraine, special commissions have been founded and elsewhere new posts of direct or of mass celebrations created to publicize such state ceremonies.

Recently the party has become impatient with the plodding lack of success by atheists to spread the message, and has held dozens of conferences to see how things could be improved. 'Spiritual liberation from the vestiges of the past and the moulding of a scientific-materialist world view is a noble task, but it's difficult and delicate. It's not enough only to destroy the believer's views -- we must demonstrate the advantages of the scientific world view,' a Lithuanian party secretary told the party's central committee in 1982. Teachers should do more to make atheism 'fascinating and purposeful', satisfy pupils' spiritual needs with patriotism and internationalism to counter what he called the increased influence and activity of the Roman Catholic church.

A great problem the authorities have found is that atheism is very dull. And religion exerts a powerful influence through the arts, especially as interest in old church music, medieval painting and religious architecture grows. In 1980 the cultural authorities in the Russian republic set up a programme specifically designed to counter the religious message in Russia's cultural heritage. This offered courses such as 'Atheism and Music', where the lecturers traced the inspiration of masterpieces to the secular principle in religious cults rather than to divine sources. The programme 'Cultural Heritage and Atheism Today' was intended to show how religion had shackled rather than encouraged art. Even musical groups such as the Moscow Chamber Chorus were encouraged to give concerts that set religious music in a secular, nationalist context.

Finding people suitably inspired for such an anti-religious crusade is also not easy. Occasionally the state is lucky: some believers have become born-again atheists and have made a good career turning their former fervour against 'superstitions' and 'vestiges of the past'. I once tried to interview one particularly inspired member of the Moscow Atheist Society who turned out to be a former priest. But though he happily told a news agency colleague about his new job, he proved rather reluctant to talk to *The Times*. I used to phone the atheists every week or so for the latest excuse why such an interview was not possible at that particular moment. It became something of a game as to who got fed up first, and reluctantly I have to admit that after a year's attempt I gave up.

But in spite of all this, traditional attitudes to religion and religious observances die hard. Christmas and Easter are deeply ingrained in the Russian way of life, just as Islamic holidays are important in Central Asia. At Easter indeed all state bakeries stock the dry cake, known as *kulich*, which Russians eat with a creamy paste of curds, butter and raisins called *paskha* – though the dish is now officially called 'spring cake'. And every Easter there are complaints that there are not enough eggs or cottage cheese on sale to make the traditional dishes.

The ancient custom of visiting family graves before Easter is widely observed. Some days beforehand family members go to cemeteries to tidy up. The railings that traditionally surround each individual grave are painted, leaves and weeds removed, the grass clipped and the stone crosses, often containing photographs of the deceased set into them, cleaned. On the day of remembrance families gather at the graveside and place there flowers, painted eggs and sometimes even small glasses of vodka. Occasionally, unfortunately, things get a bit out of hand. Vodka is not only left as a token for the departed, but is imbibed by those remembering their loved ones. And then inevitably there is trouble, with some unseemly drunkenness and even the occasional fight between rather riotous groups who have given offence to equally inebriated mourners on the neighbouring grave.

Soviet papers report a steady fall in the number of believers, boast that new 'socialist' rituals are steadily replacing religious rites. But this is certainly not true in Georgia and Armenia, the two southern republics that have long been the frontiers of Christendom. The ancient Armenian Church, one of the earliest in the world, is the symbol of national identity and still exerts a powerful influence. The Church has absorbed even the pagan tradition of sacrifice, and at Gueghard, a twelfth-century monastery carved into the cliffside, people still bring goats and chickens for sacrifice on Saturdays. Christianity is deeply felt by Armenians of all ages. Symbolically, when the giant statue of Stalin was removed from the pedestal on a hill overlooking Yerevan, the capital, it was replaced with a figure of Mother Armenia, holding a sword across her body. From a distance the silhouette forms the unmistakable sign of the Cross.

Christianity is equally strong in Georgia. Many of the ancient stone churches and chapels high up in the lush green mountains are now being restored, and some have even been reopened for services. One of the most moving moments I experienced in Georgia was standing in a darkened little church in early evening some miles from Tbilisi and listening to a single powerful voice of a woman chanting her prayers.

Greater tolerance is shown towards religion in these two republics than elsewhere. One important consideration is that they both are national churches, having their ecclesiastical centres within the Soviet Union. They are considered somehow as 'ours'. Believers do not look abroad for guidance or follow teachings that grew up outside the Soviet Union. Those religions on the other hand which exist principally outside the country – Roman Catholicism, Baptism and other evangelical sects – incur far greater official hostility. This is especially true of the Baptists, Seventh Day Adventists and Pentecostalists.

Baptists are one of the fastest growing sects in the Soviet Union. Many communities began only at the turn of the century and have gained strength rapidly, especially in the Ukraine. Soviet Baptists are fundamentalist in their teachings and way of life. Alcohol is strictly forbidden, parishioners are carefully registered, expected to give help and support to fellow believers and to donate a tenth of their income to the Baptist community. Soviet Baptism has a strong revivalist and proselytizing element in it – which makes it unpopular with Orthodoxy from whom most converts come. It also tends to lead to sharp conflict with the state, as many communities refuse to register officially or accept restrictions on religious education, thus making their activities illegal. Unregistered groups meet clandestinely, often in forests or private homes, and are constantly harassed. Many Baptists have been imprisoned or sent to labour camps for long terms. Georgi Vins, a leader of one such community in the Ukraine which regarded registration as synonymous with state control, was sentenced for his activities but subsequently exchanged together with several other prominent dissidents for two Russians held on charges of espionage in New York. He has spoken eloquently of the hardships of these unregistered believers, the attempts to remove children from Baptist parents and the discrimination Baptists suffer in public life.

For the registered communities, things are a little easier. Indeed some 200 new communities had been registered in the five years up till the main Baptist conference in Moscow in 1979, and new prayer houses built in several cities. About 150,000 copies of the Bible, the New Testament and hymn books had been legally imported, mainly from Canada and the United States, and a new edition of the Bible was published in the Soviet Union. There is a correspondence school for training ministers in Moscow. The strength of Soviet Baptism lies in the discipline and dedication of its adherents, whose resolve seems only to be strengthened by state opposition. Officials point out, correctly, that Baptism appeals particularly to the less educated, to peasants with strong wills who seek firm spiritual guidance. A survey of those attending the Moscow conference showed that the large majority had not completed their secondary education. Baptism also is especially appealing to women who want their husbands or sons to stop drinking, and indeed the community's success in giving new life to former drunkards is astonishing.

I attended several services in Baptist prayer houses in the Ukraine, and my overriding impression was one of abstemious earnestness. There is none of the mystery and ceremony to be found in Orthodox churches. Hospitality is warm but frugal compared with the banquets I have enjoyed in the residences of Orthodox bishops: and the involvement of the community in its beliefs is much more full-time: as I sat under the trees in the grounds of one prayer house, eating vegetable soup from trestle tables together with 300 others after Sunday morning service, a singer sang hymns and read from the Gospel while the community listened with serious attention.

Baptists are joined in a state-decreed union with Methodists, Mennonites and Pentecostalists. But the Evangelical Union, as it is known, has control only over officially registered communities. Many Pentecostalists especially exist in underground, independent communities, and are engaged in a bitter, unequal struggle against the state. Their fate has been brought to the world's attention by the so-called Siberian Seven – members of two Pentecostalist families who rushed past the Soviet guards into the American embassy in June 1978 and lived in a basement room until 1983. After protracted negotiations one daughter, who went on a hunger strike and left the embassy after hospital treatment, was allowed to emigrate; the others left their embassy refuge a few weeks later, and subsequently emigrated to Israel. The Pentecostalists, together with Jehovah's Witnesses and Seventh Day Adventists are sharp thorns in the authorities' flesh because of their refusal to recognize limitations on religious education, their opposition to military service and their hostility to communist teaching. Many leaders of these communities lead the lives of underground partisans, hiding from the KGB, printing their tracts on secret presses, sending messages to their followers even from the prison camps to which they are often eventually taken. When Vladimir Shelkov, the 84-year-old leader of a breakaway section of the Seventh Day Adventist Church died in a labour camp in the far north in January 1980, unsigned underground pamphlets with news of his death – after twenty-five years in and out of prison camps – reached Western correspondents within a few days.

Apart from Christian sects, there is one very large and influential religious community in the Soviet Union which also looks beyond the frontiers, and which has become of vital importance in recent years: Islam. The Soviet Union is nominally the fifth largest Muslim country in the world. Already there are around 45 million people of Muslim descent, and if their high birth rate continues there will be around 100 million by the turn of the century, compared with 150 million Russians.

Soviet Muslims live mainly in six southern republics: Uzbekistan, Tadzhikistan, Turkmeniya and Kirghizia, which make up Central Asia, plus the vast steppeland of Kazakhstan and the republic of Azerbaijan. Tatar Muslims also live around Kazan in central Russia; and some Crimean Tatars who were forcibly deported by Stalin during the war have made their way back to their homeland.

Of all religions Islam probably suffered most from the Bolshevik revolution. The early Soviet government saw Islam as a formidable conservative force, opposing social and political change. Mosques were closed, pilgrimages to Mecca stopped and all the madrasahs – Islamic theological training schools – were disbanded. Only after twenty years of intense persecution did Stalin relax – as he did towards Christianity – allowing one madrasah to reopen in Bukhara in return for Muslim aid to the Soviet war effort. Another training school was later established in Tashkent.

Today Soviet Muslims are under the control of four spiritual directorates based in Tashkent, Ufa in the Urals, Makhachkala in the Caucasus foothills and in Baku on the Caspian Sea. Legally responsible for all religious activity, the boards issue theological directions (*fetwas*), organize councils and conferences, receive visiting foreign Muslims and publish religious material. The position of Islam has become a matter of crucial importance in Soviet foreign policy, and the authorities do their best to ensure that Islamic revivalism in Iran and Afghanistan stops at the hermetically sealed Soviet frontiers. And significantly the chairmen of all four boards have recently been changed. Old men with limited education and cautiously reticent in their leadership have been replaced by unusually young, fully-trained sheikhs, well versed in Islamic theology and tradition, and of absolute, indeed exaggerated, loyalty to the state and to communist ideals. The head of the Azerbaijan board, for example, Sheikh Allashakur Pashayev, was elected, at the age of thirty-one, to lead the only community of Shia Muslims at a time when the Russians were showing clear nervousness at the effects of Ayatollah Khomeini's Shia fundamentalism across the border in Iran. Even the head of the most important board, the Tashkent Spiritual Directorate, Mufti Ziyauddin Babakhan has recently retired. However he was a fervent and vocal supporter of Soviet foreign policy, the holder of several state awards and the *de facto* representative of Soviet Islam at any international conference. In a book published in 1980 he said Soviet Muslims had never before lived in such freedom, and added: 'The Soviet Union is the generally recognized bulwark of peace and progress on Earth. And the Muslims in the Soviet Union see, as one of the principal forms of their struggle for peace, honest work for strengthening the economic and defence might of their country.' His successor has voiced no less acceptable sentiments.

Present day Islam is however only a shadow of the force it once was in this historic region. Before 1917 there were more than 24,000 mosques. Today there are about 300, with about 1,000 registered mullahs. Working mosques tend to be tucked away in backstreets or on the outskirts of cities. The finest and biggest – all the monuments of Samarkand and Bukhara – are now state museums. Indeed in one such museum a bar for foreign tourists had been set up at the entrance to a former madrasah. The barmen themselves seemed rather sheepish at the flagrant insult to Islam.

The two working madrasahs graduate about sixty students a year. The only religious publications are occasional editions of the Koran (six since 1945), a few scholarly books on Islamic architecture, a religious calendar in Uzbek and a glossy magazine in five languages called *Muslims of the Soviet East* intended for overseas distribution. *Zakat*, the Muslim donation to the poor, is forbidden. Only a handful of senior religious dignitaries is allowed to make the mandatory pilgrimage to Mecca.

The authorities foster two quite separate pictures of Islamic activity. For internal consumption the image is a negative one of decline and inevitable crisis, of religion as an unscientific legacy from the past, which will one day disappear. But for the outside world, Moscow is increasingly concerned that foreign visitors, especially those from Muslim countries, should come away with a good impression. Over 100 Muslim delegations travel to the Soviet Union every year. And in 1980 the Muslim boards held a four-day conference to mark the start of the fifteenth century in the Muslim calendar – though unfortunately for the organizers less than half those invited attended because of the strong feeling over Afghanistan, and the prepared communiqué endorsing Soviet policy was firmly rejected by Muslim delegations from Sudan and Kuwait.

At home, however, local campaigns against the practices of Islam are unrelenting. As with other religions, the elderly practise their faith fairly freely, but the young and middle-aged, vulnerable at pressure points in school and at work, must take risks and make compromises to be observant Muslims.

Nevertheless things are improving slowly for Islam, thanks to foreign policy considerations, the skilful pro-government line of the official Muslim leaders and a growing feeling in Central Asia that Muslim customs are an integral part of a revered heritage. Some young clergy have a chance now to study in Cairo or Damascus. A few new mosques have been opened. The restoration of Islamic monuments is being undertaken at state expense. And with the increasing importance of Islam as a political force, Soviet Muslims are being brought into greater contact than before with foreign co-religionists and visiting journalists.

Party newspapers admit that circumcision is almost universal, and that Ramadan fasts, religious marriages and burials at purely Muslim cemeteries are widely observed even by 'atheists'. As the first casualties were brought home from Afghanistan, there was overwhelming – and successful – pressure to have them buried according to Muslim ritual.

Occasional sociological surveys point to a high proportion of believers: in 1974 in the Caucasus 46 per cent of the Dagestani rural dwellers and 53 per cent of all Chechens declared themselves to be believers, as against only 12 per cent among the Russians. In the same year, only 21 per cent of the Chechens identified themselves as atheists compared with 69 per cent of Russians. Ask any Tashkent youth whether he is a

Muslim, and the answer is likely to be: 'Of course. We are all Muslims.' He might well add: 'But I am not a believer.' This illustrates one aspect of Islam that gives it a greater hold than, for example, the Russian Orthodox Church. Even the non-believers still feel themselves part of the Muslim community.

It is this feeling, touching on nationalist sentiment, that worries Moscow. As yet there is no visible anti-Russian nationalist movement in the main Muslim areas (the Tatar campaign to return to the Crimea is more local in scope). But the authorities are taking no chances with Ayatollah Khomeini. Broadcasts from Iran are jammed. Direct travel across the Soviet frontier is sharply restricted, and Azerbaijanis wishing to visit relatives on the other side have to make lengthy preparations. The word has gone out from the Muslim boards that the conservative demands of the Iranian clergy are quite inappropriate to Soviet Islam. Officials frequently assert that the teachings of the Koran are embedded in the Soviet constitution. Western journalists talking to Muslim clergy have found complete, and probably deliberate, ignorance of the revivalist mood in the rest of the Muslim world. Official Islam has striven so hard to prove its compatibility with communism (though the reverse is not true) that it has dropped or adapted many of the tenets still considered fundamental elsewhere.

This is not true of all Soviet Islam. There exists still a network of secret, mystical Sufi brotherhoods, which are fiercely fundamentalist and nationalist and operate, especially in the north Caucasus, as a parallel system to the official boards. Their existence can be verified only from denunciations in the press and specialized journals, and from occasional reproofs of 'fanaticism' from the official Muslim leaders. But as an official from the Council for Religious Affairs once told me with disarming candour: 'Don't you think our people (meaning the KGB) know all about these groups? And what can they do, apart from throw stones at the windows of Russian language teachers?'

Nevertheless these secret Sufi societies, or *tariqas*, are well-entrenched and continue a historic tradition. They bind their adherents, who may include influential officials such as collective farm chairmen, to silent obedience for life. They run clandestine religious schools teaching Arabic, and clandestine mosques in members' homes. They also organize pilgrimages to the tombs of local warriors as a substitute for the *hadj* to Mecca. The authorities regard these societies as particularly dangerous. *Science and Religion* said the home mosques supported social customs that were incompatible with modern social life, including blood feuds, the abduction of brides, the marriage of underage girls and polygamy. They also encouraged nationalist sentiments.

The future of Soviet Islam is intertwined with the future of the country's whole southern flank, an area which is likely to be the site of much future industrial expansion to absorb the manpower surplus. This will make it an increasingly important region which Moscow must ensure remains firmly under the control of the communist party. Opposition from Islam must be contained: Iran and Afghanistan stand as warnings of what might happen if religion were allowed to become too powerful. Today such a possibility looks remote. But Islam has proved itself more durable and adaptable than the early Bolsheviks expected. The dilemma for the Kremlin now is to decide whether this force can be exploited for domestic and foreign policy ends, or whether security and ideology require it to be contained – and perhaps suppressed.

The same dilemma marks Soviet treatment of Jews, though the balance here has tilted even more towards outright suppression. Ironically, the more the authorities try to quash Jewish identity and religious practice, the stronger is the demand for emigration and the more inflamed is nationalist sentiment. That in turn has led to widespread discrimination against Jews and an assumption that all Jews are potential emigrants and therefore also potential security risks.

The Russians have never quite known whether to regard Judaism as a religion or as a nationality. Officially it is a nationality, which means that it is recorded on a Jew's internal passport in the same way that the nationality of a Georgian or a Lithuanian is recorded. But unlike these other groups, the Jews do not have a territorial homeland within the Soviet Union – at least not one that has any historic connection with Judaism. In 1934 a patch of territory in the Far East in the Amur river basin was officially declared a Jewish autonomous region, and Stalin encouraged Jews to go and settle there. But Birobidzhan, as the capital and area are called, never developed into a Jewish settlement, and of the 180,000 people who live in this faraway region only about 8 per cent are Jews.

Judaism as a religion is severely circumscribed. The teaching of Hebrew is discouraged and religious observance subject to the same pressures experienced by other religions. In addition widespread assimilation, emigration and the wartime holocaust have reduced once thriving Jewish communities to small groups of mainly elderly people. The rabbi of the magnificent choral synagogue in Odessa, once the centre of an important Jewish community, told me wistfully that few people attended services there any longer, and they rarely celebrated bar-mitzvahs.

Emigration has had a destabilizing effect on the situation of Soviet Jews, and in many ways has made things more difficult for those remaining behind. On the one hand it has raised many hopes which are often disappointed, and has encouraged a restlessness among Jews who would not previously have thought of leaving the Soviet Union. On the other hand it has provoked considerable envy among non-Jews who also dream of going to the West (which is where most Soviet Jews would like to live, in spite of official claims that they are being allowed to join relatives in Israel) but have no valid grounds on which to apply for an exit visa. 'Being Jewish nowadays is not a religion, it's a passport,' is a remark that typifies this rather jaundiced outlook, one that is reinforced by latent anti-semitism that for so long used to mark Russian attitudes to Jews.

The authorities were extremely reluctant to allow emigration in the first place, and did everything to hinder applicants. But as long as the issue was linked to good relations with Washington emigration was possible. Now there is little interest in trying to repair the bad relations with the United States. And Jewish emigration, which once reached 50,000 people a year, has all but dried up.

Those worst affected by the change in climate are the 'refuseniks' – Jews who applied to leave but whose requests were turned down. Many were prominent scientists and researchers, and the official reason for denying them exit visas was that they had had access to classified information. But once anyone applies to leave the Soviet Union he is automatically dismissed from his job. And these refuseniks have been left in limbo – unable to emigrate, but unable to resume their old occupations. Willy-nilly they are outcasts, treated as dissidents and driven into opposition. Many formed themselves into a pressure group to insist on a resolution of their situation; some have been on hunger strikes, others have demonstrated in public, and issued open letters of protest. Before his arrest and sentence of five years exile, Viktor Brailovsky, himself a Jewish cyberneticist who had been refused an exit visa, organized unofficial seminars for other Jewish scientists in the same position who needed to keep abreast of the latest developments in their field. The last one he held in his cramped two-room flat in Moscow drew fifty well-known scientists from Western Europe and America – and was closely monitored by the KGB. Brailovsky also edited an underground journal *Jews in the USSR* in which he documented cases of discrimination, especially against young Jewish applicants to prestigious universities, who were consistently denied entry and marked down in their exams.

The controversy over emigration has severely damaged Soviet prestige overseas, and has made the authorities especially sensitive to charges of anti-semitism. Now and then these are vigorously refuted by a number of well-known Jews who hold top positions in the army, the party and the arts. Plenty of official publicity is given to such manifestations of Jewish culture as the monthly Yiddish magazine, the pronouncements of Moscow's elderly chief rabbi, Yakob Fishman, who died in 1983, and the complaints of Jews who emigrated to Israel, found they were unable to adapt and returned home – not without difficulty – to the Soviet Union.

One man who has turned this official sensitivity to his advantage and to that of Jewish communities in the Soviet Union is Yuri Sherling, the founder and inspiration behind a Jewish theatre group which is officially registered in Birobidzhan but which tours the country from a base in Moscow giving performances of Jewish singing and dancing. The Jewish Musical Theatre, as the group is called, was founded in 1977 and in spite of initial opposition from senior party officials has proved extraordinarily successful. Its first two productions – an opera and a musical review which drew together Yiddish songs and customs that were about to die out in Russia – was widely praised in the Soviet press, and drew capacity audiences, overwhelmingly Jewish, in the big cities where they played. Yuri Sherling, a former ballet choreographer, was prompted to create the troupe by his worries that as emigration and assimilation took their toll, traditional Yiddish culture would soon disappear. He overcame formidable bureaucratic obstacles, and the resistance of several prominent actors of Jewish origin who were unwilling to jeopardize their careers by supporting this unknown venture. Eventually he assembled twenty-five actors and dancers, recreated the old musical tradition and taught them Yiddish. In a clever move he invited Ilya Glazunov, a controversial artist who enjoys the support of Russian nationalists and has been known to voice strongly anti-semitic sentiments, to design the decor and sets for the new theatre. And he has assiduously pressed for full government recognition of the troupe.

Some Jews have accused the theatre of becoming a propaganda showpiece for the government – a charge the dynamic Sherling vigorously rejects. The point, he emphasizes, is that for the first time since Stalin's sweeping postwar measures against the Jews, there now exists again a proper Yiddish theatre group. And for all Soviet Jews, religious or otherwise, this has been an encouraging sign that the spirit of traditional Jewish culture has not been altogether lost.

Many outside visitors to the Soviet Union are astonished by the strength of all religions in the country. Belief, like so many other aspects of life in the USSR, is more demanding, more tangible, more committed than it is in the West where acceptance and affluence have dulled religion's cutting edge. Communism, which itself has borrowed many of religion's attitudes and practices, has never reconciled itself to the tenacity of religious belief in the Russian soul. But it has for tactical reasons accepted that it now has to live with what appears ineradicable. And Holy Russia, which many thought extinguished in 1917, lives on.

CHAPTER THIRTEEN

The Struggle Against Crime

A Utopian claim of early communists was that under socialism crime would disappear as the conditions which caused it were abolished. The claim became official propaganda under Stalin, but looked increasingly absurd to a world that saw institutionalized lawlessness overtake the country as the purges got under way. But it is a claim rarely repeated nowadays. Indeed, hardly a day goes by without the press reporting cases of theft, bribery, embezzlement, murder, assault and even kidnapping. The Russians have long stopped pretending that all is perfect in Soviet society, and the study of crime is now a topic of public debate by sociologists, criminologists and party officials. Crime statistics are never published, but it is clear that crime is rising, leading to mounting concern by the authorities and loud calls for harsher punishments from the public. Law and order has become an emotive issue, one that stirs strong feelings in the Soviet Union today, just as it does in most Western societies.

From almost his first day in office, Yuri Andropov has made the fight against crime, especially economic crime, the hallmark of his new regime. Vigilantes have been sent out to virtually every public establishment on regular raids to ensure that officials are doing the jobs they are meant to be. The struggle against corruption and illegal profiteering has been stepped up, questions are being asked of even high officials about the sources of their income, the police have been ordered to carry out house to house checks to find out who is engaged in 'violations of the socialist norms of social life', and repeated blows are now being rained down on the corruption and illegal private dealings that form the basis of the thriving underground economy.

It is a popular cause, and one which Andropov rightly sensed would quickly win him backing at grassroots level. In a survey published a few years ago, the inhabitants of a large provinical town were asked what aspect of public life most worried them. And the answer was overwhelmingly: crime. In the last two years before Brezhnev died, that preoccupation was supplemented by rising public anger over bribery and corruption, which had become so dominant in public life that it was almost impossible for the ordinary person to go about his daily business without having to engage in some underhand black market deal, grease a palm or offer a substantial bribe to get an official to carry out his normal duties.

Public concern over crime might seem surprising to a westerner, for almost no country has such a large police force or devotes so much time and money to internal security as the Soviet Union. In addition to the regular police, known as the *militsia* – a term introduced after the Revolution to distinguish them from the hated Tsarist police – there are numerous other forces used to watch, control and discipline the population. The Ministry of the Interior (MVD) has its own military organization, regular troops who are used in impressive numbers to keep order at football matches, guard all the exits and entrances to Red Square during the November and May parades (waiting fully armed inside the barracks just off the famous square – just in case of trouble), and break up any unruly crowds and unauthorized demonstrations.

There are also the traffic police, known as GAI (standing for State Automobile Inspection), who patrol in their cars, often smartly painted imported Mercedes, and man the checkpoints on all the main exit roads from each city. And of course there is the KGB, the Committee for State Security, a vast, dreaded, élite organization divided into various sections – the border guards, the criminal investigation department, the political and counter-espionage forces and the many undercover agents who penetrate and monitor virtually every important Soviet organization. In addition a special police force deals with the economic crimes and theft of state property, there are transport police and air security guards, specialized guards and security officers and millions of part-time volunteer police known as *druzhiniki*, who don red arm-bands, carry batons and help the regular *militsia* as neighbourhood vigilantes and stewards at crowded meetings.

Russians explain this enormous police presence as the response to the deep-seated fear of anarchy. Throughout Russian history the temporal rulers have struggled to enforce their authority on their far-flung empire, while periodic disorder has brought chaos and bloodshed to the people and opened the way to foreign invaders. Russian rulers have always lived with insecurity, seeing threats to their authority in the slightest expression of opposition or non-conformity, and this fear was enormously increased by the Revolution: not only did the Bolsheviks have to fight a bloody civil war and foreign intervention to establish their authority, but their heirs are only too aware that if one revolution could begin with a small group of dedicated conspirators, so perhaps could another. The Russian people share their rulers' fear of disorder, believing there is an explosive force in the Russian character that will sweep them into extremism and disaster if it is not tightly controlled. Nothing so bewilders the average person as the vision of social chaos which is how the permissive society in the West is made to appear. Most dissidents have just as strong a belief in rigid social control as the rulers whose political system they oppose. There are few liberals with a genuinely tolerant view of opposition and political pluralism.

Given this fear of anarchy and the extraordinary efforts the state makes to enforce social and political discipline, why is crime on the increase? Serious Soviet analysts now recognize that crime is not simply the 'remnants of bourgeois mentality' as it used to be portrayed, but is rooted in social conditions. And many things are now changing for the worse. Since the war millions of people have moved into the cities, and with the influx have come problems long familiar in the West: rootlessness, loneliness, alienation, boredom, stress, overcrowding and so on. Enormous efforts have been made to relieve the housing shortage, one of Stalin's most bitter legacies, but ironically these have often had other unfortunate results. Khrushchev ordered a crash programme of flat building, but buildings hastily put up in his time were so cramped and shoddily constructed that many have become virtual slums already: mean entrances, ill-fitting doors and windows, poor plumbing, crumbling staircases and leaking roofs. They are known derisively as 'Khrushchev flats'. And whereas many of today's brick-built blocks are very much better designed and offer people a reasonable amount of living space without having to share kitchens and bathrooms, there is little sense of community in the vast, bleak estates of modern tower blocks that now ring Moscow and the large cities. (A famous Stalinist professor once told me how she looked back with nostalgia to the tough old days when she lived in a communal flat, with a woman who acted as her personal maid in the room next door. 'There was such a feeling of community, such togetherness,' she said.) As old people move into flats of their own, they are no longer able to help in the upbringing of children, and with the high divorce rate and most women working, children have less chance nowadays of a stable family background. Old-fashioned values have weakened, and social amenities have not kept pace with the burgeoning urban population. Vandalism and drunkenness are common in the tower block estates, and many Russians are seriously worried by youthful hooliganism.

Ironically crime has also increased at a time when material prosperity has never been higher, nor the law more fairly enforced – two of Brezhnev's main achievements. But many people now think the law too lax. Although punishments seem harsh by Western standards, they are less draconian than they used to be. And with so many laws and regulations, almost everyone breaks some rule in the course of daily routine. Public respect for all laws and for the principle of legality is thereby diminished. For example, few people take any notice of the lights at pedestrian crossings, although a policeman invariably standing nearby whistles furiously at anyone stepping out into the road before he or the lights have given the go-ahead. But beyond a reprimand and a torrent of official abuse, errant pedestrians are rarely punished. And so they step out again into the road around the corner in the hope that this time no one is watching.

Material prosperity has increased the temptation to crime, as Russians have begun to covet the good things of life but are frustrated by shortages and unfulfilled expectations. Indeed it is the state's inability to supply the consumer goods it has long promised that lies at the root of most crime in the Soviet Union nowadays. For in the communist system virtually any attempt to circumvent the cumbersome workings of the planned economy falls into the realm of criminal activity. And the big rise in crime in recent years has not been in murder and violence – though this is more common than a generation ago – but in economic crime: bribery, extortion by petty officials, embezzlement in factories and offices, and especially the flourishing 'second economy' where the black market and private enterprise make up for the deficiencies of the state system.

The only trial I ever attended in Moscow – apart from various fruitless attempts to get into the courts where dissidents were being tried – was of a group of young men accused of something that in the West would not be considered criminal at all: speculation, the private purchase of goods and resale at a higher price for personal gain. Under article 154 of the criminal code of the Russian Republic it is a crime carrying a maximum penalty of five years' imprisonment. In many ways it was a typical trial, held in a little courtroom that looked like any ordinary Soviet office: the walls painted light green, the door padded to keep out the noise of the passage, three ceiling lights, double windows with one ventilation section open, a bare wooden floor.

Rows of benches began to fill up just before the hearing with about twenty spectators, mainly women. Some were pensioners, others with gold teeth, black shawls and olive skins had come to Moscow from the Caucasus especially for the case. A policeman in the usual grey uniform and winter fur hat with the Soviet emblem on it went to the defendants' box at the side of the room, and routinely ran his fingers round the ledge and under the seat looking for concealed weapons. The two lawyers sat at a table in the middle of the room, their brief-cases open, talking to the prosecutor. Glancing in my direction, he cautioned them in a low voice that there was a foreigner in court (I had arranged to attend the trial in advance with the Ministry of Justice).

The defendants came in, escorted by six burly policemen. A woman of about twenty-four appeared first, a Chechen from the North Caucasus. She wore a white shawl over her head and kept her eyes down. Three young men followed her, and were shut in the defendants' box. One policeman stood guard and the others sat a few feet away. Then the clerk called out, 'Stand.' The door at the end of the room opened and three men in suits came in and took their places on high-backed leather chairs on the dais. The man in the centre, aged about forty, was the judge, those on either side the two 'people's representatives', who in Soviet law are the equivalent of the jury. In fact they rarely go against the judgement and wishes of the professional judge.

It was the second day of the case, the turn of the defence lawyers. The first stood up to argue that the charge of speculation against his client, Vladimir Troyanovsky, had not been proven. The case against him was strong however. He was a fourth year student at the prestigious Plekhanov Institute of Economics in Moscow. The previous year he contacted a foreigner, apparently from the Middle East, who proposed selling him boxes of Japanese scarves on the black market. Troyanovsky telephoned a friend, a young Chechen named Jimaldayev living in Moscow, who said he knew two women from Grozni, capital of the North Caucasus, who would be able to dispose of the scarves. Troyanovsky proposed buying them for 9.50 roubles each; Jimaldayev would sell them to the women for 11 roubles.

On March 8, a public holiday when all Moscow was celebrating International Women's Day, the two women were outside Troyanovsky's apartment, loading the boxes into a car belonging to a friend. A policeman asked them what they were doing. They said, fairly plausibly, that the boxes had flowers in them. The policeman investigated, saw the scarves and found 13,000 roubles in the glove compartment of the car. They were all arrested.

Troyanovsky's lawyer argued that to prove speculation you had to show that the articles were actually bought. It was not known whether the mysterious foreigner – who was apparently also arrested but expelled from the country before the case came to court – had been paid. In any case, the scarves were unobtainable in Soviet shops, so it was impossible to know what the real price should have been. But perhaps realizing his case was weak, the lawyer began to appeal for clemency. Troyanovsky came from a good family – his mother worked in the state publishing house of political literature. He had gone to a special school for bright children, served in the army with distinction, and was doing well in college. He regretted what he had done, and had already served twenty-one months in prison awaiting trial. The prosecutor had demanded the maximum sentence of five years; but surely he could be set free now.

Jimaldayev, a handsome young man wearing a smart brown jersey, sat with his chin on his hand. His lawyer tried to put all the blame on Troyanovsky. My client, he argued, had nothing to do with the scheme. When they had all met on March 7, it was Troyanovsky who had persuaded them. The lawyer spoke for forty-five minutes, and provoked an outburst from Troyanovsky's lawyer: 'You cannot blacken my client's character; you don't know him. It's not your business.' The judge, who had spent the time making occasional notes, mildly reproved them both. He then asked one of the accused women, who was sitting with her parents on the spectators' bench, whether she had anything to say. She mumbled apologies. And Troyanovsky? He wanted a five minute break to collect his notes. The court adjourned.

In the afternoon the prosecution and defence summed up their cases. The following day the court gave its verdict. The accused were all found guilty. Troyanovsky got the maximum term – five years. He had just over three left, to be served in a labour camp under the 'ordinary regime'. Jimaldayev got three years, the owner of the car got two years, as did the two women. But two months earlier the government had declared an amnesty for all women with young children who were imprisoned. They both fell into that category, and so both were released immediately.

The trial appeared to be perfectly fair, the sentences in accordance with the law. And yet I could not help feeling it was hard on the young men, for millions are daily engaged in similar black market dealings and manage to protect themselves either with a bribe or by pulling strings.

Shortages are endemic in the system, which opens the way for all manner of corruption. And in spite of the much trumpeted cleaning-up campaign now under way – which had already begun before Brezhnev's death – the authorities are powerless to stamp out the black market altogether and the corruption associated with it.

The difficulty lies in deciding where to draw the line between criminal corruption and the system known as *blat*, which means using your influence and connections to get what you need. If you have *blat* in Soviet society you can manage nicely. If you do not, you are for ever walking away disappointed as that last pair of imported shoes is sold, there are no tickets left for the theatre, the aircraft is fully booked and the obstinate old man at the restaurant door insists there are no free tables. *Blat* is not necessarily corruption, but rather the repayment of favours. Like Sicilian godfathers, Russians remember obligations, and know when it is appropriate to repay them. With *blat* most of life's daily obstacles can be overcome. A relative might work in the shop where the shoes are sold: she can not only put aside a pair for you, but also purloin an extra pair which you can then donate to someone whose acquaintance you need to cultivate – perhaps a doctor who will take a bit more time over your case, or a seamstress who can run you up a nice dress privately during her working hours.

No money need change hands. Straight bribery – necessary if, for example, a GAI inspector flags down your car late at night on the pretext that you crossed a white line or were in the wrong lane – is a different and more serious matter, that nowadays carries stiff penalties. *Blat* depends more on an unspoken understanding that a little help in speeding up the bureaucracy or avoiding a lengthy queue will be repaid by an equal favour. It is not solely a question of political influence – though a cousin in the party apparatus will certainly see that his relatives are properly looked after, even if they are not allowed themselves to use the party shops, or get their medicines from the 'Kremlin clinic' that treats the top people.

The real position of power – until the latest campaign made it too risky, at least for a while – is a job in a big shop, or, better still, in a warehouse as a wholesale distributor. To illustrate the point a paper once ran a series of satirical imaginary letters from a supposedly naive girl in a warehouse who was deluged with all kinds of favours from the chic and the famous. Their sole aim, as was clear to all except her, was to lay hands on leather jackets, imported trousers or smart blouses. She found that she and her friend had an entrée to all the exclusive clubs –

the Union of Artists, the Union of Writers, the Union of Cinematographers and so on – where she dined in style in the club restaurants, met actors and singers and enjoyed the attentions of the top 'People's Artists'. But she professed surprise that they all wanted to invite her to their homes at the end of each quarter – 'just when we are so busy in the warehouse with the new deliveries'.

She originally became caught up in their world because she decided, the newspaper satire added, to write a thesis on the phenomenon that makes *blat* both possible and essential in the Soviet Union – the chronic shortage of consumer goods. Such goods which disappear within hours of being put on the counter are known as 'deficit' items. As part of her thesis the girl naturally talks to a figure all Russians recognize as the epitome of the wheeler-dealer – the Georgian. Anyone from this notoriously corrupt Caucasian republic is immediately suspected of shady deals, black market trading and consequently enormous wealth. And in the satire the Georgian praises 'deficit' as the very stuff of life. Without such shortages, he says, no one would make any money. He goes on to describe a typical chain of deals.

'Supposing you want tickets to the ice-hockey final. What would you do? Go and buy a red fox hat for the cashier at the office? No, that's not the best way. Ask Volodiya? No, I prefer to keep him in reserve for the time when I need an air ticket. So, first go round to my cousin who works at the bakery where you can buy fresh Georgian bread. Come back a few hours later and he'll give you all you need – with only a few roubles extra for "service". Take this bread across the road to the council offices. There's a man there who adores our bread and he has a wife who works in the stockroom taking orders for spare parts for cars. She'll get you an accelerator pedal. I know that the husband of the woman in the hairdresser's has been searching for one everywhere for his car. You can get a voucher for a magnificent hair-do in return. Take that along to the shop, exchange it for the red fox and then off you go to the ticket office and the rink to get some choice seats. Easy really.'

But *blat* can easily become too blatant. The unsolicited favour has little to distinguish it from a bribe. And many people whose favours or services are needed have come to expect such offerings, indeed count on them to supplement their meagre incomes. All too frequently they refuse to pay any attention to the client who does not slip something substantial under the counter. Even those who come to their jobs with good intentions are quickly corrupted. One paper chronicled the unhappy history of a woman food sorter, married for sixteen years to a government chauffeur, who was promoted to the key job of supervising wholesale food distribution. She faced a sudden avalanche of bribes and gifts. People began bringing boxes of chocolates to their home, and she started returning late in the evenings, drunk. 'I was invited out,' she told her husband simply. Indeed she was. The managers of all the shops to which she distributed the produce did their best to ensure their establishments got the pick. Someone would come from a shop with an invoice, bringing also salami, a joint of meat and a tin of stew. She accepted whatever she was given, and her appetite grew. She started making a distinction between 'her' shops and those that did not give anything, and retailers who failed to offer a present went away empty-handed. She worked until late at night securing supplies for the obliging stores, and in return was given dozens of bottles of vodka, among other things. During business hours the head of the local trade union branch would sit demurely opposite her as though he hardly knew her. But when the clients had gone, they would open their gifts, have a few swigs and sing and drink until the late evening. And so it went on. She used to be up half the night drinking with people from her office. Her husband remonstrated, but realized she would never be punished by her drinking companions. At holidays a shop manager would graciously offer her his office car stuffed to the roof with parcels, boxes, tins and bottles, including thirty or forty bottles of spirits. She told her husband: 'Every-one around here respects me, and that's why they bring presents. If you don't like it, you can clear out.' And so he did, writing to a paper to explain why.

The case is typical. And it is often the top officials who encourage such corruption by soliciting 'gifts' and discount purchases from local establishments without giving shop managers any leeway to make up the consequent drain on their budget – with the result that the shops have to shortweight customers or find some other illegal way of balancing their books.

Currying favour with bribes is taken for granted in daily dealings, as the following instances, quoted anonymously by a newspaper, make clear. The deputy head of a school: 'Of course if a teacher has been teaching for many years there's nowhere left in her flat to put presents. At the start of the year, a vase; on teacher's day, another vase; and then more on her birthday, Women's Day, speech day, the end of term. You know, among parents and children there's sometimes a competition to see who can give the most generous presents. And the teacher? Well, she gets used to it, even though there's a hint of bribery which is sometimes quite obvious.'

The sick child's parents: 'How can I not bring a box of chocolates to the doctor, or a nicely wrapped bottle of brandy? It's the done thing – like saying thanks for your trouble. There are several ways of treating a patient: with special attention, or just normally. So what's wrong?'

The chief accountant: 'You have to respect and please the auditor. For instance, I know there are no financial irregularities, but still I am afraid. If he wants, he can always find something wrong. I don't know whether it's a present or a bribe – a bribe I suppose. If he's not given anything, the auditor can always hint at what he would like.'

The farm manager: 'I won't elaborate. I'll just give you the facts. We took a tractor engine to be repaired. When I sent a mechanic to collect it, he came back without it. When I asked him the problem, he said: "In return for the engine they want a sheep." So we had to slaughter one and send him back with it. In the old days they would fix things for a bottle of brandy. Now they want a sheep. What it will be next I don't know.'

The council chairman: 'I don't like talking about such things, but if you don't mention my name I'll tell you frankly, because I've had enough. This person you have to take out to supper, that one for a day's hunting, and the other one for a sauna. Naturally it all costs money, and who is going to pay? We're not doing this for ourselves, but for our region.'

The worst thing of all, the paper commented, was that in the end it was the state that had to pay for all the bribes, as no one paid from his own pocket. The money was always found, one way or another, from the factory or office funds. Using these to buy presents amounted to plain stealing. The article, memorable for its frankness, also complained that often people had to be bribed to do their jobs properly, such as the obligatory five-rouble note for those who cleaned and prepared the baths and massage rooms in health resorts. In other cases people such as financial inspectors had to be bribed to stop them being too conscientious – lest they discover the frauds and embezzlement practised in so many establishments in order to build up enough funds to pay for all these enforced gifts. Would the country be any worse off if no one offered bribes? the paper asked. Would doctors, teachers and wholesale distributors not do their jobs properly as laid down by the law instead of giving time and attention to some, while neglecting others? It is a question Andropov must have asked himself many times as head of the KGB. Now he has a chance to enforce some answers.

But in the Soviet context the temptation to exploit one's position is almost irresistible, and most people take it for granted that with power goes privilege and the chance to feather one's nest. Of course people grumble and complain that 'they' have access to what they want. But instead of protesting, Russians tend either to curry favour with the privileged in the hope of themselves getting hold of some of the sought-after benefits, or to make sure that they elbow their way to the top and enjoy the fruits of success.

One man once made a lot of money as a confidence trickster playing on these attitudes to power and privilege. He went to the Black Sea, posing as a minister, and booked himself into one of the best hotels. He ordered caviar, brandy, tasty delicacies to be brought to his room. He asked for imported cigarettes, and ordered two suits made up for him in a local tailor's. He refused to pay for anything, behaving with an arrogance that was accepted as quite natural for a man in his position. And indeed he was only caught after he had accused the unfortunate tailor who tried to claim his money of libelling him and had him jailed for a year. The tailor appealed and the higher court found that no one had ever bothered to question the credentials of the 'minister'. 'Is this how our people expect a minister to behave?' *Literaturnaya Gazeta* asked indignantly. The answer was clearly yes.

Unfortunately wrong-doing by real ministers and senior officials is all too common. Usually such things never reach the papers, for the party has always been obsessively anxious that nothing should spoil its image as the embodiment of the nation's wisdom and morality. But occasionally the most blatant offenders are exposed in an effort to warn others. One such case was the mayor of Sochi, the main Black Sea resort. He once agreed to write an article for *Literaturnaya Gazeta* about the evils of smoking, but was late in handing in his article. Each time the paper telephoned, it was told Vyacheslav Voronkov, the mayor, was 'busy'. But finally the article arrived, a long diatribe against the evils of smoking.

Four years later the paper, not a whit abashed, disclosed that far from being busy in his office, Voronkov had been entertaining officials in his luxurious sauna, wining and dining them and cajoling them to agree to the appointment of one of his cronies as the director of an important local factory. The mayor turned out to be the chief bribe-taker in Sochi, a man who spent his days intriguing, his evenings meeting corrupt clients, and his energies hiding the gold, jewellery and immense fortune of thousands of roubles he was illegally acquiring. He was tried and sentenced to thirteen years in jail.

Like many others caught in the net of corruption, his career began well enough. A graduate from a Moscow civil engineering institute, he was a factory director in Sochi at the age of thirty, deputy mayor at thirty-two and mayor a few years later.

But on his first day in office he found a collection of the finest brandies on his table, with a note wishing him all the best. At home, he found a hamper bulging with fruits and delicacies, offered by the local wholesale supplier of meats and ham. On his first official trip to Moscow, his suppliers followed him with suitcases of wines and food, sending them up to his de luxe hotel suite.

He soon came to expect such gifts, and sent the mayoral car and chauffeur to the factories and restaurants of Sochi to collect caviar and other choice items. In return he used to hand out whatever his office could arrange – flats, jobs, cars, theatre tickets; the director of the fish shop that kept him in caviar got a new flat.

After a while, tiring of waiting at home, he went out in search of clients, meeting them in back streets at night. The going price for a factory manager's job or a new flat was about 1,500 roubles. He found an accomplice, Nikolai Remiz, and while the mayor was delivering homilies at political meetings on the need for a 'principled state approach' to problems, Remiz was out looking for new clients.

The partnership came to a sudden end when Remiz had his portrait displayed in town on Victory Day as a war veteran. Someone wrote underneath 'Bribe-taker No. 1'. Some weeks later one of the mayor's clients was arrested for drunken fighting in a restaurant. The mayor tried to get the local newspaper to suppress the story, but failed, and finally an investigation was inevitable.

Ironically, almost a year before the story appeared, a British news agency colleague was approached once by two men who came to Moscow and insisted on meeting him for a talk in the street. The pattern seemed all too familiar: each month dozens of sad figures, at considerable risk to themselves, approach Western correspondents to relate a story of unfair dismissal, official arbitrariness and petty oppression. Occasionally they have news of genuine political interest, and so correspondents usually spend time listening to them. On this occasion my colleague met the men, one of whom said he was deputy prosecutor in Sochi and had been sacked and threatened for trying to reveal an important scandal involving the mayor and other senior party men. . . . It all sounded like one of those familiar tales, impossible to check or substantiate. My colleague kicked himself when he read the story in the papers later.

Large scale fraud or embezzlement, the stealing of state-owned property or the siphoning off for private use of supplies intended for factories and state-run enterprises is the most serious form of economic crime, and it is not uncommon for the worst offenders to be shot. But ordinary Russians do not judge this nearly as harshly as crimes that affect them as individuals. People will happily purloin wood, tools, cement and bricks to repair their flats but would not dream of stealing a single kopeck from their neighbours, and are scrupulously honest in their relations with their fellow men. The state is too vast, too impersonal to be seen as a victim. And indeed, it is hard often to see who actually suffers directly from the 'misappropriation of socialist property', as pilfering is known.

Conversely it is state arbitrariness towards individuals and injustice committed by petty officials in the name of the state that most angers people, who have no hesitation in protesting. One such case, for example, was reported from central Russia where a veritable scandal had been caused by officials' attempts to make up for their shortfall in agriculture at the expense of individual citizens. The police set up checkpoints at the boundaries of the local administrative region, and stopped all trucks and cars. Anyone found carrying potatoes above a very limited quantity across the boundary line had them confiscated, although they had been legally bought in the peasant markets, on the pretext that the buyers had more than they needed for their own consumption. No compensation was given, and what was confiscated was added to the potato harvest from the state farms, thereby boosting dismal production figures. There was a colossal row, details were published in the press and the racket was stopped. But not always do such things get publicized or curbed.

Ordinary Russians were shocked and angered by this story. But a much more serious case of fraud, which led to one of the most widespread purges at the end of the Brezhnev era and involved the dismissal of hundreds of officials and even the execution of a deputy minister, led to considerable gossip and scandal but did not really affront anyone or provoke personal indignation. This was the celebrated caviar fraud. About 200 people in the Ministry of Fisheries were involved in packing the celebrated delicacy in tins that were marked as herring.

These tins were then sent to the West where they were opened, the caviar was retinned, and the profits were divided between the Soviet officials involved and the Western partners in the fraud. The earnings of the Russians were banked abroad and kept by officials for their personal – and highly illegal – use on business trips to the West.

The fraud was discovered because, typically, there was a mix-up in the distribution and the counterfeit herring tins were mistakenly diverted to the home market. Many a Russian got a pleasant surprise on finding that his tin of herring contained something of considerably greater rarity. But unfortunately for the perpetrators, one or two tins fell into the hands of the police who ordered an investigation. The scale of the operation, involving pay-offs all the way down the line, and reaching into the senior echelons of the Ministry of Fisheries, shocked the authorities. The elderly minister was forced to retire. Hundreds of people were arrested and questioned. For two years the matter was successfully hushed up, although rumours began to spread. And when it was finally revealed that a deputy minister had been executed, no word was ever published about the fraud itself, nor was it ever disclosed who the Western collaborators were.

Ironically this was another occasion when Western correspondents could have stumbled on the story if they had known what was involved. For soon after the investigation began, a Canadian woman was arrested at Moscow airport for attempting to smuggle jewellery out of the Soviet Union. She was detained in Lefortovo prison for two weeks and then the case was dropped and she was expelled. But after her release she told the Canadian embassy that she had met dozens of Russians in the prison who all seemed to be from the Ministry of Fisheries and who appeared to have been involved in some colossal fraud. Nobody followed up her story, and nobody remembered it until news of the caviar scandal leaked out two years later.

Corruption on this scale worries the government more than the ordinary person. It is petty corruption that is more fiercely resented: the knowledge, for example, that you cannot get your son or daughter into a good university without pulling strings, that once there they may have to offer a bribe to the examiner if they want good marks, that what matters even in the respected academic world is whom you know rather than what you know. Every year the papers publish details of parents who have handed over sums of two or three thousand roubles to guarantee a place in this or that university faculty, denounce 'fixers' who advise would-be students where to apply and perform the necessary introductions.

Education can be a very profitable enterprise, for private lessons are permitted by law and teachers can earn at least 10 roubles an hour giving after-hours instruction to pupils in need of special coaching before examinations. But those who speculate on their academic position earn people's especial contempt. The director of correspondence courses in the Central Asian oasis town of Urgench was arrested in 1981 for selling diplomas, and was found by police to have an Aladdin's cave of ill-gotten gains at home: 3 cars, 23 dinner services for 380 people, 74 suits and 149 pairs of shoes.

But while crime of this kind might pay, it is hard to enjoy its fruits in the Soviet Union, for ostentatious living immediately provokes suspicion and can lead to an investigation. So today's millionaires in Russia lead double lives. One example, detailed in the press, showed the lengths to which they have to go.

He always goes out looking like an ordinary plumber. His wife shops in the market far from her home where no one knows her. When anyone knocks at the door, the family hastily hides everything in sight while the wife pretends she cannot open the lock. Only once a year, when they go on holiday to the Black Sea, do they live in the style they can afford. They hire a flat in Sochi, live it up and squander money. But every evening they telephone a relative in their locked and shuttered home to see that everything is all right. And no one would suspect that this family lives off a golden fountain of illegal earnings.

Some people, especially from the Caucasian republics, take risks and revel in their wealth. When the family goes to Moscow, a private taxi waits outside their hotel. The chauffeur is sent on dozens of errands – to the market for flowers for the receptionist, to the café for mineral water, to the bakery for special cakes. They act like the old aristocracy. Whenever they arrive people scurry round to compete for custom, offering chic and expensive furniture, imported toilet bowls – the acme of fashion and the yardstick of success for the parvenu – as well as matching pastel baths and basins. Two cars carry their purchases back to their secret treasure-store in a village outside the city. A huge well-packed container is sent to the station with furniture supplied on the strength of a special stamp in their Moscow residence permits. No matter that the law forbids its export from the city: wads of banknotes circumvented that difficulty.

Such wealth is impossible to acquire by legal means, as even top

salaries would not allow such a life-style. The common assumption is
that somewhere there is a link to the profitable black market. But few ask
questions, and apart from snooping neighbours, anonymous letters of
denunciation and accidental discovery, the authorities have no cause or
time to investigate every citizen who goes to an expensive restaurant.
There have been calls for the equivalent of a tax return, so that a quick
check could be made on those apparently living beyond their legal
means, and newspapers have suggested that anyone making a large cash
purchase – such as a car – should first show how he got the money.

When the secret millionaires are unearthed, the papers make much of
their miserliness, their secret hoarding of useless wealth. The director
of a social security office for industrial enterprises in Azerbaijan, for
example, who made a lot of money diverting cars intended for invalids to
the garages of perfectly healthy people, was found on his arrest to have at
home gold weighing 34 kilograms. He had of course the requisite
imported toilet bowl, and had decorated his town residence with antique
pictures and *objets d'art* which he kept in glass display cabinets. In his
country dacha he had built a swimming pool and had his own orange
grove. But he was nonetheless a prisoner of his wealth, unable to enjoy it
beyond the confines of his various homes.

One area of crime that carries especially harsh penalties is the
smuggling and illegal exchange of foreign currency. Russians are strictly
forbidden to hold any money other than roubles, whose official exchange rate is artificially fixed for tourists and foreign businessmen and
which cannot be taken in and out of the country. The penalties for
changing money on the black market are severe – eight years in a labour
camp. But even within the Soviet Union Western convertible currency is
so sought after that speculators and black marketeers are ready to risk
being caught by the KGB – who automatically investigate crimes
involving currency – in order to lay hands on dollars, pounds and marks.
For with these they can buy goods in a network of hard-currency shops
which stock imported food and drink, radios and electrical items and
clothes for sometimes a quarter the price on the open market – if they
are even available.

These shops, known as *Beriozka* (birch-tree) shops, are tucked away
in back streets, with drawn blinds and police lurking nearby, and are
intended only for foreign residents and tourists, whose currencies are so
eagerly sought to fill the state coffers. Until 1981 Russians were often
able to bluff their way into these stores, especially those which accepted
special coupons that diplomats could buy at the state bank. But the

abuses became so blatant, with Russians buying goods in these shops and reselling them for many times the price on the black market, that a crackdown was enforced. The issue of coupons was restricted to diplomats (previously they were also available to journalists and businessmen in Moscow), Russians were not allowed in the shops any more and identity cards were demanded at the door.

Foreigners, especially third world diplomats and students, were often the source of the corruption. They used to buy imported cigarettes by the boxful in the hard currency shops and then resell them on the black market for roubles at enormous profit. Often it was only in this way that some African embassies in Moscow could make ends meet. And the open currency violations and trading in Western goods by students at Lumumba University, a university established in Khrushchev's time to train third world students, contributed much to a growing dislike of foreign students and tended to fuel latent anti-black racialism.

When still head of the KGB, Andropov did much in his final year to try to stop all this. Foreign currency shops were raided and those illegally in possession of foreign currency arrested; customs regulations were tightened up to try to prevent the profitable smuggling out of the country of gold, precious stones, icons and antiques; the most notorious foreign students engaged in currency transactions were arrested and sentenced to several years' imprisonment; and the press waged a propaganda campaign against the hangers-on, especially prostitutes, who acted as links between foreigners and the black market.

One such inhabitant of the Moscow *demi-monde* was 'Madame Shura', a brunette well known to the regulars at the comfortable old National Hotel. She was always there at midnight, when the cloud of smoke hung low in the dim light of the bar, and the tired businessmen were killing time and buying drinks for the Russian women who had somehow penetrated into the hard-currency bar. She felt at home among the foreigners.

One night, however, she was more than usually anxious, on the look out for an elegant man with a raincoat over his arm who eventually appeared at the door, walked purposefully over to her and handed over a wad of green banknotes wrapped in cellophane. Silently and deftly she opened her bag and handed him roubles in exchange. The other drinkers noticed nothing as the stranger then disappeared.

Stuffing her foreign currency into an empty cigarette box, she glanced round the room and as she was leaving, slipped the packet into the pocket of a red-haired man who had been sitting beside her and had got up to see her out. She intended to ask for her 'cigarettes' back in a safe place outside. But as they were hailing a taxi, they were arrested. At the police station she denied any illegal transaction. But the red-haired man produced the packet and its contents and swore she had put it in his pocket. Witnesses were called who had watched the exchange in the bar.

Illegal currency dealing turned out to be not the only business Madame Shura had going. Pictures, icons, caviar, antiquities, precious stones – she sold them all to those foreigners who knew which bars to frequent. She had never wanted to hold down a job. A school drop-out, she had sold toys in Moscow's main toy-shop, worked in a café, helped at a hairdresser's before drifting into the world of the bar girls in the big hotels. She soon learned the black market rates for foreign currency and who was after gold or icons.

She began to live well, throw big parties, hire her own chauffeur, look chic at the fashionable resorts. At one encounter she met a Scandinavian and worked her charms to persuade him to marry her. She knew this would make it easier to gain access to the foreign-currency bars. It was also an escape route out of the Soviet Union if necessary. He began to doubt her affections, however, and she curtly told him to find her another foreigner to marry. He did, and got his reward in cash. After the honeymoon Mrs Kristiansen, as she became, returned to business. Her husband conveniently returned to Scandinavia and she filled in time as a prostitute and set up a partnership with a former criminal from Soviet Central Asia.

They sold a Canadian an old master painting for $15,800 in cash. They collected icons, gold and antiques from second-hand shops, arranged meetings with middle men in a flat and sold the objects – whose export is forbidden under Soviet law – to eager foreigners willing to take the risk. Their underworld 'corporation', trading in roubles and dollars, moved on to diamonds, generally making their deals at the bar of the National Hotel. At one time her partner sold seven diamonds for 100,000 roubles (£66,000).

When caught, she was tried and sentenced – though to the surprisingly short term of six years, considering the sums involved. Her partner was given ten years.

Crimes of this kind are only possible in the big cities. In the villages, where foreigners never penetrate and no one knows what a dollar looks like, crime is more primitive, more universal: drunken assault, theft, swindling, the occasional murder. The crime rate is probably no higher than in any peasant society, though the harshness of life in these remote areas often makes justice a rather rough instrument for dealing with the grisly effects of drunken brawls: the most common instrument of assault, and indeed of murder, is the ordinary axe.

The state worries less about this than about criminal movements that have dangerous implications for security: nationalism, overt or under-ground, religious opposition to secular authority, anti-communist con-spiracies, private enterprise and the vestiges of tribalism, especially in the southern republics and traditional Muslim areas. Even nowadays bandits and outlaws still exist in the forests and desert wastes, evading capture and living like old-fashioned desperadoes.

As a foreigner I had little personal experience of crime in the Soviet Union: I was never robbed, never attacked in the street (though several Westerners have unpleasant stories of being mugged and robbed), never personally threatened. Of course there were unpleasant incidents: I arrived outside the Intourist hotel only half an hour after a deranged escapee from a mental institution had chopped three elderly Swedish tourists to bits with an axe; I went to the barricaded street outside the office of Finnair where a man had burst in with a shotgun and held the employees as hostages in an attempt to get a plane out of the country; I remember the time when police sharp-shooters were brought into a block of flats where foreigners lived to try to capture a man who had seized a young girl and violated her. But such incidents would hardly raise an eyebrow in New York. Only because it was Moscow did the world pay any attention to what were sadly predictable crimes in any big city.

But there was one whole area of crime – or so it is officially designated – from which neither I nor any foreigner could escape: political dissent. There were countless cases of brave people who saw an injustice, spoke out and were punished or persecuted for their views. Although I spent less time with dissidents and knew less about the various movements than many of my Western colleagues – believing that the West probably has an exaggerated view of the importance within the Soviet system of these groups and that it was a mistake to concentrate on their plight at the expense of other aspects of life in the Soviet Union – I must have spent many, many hours with men and women who had deliberately put themselves at risk, who wanted only justice for their country and society but were condemned to injustice and suffering.

The story of attempts by Andrei Sakharov and other notable figures to publicize the regular infringements of human rights and personal liberty is one that has been well told already. The West has rightly made the plight of individual Soviet citizens – Orlov, Shcharansky, Ginzburg and dozens of others – a matter of international importance, for the treatment of these people is not only a test of Soviet good faith in sticking to agreements negotiated in Helsinki on human rights, but it is a yardstick by which the Soviet system should be measured.

For this reason the Russians are acutely sensitive about dissent. The authorities go to absurd lengths to pretend there is no such thing as political opposition, while pursuing a relentless crackdown on all those who threaten to offer the slightest challenge. And those whose cases have become too well known abroad are systematically portrayed as ordinary criminals, as traitors or as opportunists whose motives are mercenary and loyalties questionable.

I often wondered why the authorities were so anxious to hold trials that were clearly rigged from the outset. Every Western correspondent knew that the outcome of the trials of Anatoly Shcharansky or Yuri Orlov was never in doubt. And it was also perfectly clear that no ordinary person, and certainly no Western diplomat or correspondent, would be allowed into the court during the trials. Yet the official media insisted that the trials were 'open', emphasized the correct legal procedure that was followed and the opportunity given to the dissidents to defend themselves. The KGB evidently was uneasy at overstepping some clearly defined mark. For it had no intention of allowing the throng of Western correspondents who gathered on the pavement outside the courthouse where Shcharansky was tried in 1978 to find out what was happening inside; and yet it did not stop Shcharansky's brother from giving briefings on the day's proceedings, or forcibly break up the gathering of supporters, including Dr Andrei Sakharov – two years before his own exiling – who held a daily vigil outside the court.

Looking back, it is clear that the policy of playing it softly, avoiding confrontation with the Western press – except when journalists were far from their colleagues – varying the approach and concealing the mailed fist beneath a velvet glove was extremely clever. The unfavourable publicity abroad was kept within limits; the apparent meticulous legality with which the trials were conducted could always be cited to counter Western charges; and, most important of all, the message went out to other ordinary Russians that while dissent would not be tolerated, there would be no return to the dark days of arbitrary arrest, mass terror and summary punishment. The rule of law was to prevail, at least in form.

And form for many Russians is as important as substance. In so many fields what matters is whether the prescribed rules and rituals have been followed, whether the appearance of things is acceptable. I was reminded, as I hung around on that dusty pavement on a hot week in the summer of 1978, of a scene I had witnessed in an Orthodox Church in Minsk in 1968: two old women who had come to pray saw each other as they were crossing themselves before the icons. 'Hello,' one said, cheerfully, 'how are you?' and in the same breath intoned the ritual responses and prayers. There followed a long conversation – about the price of oranges, the health of their families, their complaints about some mutual friend, gossip about the neighbours – all interspersed with their devotions, which were conducted completely automatically with no visible interest in the real meaning. They probably left the church fully satisfied their obligations had been fulfilled. The form was preserved, even if the spirit had been forgotten.

On the whole the gradual elimination of dissent effectively prevented any welling up of public or even private sympathy for those who were arrested, exiled or silenced. Few ordinary Russians understand or support political dissidents. The working masses in whose name these intellectuals were struggling knew nothing of their cause, and fully supported the officially fostered view that such people were renegades, anti-Soviet elements whose interest in making their cause known to the West was to enable them to emigrate. I remember when a Jewish couple briefly put out a banner on their balcony in a block of flats on Gorky Street, a main street in the centre of Moscow, calling on the authorities to allow them to emigrate. They were of course swiftly made to take it down and subsequently arrested. But the knots of people who gathered to watch – not including the plainclothes KGB toughs who always arrive swiftly on the scene to intimidate any would-be sympathisers – were harsh in their judgements, showing no sympathy for the Jews' demand.

Most Russians want nothing to do with political dissent because of the risks involved. They will happily listen to – and tell – anti-communist jokes as long as there are no strangers around. And in private Russians are often bitterly critical. But there is always that tell-tale glance over the shoulder, the lowering of the voice when the dreaded initials 'KGB' are used, the sudden retreat and contradictory expression of loyalty when they realize they have gone too far.

I saw the embarrassed public reaction to touchy political topics during a bizarre discussion at a polyclinic, where I had gone with Roy Medvedev, the Marxist historian who was expelled from the party for his resolute anti-Stalinist views and the publication of his magnificent book

Let History Judge in the West. A colleague and I had gone to his flat to talk to him in 1980 about his quixotic decision to try to stand as an opposition candidate during the elections to the Supreme Soviet. We met him, one side of his face muffled in a bandage, leaving his flat to go to the polyclinic because of his very bad toothache, and offered to drive him there in order to find time to talk. When we arrived – in my car – I expected he would discreetly get out before the foreigner's number plate was spotted and break off the discussion. But not a bit of it. 'Come on in,' he said, as he checked in at the receptionist's desk. And he went on talking as we went upstairs to the crowded waiting room. It was extraordinary watching the reaction. 'Well of course our system is meant to be democratic, so I'm just testing the principle,' he said. 'I know in your countries it's quite different. Of course the authorities don't like what I'm doing, but they have to find a legal way to stop it . . .' he said, much to our embarrassment as all eyes turned towards us. Roy seemed oblivious of the titters and surprise he was causing. Old women frowned and moved away, some middle-aged people made much of being particularly engrossed in their newspapers. Two youths nudged each other and motioned at us with a grin. Such things were simply not said in public.

Medvedev is a towering figure, a warm, gentle man of penetrating intelligence and quiet, patient good humour, who has never seen himself as a dissident and yet has had to struggle against various official attempts to prevent him writing his books on modern political history or seeing Western journalists. His twin brother, Zhores, was incarcerated in a psychiatric hospital, and Roy fought hard – and successfully – to rouse the conscience of the world and have him released. Zhores, deprived of his citizenship, now lives in England, but Roy continues to live quietly in Moscow. He has been bitterly denounced by other dissidents because of his unshaken belief in Marxism-Leninism and his refusal to 'speak out', to sign petitions or to break the links he still maintains with friends in the party.

He lives on the knife-edge between tolerance and suppression, and in the stricter atmosphere of Andropov's regime there have already been attempts to silence him. 'I am not a dissident,' he told me some years ago, 'but unfortunately "they" think I am.' It is a remark that has been made by dozens of others who have fallen foul of the authorities. And most of them have already paid a harsh price. Now, as before, dissent is, for the rulers of the country, still a very serious crime.

Epilogue

So much to do, so little time – that was the verdict of all the concerned officials and intellectuals I spoke to eight months after Brezhnev's death. They had nothing but admiration for the new mood of purposefulness at the top, for the changes introduced in the first few months of the Andropov regime, and for the results – better food supplies, a noticeable drop in corruption, especially among the police and public officials, greater output and encouraging signs that the economy was responding to the campaign for tighter labour discipline and responsible management. But was there time for rejuvenation when so many elderly party officials had to be eased out of their posts? Could the necessary changes in entrenched ways and habits be forced through, or would the new drive for efficiency run into that great destroyer of all initiative, the faceless, formless, conservative bureaucracy? And above all, would the outside world give Russia a chance to tackle the tasks at home, or would the worsening international situation preoccupy the leadership?

On the surface, of course, everything seems much the same. Moscow in the summer has a warm, dusty, lazy feel: pensioners sun themselves on benches under the lime trees, pigeons peck around near puddles and refuse containers in the courtyards, convoys of buses flying little red flags take the city's children, scrubbed and neat in their Pioneers' uniforms, out to the freshness of the countryside where they will spend six weeks in the summer camps. Crowds of Western tourists are chaperoned from their Intourist buses around the Kremlin churches. Moscow's intellectuals disappear to bask away the summer in their dachas. In Gorky Park the famous big wheel slowly revolves, carrying children and courting couples high above the skyline, sailors queue up to buy ice-creams from stout, white-coated women in charge of trolleys and rickety kiosks, enthusiasts sit at tables under the poplars playing chess, and crowds meander along the paths beside the river in Moscow's first and best known park of rest and culture – one that in summer seems a far cry from Martin Cruz Smith's frozen winter landscape where bodies under the snow start off a thriller of international intrigue.

On the streets too crowds still throng past the lowly, pastel-painted buildings of the old city centre, jostling, hustling, stopping at the occasional makeshift stall to see what books are on offer or inspecting the latest batch of shirts on sale. As always the metro rumbles every three minutes through the spotless, magnificent marble stations with their chandeliers, bronze statues and mosaic murals, still as crowded as ever, still one of the world's most efficient and cheapest underground railways. Here you can see faces from all parts of the Soviet Union, as soldiers in uniform, corpulent old women, chicly dressed office workers and youths in leather jackets line the lengthy escalators in a ceaseless flow that gives a strong sense of the mighty city's vast and varied population.

The rhythm of life seems unaltered. Indeed the new regime has made little difference to the lives of most people. Even the short, sharp shock of the discipline campaign in the spring of 1983 that emptied the bath-houses and barbers' shops and sent skivers scurrying back to work has subsided as people again find time to attend to their personal affairs, cultivate their connections, pursue their schemes for getting hold of the luxuries that lighten and brighten their lives. 'Oh, all those shop raids only lasted a month,' a friend said. 'It's back to normal now.' And with that spontaneous wit that generates a joke for every new event, he told me the one that circulated as the efforts to improve punctuality in offices and factories got under way. The phone rings in the flat of Ivan Petrovich. His wife answers it. 'Where's Ivan Petrovich?' an urgent voice asks. 'This is his office calling. Is he still at home?' 'My husband has just passed away,' his wife replies tearfully. 'Oh thank goodness,' the voice says, 'we thought he was late for work.'

But this is only the surface of things. Within the party apparatus, among the senior officials, the mood is very different. Gone are the days of drift and cronyism. The fight is on against personal profiteering, the abuse of privilege. The peremptory dismissal of Nikolai Shcholokov, the former minister of the interior and one of Brezhnev's closest associates, was a clear warning not only to the faction that opposed Andropov, but to all senior officials. A corrupt party secretary in Krasnodar was also dismissed and others have been publicly rebuked in *Pravda* – 'their last chance to put their houses in order,' as a party member told me. The new regime has first to tighten up, to streamline the unwieldy party apparatus and impose its insistence on proper performance before it can begin to see how and where reform should be introduced.

Change in Russia has traditionally come from the top, and this is still the case. Soviet officials are sensitive to the wishes and commands of those above them, less so to the interests of those lower down. But the chain of command is lengthy, and it takes a Herculean effort to ensure that the decrees from above are actually carried out at the lowest level where it really matters. Naturally there is no contradicting an edict. Russians do not argue with authority, even that of a ticket inspector or a sales assistant. Instead they tend to comply with apparent meekness, giving a display, if necessary, of enthusiastic approval. But if the order goes against their wishes or overturns an established pattern, they usually manage to nullify its effect by a gradual reversion to the old ways. To force through change demands not only unquestionable authority at the top, but constant vigilance to ensure that the order sticks long enough to be accepted as a new way of doing things. And this is where Andropov faces his toughest challenge. The days of overnight purges, iron decrees enforced by threats and under duress are gone. Soviet society is now too complex to be amenable to such methods, too diverse and developed for any return to rigid authoritarianism. The leadership has not only to take powerful interest groups into account, but it has to win backing for its policies all the way down the line.

One way of doing this, as is already clear, is to tighten ideological discipline, increase the party's cohesion. The effect is immediately and especially noticeable in the arts. Soviet intellectuals are nervous. On the whole they support the attempts to galvanise their country into action, but not at the expense of the increased freedoms to experiment and criticise – freedoms that were won almost by default in the final, lax years of the Brezhnev era. And the new policies are always subject to the crude interpretation of minor functionaries. In the cultural field this has produced some bizarre results. Within days of a tough ideological speech by Konstantin Chernenko, the defeated rival for the party leadership after Brezhnev's death, officials responded to his criticism of Western influence and pop music by cancelling an invitation to a French pop group. A notice was put in the local Moscow paper explaining that for technical reasons the advertised concert would not be held. However, the cancellation came too late; the group was already on its way. And so when it arrived, there was something of an official dilemma, and in the end another notice had to be put in the paper saying that the concert would after all take place.

In the battle to win hearts and engage minds the new leadership has had to do something to lessen the credibility gap between rulers and ruled. Cynicism is the enemy of enterprise, and especially so in the Soviet Union. Nothing so damaged Russians' faith in their system as the inflated promises of the past. Like wonder drugs, policies and projects were touted by propagandists as quick-fix solutions to temporary difficulties, harbingers of future plenty. In my first few months as a correspondent in Moscow I was swept away by some of the claims. I remember enthusiastically reporting a project in Odessa to cultivate oysters, which, it was claimed, would soon be so productive that oysters would no longer be a rarity but the daily fare of the common man in the Black Sea port. Other more jaundiced colleagues had already acquired the necessary scepticism, dismissing the claim as another *skoro budyet* type of story. This phrase, meaning 'There will soon be . . .' comes from countless official forecasts, and is repeated by ordinary Russians with heavily ironic overtones.

Some official claims were totally spurious. I remember one that excited my editors on *The Times*. A report said scientists in Siberia had built a prototype village in the far north covered with a huge glass dome for insulation, as this was found to be cheaper for temporary oil exploration settlements than putting up individually heated buildings. It conjured up a fascinating image of a space-age settlement. But I ran into vagueness and hesitation when trying to commission a photograph from Tass. And eventually I learned that the glass-dome village – though long a fantasy of Siberian scientists – simply did not exist, and the Soviet journalist who had invented the story was sacked. It is not only the febrile hacks of Fleet Street who produce some improbable fantasies.

The dropping of most such claims (though not all; even in 1983 reports were being put out of a man who had invented motorised boots, a present-day version of the giant's seven league boots) and the overhaul of the propaganda apparatus has been an important priority for the new regime. The papers have become more factual. On several occasions in 1983 they reported serious accidents that would certainly have been suppressed in the past – the ramming by a passenger ship on the Volga of a railway bridge involving serious loss of life, an accident at the Atomash plant producing nuclear reactors. The press has also carried reports of the discussions at the Thursday meetings of the Politburo, whereas in the past it was scarcely acknowledged that the Politburo met each week. Unfortunately as part of their new seriousness the papers are now carrying less satire and fewer reports of shenanigans in the provinces – possibly because most readers simply had a good laugh and failed to draw the appropriate moral.

In the drive for efficiency more honesty is being demanded of officials, even if – or especially if – they have bad news to report. Nothing is so devastating to long-term planning than the self-deception of optimistically 'adjusted' statistics, producing false hopes that are inevitably destroyed by reality. A joke about cows sums up the phenomenon. A collective farm was set a target of rearing ten calves one year, but due to bad weather and poor management managed to produce only two. The farm director, frightened of the ignominy such a result would bring on him, reported to the local party committee that the farm had produced four. The party was equally horrified by this result, and in its report to the regional committee adjusted the figure to six. They in turn changed it to eight before sending it on to the republican capital. There the party secretary informed the Central Committee in Moscow the farm had fulfilled its plan and reared ten calves. But the Central Committee thought a little extra effort would encourage the others, and when the results finally got to the Politburo, they showed a healthy overfulfilment: twelve calves instead of the decreed ten. 'Good,' they said, 'we can give two calves to the developing countries and keep the rest for ourselves.'

I told the joke to a friend who had once been the director of a primary school in the provinces. 'Well I had the same experience, not with cows but with hot school dinners,' he laughed. His school had been ordered to produce 360 dinners for the pupils, but he had insisted the kitchens were too small and could supply only half that number. The local authority overruled his objections however, and recorded that the school was supplying 360 dinners. When an inspection team arrived they discovered the shortfall. And the director and his colleagues had the painful experience of hearing themselves publicly lambasted by the party committee for failing to meet their target.

In many ways the new openness about the real situation facing the country is an attempt to prepare Russians for difficult times ahead, and to shake their complacency. For both the strength and the weakness of Soviet society is its extraordinary stability. Westerners accustomed to the rapid turnover of ideas, fashions, people and leaders find it hard to appreciate how settled the pattern of life is in Russia. People hold jobs for a very long time, take it for granted that their circumstances and the conditions around them will remain much as they are for many years. Andrei Gromyko's record tenure of office as foreign minister is symbolic and hardly exceptional. A British diplomat's wife was once flagged down by a policeman on point duty for contravening a roadsign. Trying to bluff her way out of it, she insisted the sign must be new as it had not been there the previous week. 'Listen,' the policeman replied patiently, 'I have been on point duty on this spot for the past eighteen years, and that sign has always been there.' So astonished was she that she could make no reply.

Such stability has the advantage of ensuring continuity. At the higher level, planners and diplomats can take a long-term view, compensate for the lack of easily available information and archives with their own lengthy personal experience. Few statesmen have ever had the grasp of detail, fixity of purpose and patience of Mr Gromyko. Western foreign ministers might argue over what was decided about the postwar division of Europe at the Yalta conference; Andrei Gromyko was there. (Tourists to Livadia Palace, where the famous 1945 conference was held, always look with wonderment at the oil painting of the meeting between Stalin, Churchill and Roosevelt, where the unmistakeable figure of Gromyko, black-haired but scarcely changed, can be seen in the background.)

The disadvantage is the tendency to staleness, the hostility to innovation and corrections of course and the difficulty of bringing fresh blood and fresh ideas into the body politic. At the lower level, the lifelong job security dampens ambition and leads to boredom and routine.

If and when the older generation is replaced in the Politburo and the party apparatus, will policies change? Will the postwar, post-Stalin men, better educated, better fed and clothed as children, more broadly rounded in their outlook, take their country along a different path? Most experts think not. For not only is the new generation schooled in the ranks and thinking of the party, but it too will be faced with such an array of conflicting interest groups and problems so intractable that any radical disturbance of the present brittle balance is likely to provoke incalculable upheaval. And that is the last thing any new leader will risk. Domestic change, most urgent in the economic field, is more likely to come so slowly as to be imperceptible, allowing ideologists to present it as the continuation of previous orthodox policies. Those Western Sovietologists who predict the imminent collapse of the economy and radical changes forced by crisis underestimate not only the basic stability of the system, but also the vast difference that would be made if things as they now are were simply made to work properly. Soviet economists delight in calculating the extraordinary boost in output there would be if all workers turned up on time on Monday mornings, sober.

However, though Russia is, and traditionally has half wanted to be, a self-contained world, what happens outside matters – far more than most people in the West realise. For to many ordinary Russians the state of relations with the United States and Western Europe is of direct and personal concern. When things are bad, as they are now, old fears and attitudes surface. Russia retreats into its fortress, the military step up their influence and spending and the hardline ideologists play on latent xenophobia to whip up fears of encirclement. And this brings a general clampdown that affects all kinds of people in dozens of different ways. Travel to the West becomes more difficult as tourist groups go elsewhere, scientific and cultural exchanges are cut back, fewer Russians attend seminars and international gatherings. Emigration, though a relatively new and unaccustomed phenomenon, virtually dries up. It becomes harder to obtain Western books and journals, fewer Western films are shown, broadcasts are jammed, contact with overseas visitors is more difficult and more dangerous. Contracts that might have brought the Russians the things they dream about – jeans, hamburgers, pop records, French perfume, good material – remain unsigned. Campaigns for ideological vigilance mean extra unwelcome hours spent at political harangues, more licence for snoopers and nosey neighbours who turn their petty quarrels into matters of political significance.

More fundamentally, the breakdown of détente means that association with the West again means association with the enemy. And therefore things of no strategic or ideological importance become tainted, simply because they are linked to the Western way of life. Why should the party leadership be so concerned about pop music? What does it matter that jeans and T-shirts are typically American or that the jargon of the gilded youth is filled with English? It matters because in times of tension these things are thought to undermine patriotic feeling, nationalistic rallying around the flag. And indeed they do. As one Russian pointed out, the great threat to the leadership and to the Soviet system in general comes not from new Nato missiles, but from the all pervasive influence of the West. Americans think little and know less about daily life in Russia; Russians, on the other hand, think incessantly about life in the West. And whereas during détente such curiosity was permissible, a new cold war has erected barriers around whole areas of ordinary experience.

Actually it is untrue to say all Russians are affected by a breakdown in East-West relations. It is only the educated inhabitants of the big cities, the growing middle class, who have any concept of the world beyond the Soviet frontiers. But they wield a disproportionate influence on the intellectual and political life of the country. Now, as before, Soviet society is still a pyramid resting on a very large base, the *narod*, the vaunted masses in whose name the country is governed but who play so little part in its government. Their lives are unaffected by big power politics. Their mental framework is that of Soviet society in which they have grown up and to whose values they owe allegiance. Shortages of food, the demands of the local factory bosses, the availability of rural transport are of more concern to them than what Western publications are available in the big cities. For the older generation the war was the first and only time the outside world was thrust so brutally on them. For young people, national service is the only time they have been taken away from their home communities and brought into contact with other ethnic groups, if not other countries.

Yet even in these rural communities there is a feeling of belonging to a vast country, pride in the Soviet Union's position as a world power. It is a feeling reinforced day in, day out by radio and television, by the message of the party, by such publicised areas of achievement as the space programme. Belonging to a superpower is a source of pride that compensates for daily grumbles about shortages and hardships. And the less people actually know of the outside world, the fewer their doubts and feelings of inferiority. It is a pride inculcated from above that then wells back up again and determines many of the Kremlin's reactions, the attitudes that govern Soviet relations and negotiations with other countries.

The general ignorance about the reactions of these other countries to themselves, an ignorance compounded by official insistence on depicting Soviet actions in nothing less than shining colours, reinforces a naturally ethnocentric view. Most Russians simply cannot imagine that they could ever be in the wrong, that their country could ever do something unacceptable to the rest of the world. They do not see and cannot agree that the Soviet Union was responsible, even in part, for the breakdown of détente. And even if some better educated people have doubts about Afghanistan or other Soviet policies overseas, natural patriotism tends to assuage these. People see the West, and especially the United States, therefore as the guilty party that deliberately engineered the destruction of good relations at the end of the seventies. It is up to the West, most people think, to make friends again.

The Kremlin, whether or not it really shares this officially sanctioned view, knows that the world is too dangerous for a diplomatic sulk. How to restore a working relationship with the West – and with China – must therefore remain one of the principal preoccupations of the leadership. But as Russians themselves were asking in the summer of 1983, does Andropov have the time, stamina and personal authority to do this? He clearly has the will, but does he have any room and freedom for manoeuvre? More importantly for the Soviet Union, how constricting will the perception of a threat from the West be in the attempt to introduce change and reform at home?

These questions sound sombre, and point to difficult times ahead. But they also sound familiar. They have indeed been asked in the past – twenty, fifty and even a hundred years ago. The same dilemmas have beset Russia before, the same Gordian knots of geography, history, economy and ideology have waited to be cut, and the same attitudes have governed the rulers' responses. To ask where the Soviet Union is going poses a question that cannot be answered. But to ask where it has been and where it is now is not only essential, but is the only way that any understanding can be gained of Soviet perceptions. And the most striking point to emerge, in my view at least, is the sense of continuity, the unchanging nature of the country.

Nowhere so aptly and so beautifully sums up Eternal Russia than a few acres surrounded by a high brick wall at the side of one of Moscow's ancient complexes of gold-domed churches. The cemetery at Novodevichi is a quiet and moving record of Russian history: its writers and poets, generals and explorers, heroes and rulers.

Symbolically, the famous men and women of pre-revolutionary times rest together with citizens of the post-revolutionary Soviet state. There is Gogol, with a gold-lettered inscription and appreciation of his work from Stalin's government in 1951. Chekhov is buried in a simple square marble grave at the end of a row, the area within the railings beautifully tended by anonymous admirers. Along one wall is a modernistic representation of an airship, with the portraits of all those who perished in its destruction below. Russia's pain is also cruelly but silently felt in the white marble column into which is carved the young and beautiful head of Nadezhda Alleluyeva, Stalin's wife who committed suicide at the height of his harsh collectivisation programme. It is inscribed with a dedication from simply 'I. V. Stalin'. There are the heroes of the war – one minister of military communications is carved with almost comic realism holding a telephone to his ear – and the heroes of Soviet space shots who perished in accidents. Famous doctors and scientists are there. So too is Anastas Mikoyan, the great Bolshevik survivor, and, of course, Nikita Khrushchev. Above his grave is a modernistic marble pediment, with a bronze statue of the famous bald, peasant's head above it. Ironically, it was carved by a man famous for his public row with Khrushchev over modern art – Ernst Neizvestny, who himself has since emigrated.

Novodevichi Cemetery unifies and typifies Russia. It is somewhat shabby, shaded by trees that give it a quiet, country feel. There is both beauty and bombast there, achievement and sycophancy. Of course, nowadays it is out of bounds to most people, and only open to the relatives of those interred. In Brezhnev's time there were worries that too many people came to pay homage to Khrushchev. Of course also Soviet intellectuals regard it as a place of pilgrimage. And of course when I went there, on my last day in the Soviet Union, I got in, concealing my foreignness, through friends of friends who themselves obtained entry by *blat*.

Index

ABOUT THE AUTHOR

Michael Binyon read English and Arabic at Magdalene College, Cambridge. He graduated in 1967 and became the first British teacher in the Soviet provinces when he taught at the Minsk Pedagogical Institute under the auspices of the British Council from 1967 to 1968. He then joined the London *Times* and worked in their Washington, D.C., bureau from 1975 to 1977. He was the *Times*'s Moscow correspondent for the next four and a half years and moved to their Bonn bureau in 1982. He is married and has two children.